ENTREPRENEURIAL JOURNALISM

Entrepreneurial Journalism explains how, in the age of online journalism, digital-savvy media practitioners are building their careers by using low-cost digital technologies to create unique news platforms and cultivate diverse readerships. The book also offers a range of techniques and tips that will help readers achieve the same. Its opening chapters introduce a conceptual understanding of the business behind entrepreneurial journalism. The second half of the book then presents practical guidance on how to work successfully online.

Topics include:

- advice on launching digital start-ups;
- how to use key analytics to track and focus readership;
- engaging with mobile journalism by utilising smartphone and app technology;
- developing revenue streams that can make digital journalism sustainable;
- legal and ethical dilemmas faced in a modern newsroom;
- the challenges of producing news for mobile readers.

The book features leading figures from the BBC, Google and the *Guardian*, as well as some of Britain's best entrepreneurial reporters, who offer advice on thriving in this developing media landscape. Additional support comes from an online resource bank, suggesting a variety of free tools to create online news content.

Entrepreneurial Journalism is an invaluable resource for both practising journalists and students of journalism.

Paul Marsden lectures at Leeds Trinity University, UK. He specialises in online journalism, teaching trainee journalists how to build news websites, use technology to tell stories in inr _____ an audience and generate incon

ENTREPRENEURIAL JOURNALISM

How to go it alone and launch your dream digital project

Paul Marsden

Routledge
Taylor & Francis Group

LONDON AND NEW YORK

London Borough of Enfield		
91200000596619		
Askews & Holts	Mar-2017	
070.4068	£26.99	

For a
pleas

First published 2017
by Routledge
2 Park Square, Milton Park, Abingdon, Oxon OX14 4RN

and by Routledge
711 Third Avenue, New York, NY 10017

Routledge is an imprint of the Taylor & Francis Group, an informa business

© 2017 Paul Marsden; individual contributions, the contributors

The right of Paul Marsden to be identified as author of this work has been
asserted by him in accordance with sections 77 and 78 of the Copyright,
Designs and Patents Act 1988.

British Library Cataloguing in Publication Data
A catalogue record for this book is available from the British Library

Library of Congress Cataloging in Publication Data
Names: Marsden, Paul, 1984–
Title: Entrepreneurial journalism : how to go it alone and launch your dream
digital project / Paul Marsden.
Description: London ; New York : Routledge, 2017. | Includes bibliographical
references and index.
Identifiers: LCCN 2016030691| ISBN 9781138190351 (hardback : alk. paper)
| ISBN 9781138190368 (pbk. : alk. paper) | ISBN 9781315641096 (ebook)
Subjects: LCSH: Journalism--Management. | Journalism--Vocational
guidance. | Online journalism. | Journalism--Technological innovations.
Classification: LCC PN4784.M34 M34 2017 | DDC 070.4068--dc23LC
record available at https://lccn.loc.gov/2016030691

ISBN: 978-1-138-19035-1 (hbk)
ISBN: 978-1-138-19036-8 (pbk)
ISBN: 978-1-315-64109-6 (ebk)

Typeset in Bembo by
Servis Filmsetting Ltd, Stockport, Cheshire

Printed and bound by CPI·Group (UK) Ltd, Croydon, CR0 4YY

CONTENTS

List of illustrations   *vii*
List of contributors   *ix*
Acknowledgements   *xi*

Introduction   1

1 What is news and what is journalism in 2016?   4
  Rebecca Whittington and Catherine O'Connor

2 The business of journalism   22
  With Andrew Youde

3 Innovation   40

4 Building your idea   56

5 Being an entrepreneurial journalist   70
  With Wayne Bailey

6 Starting your website and writing online   91

7 Engaging, measuring and reacting to your audience   109

8 Your smartphone as your best reporting tool   124
  With Lindsay Eastwood

9 Using social media to promote your work   147

10 The boundaries you must not cross and remaining ethical
    in the journalistic Wild West   163
    With Nigel Green

Index   *179*

ILLUSTRATIONS

Figures

1.1	Growth of smartphone news use	12
1.2	Top social networks for news	13
1.3	Proportion who paid for online news in 2015	14
1.4	Yearly median payment for online news	15
2.1	Christian Payne	31
3.1	'Where's Damascus?' An interactive game devised by UsVsTh3m	47
3.2	'Jeremy Hunt's realistic A&E crisis simulator'. An interactive game devised by UsVsTh3m	47
3.3	Martin Belam	48
4.1	Daniel Ionescu	64
5.1	Matt Cooke	71
5.2	Joanna Abeyie	78
5.3	The feedback cycle you should follow in the early stage of your site	80
5.4	Breaking down your audience in terms of age, gender and ways they access your site helps potential advertisers	83
5.5	Making your headline audience figures available, especially if they are broken down geographically, is also extremely important	83
5.6	Graham Poucher	84
6.1	Tom Rostance	101
7.1	Stuart Heritage	117
8.1	Image of cups that demonstrates how to focus a smartphone camera	128
8.2	Nick Garnett	130
8.3	This is how you shoot video using a monopod	132
8.4	Bracing yourself can provide stability while shooting video	132
8.5	How to adjust the exposure on the camera	133

8.6	Avoid shooting into the light	134
8.7	The slider on the smartphone allows you to zoom.	134
8.8	Think about what is in the background of your shot	135
8.9	This is good framing for an interview	136
8.10	Here the interviewee is too far to the left	137
8.11	Your interviewee needs to be looking at you	137
8.12	Your interviewee needs to be on the same level as you	138
8.13	These are your choices when you import footage	139
8.14	This is how your timeline will look when you are editing footage	140
8.15	This is the transitions menu	141
8.16	This menu appears when you are about to record a voice-over	141
8.17	Christian Payne	144
9.1	Anna Doble	149
10.1	Gavin MacFadyen	165
10.2	Ruth Collard	166

Tables

5.1	Conducting a STEP analysis	74
5.2	Conducting a SWOT analysis	74

CONTRIBUTORS

Wayne Bailey teaches across a number of professional education programmes and specialises in higher education practice and business enterprise in education. His research is particularly focused on the internationalisation agenda and the impact this has on teaching within the higher education sector today. Effective HE marketing in both home and international markets is also a key focus of his research.

Lindsay Eastwood joined Leeds Trinity University in 2008 after working as a journalist for eighteen years in both print and broadcast media. She has been a reporter at the *Craven Herald*, *Watford Free Observer*, *Yorkshire Evening Post* and ITV Yorkshire. She now teaches news writing and video journalism skills.

Nigel Green began his career as a trainee journalist on the *Sheffield Star* in 1985. He has since worked for a wide range of national and regional newspapers, as well as ITV Tyne Tees. Nigel specialises in crime and investigative reporting but has also covered assignments in war zones, including Afghanistan and Iraq. He is currently an Associate Principal Lecturer at Leeds Trinity University, where his main role is teaching media law.

Catherine O'Connor is Head of the School of Arts and Communication at Leeds Trinity University. Prior to joining the university she worked as a journalist in the regional news media, including the *Halifax Courier*, *Yorkshire Evening Post* and *Telegraph & Argus*, where she was Deputy Editor.

Rebecca Whittington was a reporter, news editor, editor and video journalist for some of Yorkshire's top newspaper and digital titles, including the *Yorkshire Post* and *Yorkshire Evening Post*, before joining Leeds Trinity University as a graduate teaching assistant in journalism and embarking on a Ph.D. measuring the impact and efficacy of digital reporting tools in regional UK newsrooms.

Andrew Youde is Head of Division (Academic and Professional Studies) in the School of Education and Professional Development at the University of Huddersfield. Before taking up this post he was Head of A-Level Business and Economics at Huddersfield New College.

ACKNOWLEDGEMENTS

This book is the product of a year's worth of research, which wouldn't have been possible without Leeds Trinity University giving me the time to write it. For that I owe my boss, Catherine O'Connor, and my colleagues, who have either contributed, offered to proofread or covered aspects of my teaching, a considerable amount of gratitude.

Thank you to Karla, Talor, Haydn and Richard for putting up with me for the last few months while I completed it and Frances for her help pulling it all together. Thank you to Trinity Mirror, the Reuters Institute for the Study of Journalism and The Lincolnite for letting me use images of their work. I should make it clear that this book is not affiliated with nor supported by Apple.

Finally, thanks to all the contributors – including Dan Evans and Josh Stead for their input – and interviewees who have added their expertise to the project.

Paul Marsden, June 2016

INTRODUCTION

There has never been a better time to be a young journalist. And this is why.

Traditionally journalism graduates had their future mapped for them. They would leave university and progress to trainee roles in large news organisations, as I did myself in 2005, and they would progress within that structure.

As a trainee in a regional newspaper you were told in several years you could become a senior reporter, then possibly a specialist reporter or a sub, then maybe a news editor and possibly even one day the editor.

This model of progression fits the 10,000-hour rule identified by researchers as the 'magic number' to become an expert in a skill, in this case producing a newspaper. As journalist Michael Gladwell says: '[Ten years is] roughly how long it takes to put in ten thousand hours of hard practice. Ten thousand hours is the magic number of greatness'.[1] It turns out that practice pays off.

Now, there are a lot of experienced journalists out there with more than ten years' experience working on newspapers, just as there are plenty with that level of experience of broadcasting on radio or television.

However, how many people have spent ten years producing truly digital journalism? The implication of Gladwell's point is there are remarkably few journalists who have. Some of the best are featured in this book.

The requirement for new skills is clear in the leaked innovation report produced by the *New York Times*, one of the world's leading newspapers, which argues that 'to help change the culture [of the organisation] we need better digital talent'.[2] But the fact that so few people are experts in digital storytelling is fantastic for young reporters.

They are new to the industry, so should have the drive required to put 10,000 hours into the development of new skills. Technology has levelled the playing field.

They are also aided by the fact they are among the first generation of digital natives to become journalists. They were children who grew up doing their homework on computers rather than having to learn how to use them to do their jobs like older generations. Their daily use of a variety of digital platforms has also made them more innovative and adaptable towards their deployment of these.

It is highly likely they will have experience of producing their own media on a regular basis, a task that was much harder twenty years ago when you had to find an alternative printing press or a broadcaster that would let you have a go.

A perfect breeding ground for entrepreneurs

The lack of experts is why digital journalism feels so unsettled, slippery and exciting as a concept. Imagine studying English without an English literary canon. Where do you go when there is no Shakespeare to idolise or comprehend? We are in essence collectively writing the first chapter.

The liberation, experimentation, and no small degree of chaos that the internet has introduced into journalism has wreaked havoc with some of the longest standing news groups across the world. As James Harding, director of news and current affairs at the BBC, points out: 'The internet has ripped a hole in the business model of many great news organisations'.[3] It has left historically well resourced but often slow-to-adapt legacy (pre-internet) publishers slugging it out on a complex battlefield full of individual specialist bloggers.

But by far the biggest challenge to the establishment is coming from insurgent digital-only ventures, which are hungry for growth. Two of the market leaders in this area, Buzzfeed and the Huffington Post, have succeeded due to their focused business plans, which have sought viral growth. Therefore a key aspect of this book will investigate how you can be successful in drawing up a plan to attract your target audience online.

It is important to remember the modern journalistic landscape is tailor-made for young entrepreneurial journalists, primarily because you aren't starting from anywhere near as far behind the industry and its experts than you used to be. The continual evolution that technology is providing supports the viewpoint of American academic Jeff Jarvis that we 'don't even know what the internet is yet'.[4]

Jarvis compares the development of the internet to that of the printing press, saying it took fifty years after its invention by Gutenberg for the book to take on its own form. The first newspaper took a further century. He argues:

> This is just the beginning ... our students are the ones who are going to invent this future and the best skill we can give them is the ability to think like an entrepreneur, like Gutenberg, and to find opportunity because we don't know.[5]

You have the opportunity to tell stories in more ways now than you've ever had previously in the history of journalism. You've got more tools at your disposal, across any kind of format. The difficultly comes in the fact that you have to choose your way of doing it, and this involves developing your own path – not only when it comes to producing the content, but distributing it, building an audience and developing a sustainable business model around it. Yes – it turns out that to survive you need to generate revenue.

There are more options than ever. This means that there are different ways to be successful. It is not easy, definitely not – money is scarce and the contrasting priorities of journalists and the platforms they rely on are producing an unstable relationship. A change of approach in Silicon Valley increasingly leaves newsrooms reeling while they figure out how to rebuild their methods of working. But now, more than ever, it's about making the right choices, knowing when to stick or twist when technological innovations occur. This book aims to help you do that.

Now you are aware that you've less ground to travel, and a much bigger chance of creating a successful news website if you devote enough time, energy and passion to it, we shall begin.

Notes

1   Gladwell, M (2008) *Outliers: The Story of Success*, St Ives: Penguin.
2   *New York Times* (2014) *Innovation Report*.
3   Harding, J (2015) *The Future of News*, BBC.
4   Jarvis, J (2015) International Journalism Festival, Perugia.
5   Jarvis, J (2013) World Journalism Education Council, Mechelen.

1

WHAT IS NEWS AND WHAT IS JOURNALISM IN 2016?

Rebecca Whittington and Catherine O'Connor

Where have we come from?

The creative opportunities for storytelling have never been greater – journalists can use technology and platforms to innovate, enhance and engage. But to reach this point, the news media has been through vast and fast change of a scale and pace which has framed innovation within a debate that swings from despair about the looming death of journalism, conversely to the means of saving the same industry.

The advent of the internet opened up an array of publishing opportunities for journalists – but it also ingrained in audiences the idea that news could be accessed for free. Decades down the line the issue of who pays for the news – and how to encourage consumers to pay for online and digital news – remains one of the core challenges facing the industry.

Newspapers lurched from one plan to another in terms of how they should react to the arrival of the internet and, for writer Clay Shirky, the principal issue was that all ideas generated amounted to the same thing – 'here's how we're going to preserve the old forms of organisation in a world of cheap perfect copies!' This led to an assumption that the basic organisational form of newspapers was sound and only in need of a digital facelift.[1]

It was an assumption that left the industry resolutely tied to an 'old' method of production and distribution while not responding robustly enough to fast encroaching technological developments – and struggling with what the change meant for their business models. News organisations might have made sure they were 'present' on new platforms and via new means of access but the modus operandi tended towards replicating the print product rather than rethinking the product for the platform.

For those looking in from the outside, it might be hard to decide which mast to nail their colours to in the 'life v. death' debate about journalism. Those with long-held experience on the inside might despair that decisions about how to secure the future are being held in the context of excitement that footage of rubber bands being used to explode a watermelon attracted 10 million views for Buzzfeed.[2]

According to *New York Times* lead media writer Jim Rutenberg,[3] 'executives who run news organizations almost universally say that we'd all better find our own watermelons – and find them yesterday'.

Rutenberg talks about the 'rushed panic' in which huge changes are being made to the content news organisations generate and the way their content is presented in an effort to 'draw big, addicted audiences'.[4]

As *Guardian* columnist John Naughton points out, we have shifted from a pre-internet age where information was scarce to having an 'unmanageable abundance of information' but where time and attention are scarce, resulting in a battle between traditional media and online media, the latter coming out on top in terms of 'grabbing more and more of people's time and attention'.[5]

Crumbling power bases

Technology has cracked open the news market, given the means of content delivery to all, fractured once powerful revenue streams, and left industry behemoths struggling for control and fighting for their futures.

Futurist Ross Dawson drew up a 'newspaper extinction timeline' in 2010, predicting that newspapers in their current form would be insignificant in the US by 2017 and in the UK by 2019, although his forecast did point out that newspapers becoming insignificant was not the same as the 'death of news-on-paper'.[6]

The UK did witness its first casualty in 2016 when the *Independent* stopped its printed product, although the company was extolled for its new position as the first UK national newspaper 'to embrace a global, digital-only future'.[7]

Almost in tandem with the closure of the *Independent*, Trinity Mirror announced a February 2016 launch for *New Day*, the first new national newspaper to hit UK streets for thirty years. Targeted at a 'time poor' audience, it spurned the idea of running a parallel website but aimed to engage readers in dialogue on social media.[8]

Despite a promotional print run of around 2 million copies and a £5 million TV advertising campaign, *New Day* closed after just ten weeks, having failed to achieve only around 30,000 of the 200,000 daily sales it had hoped for.[9]

Rewinding back to January 2001 shows the scale of the long-term decline in circulations. Then, the UK's ten major national newspapers sold on average 12.06 million copies a day, according to Audit Bureau of Circulation (ABC) data,[10] but that figure has now more than halved. By April 2016, the remaining nine major daily national newspapers sold on average a total 4.87 million copies a day.[11]

Figures detailing online access to news are more positive. ABC data published in May 2016 detailing users year-on-year showed some substantial increases. *Mail Online* maintained its position as the UK's largest national newspaper website recording an increase in unique daily users of just over 3 per cent. The *Guardian*, in second position in terms of its website, returned a year-on-year increase of more than 21 per cent and the *Independent*, apparently not dented by the loss of the print product, recorded an increase of just above 24 per cent.[12]

In addition, the National Readership Survey (NRS) suggested in early 2016 there had been significant growth in the monthly reach for national newspaper titles, with most of that growth coming from mobile devices (although a change in NRS methodology had itself pulled in more mobile readers).[13]

The NRS estimated most national newspapers had double the number of readers on mobile devices compared to desktop computers. The survey showed that the *Daily Mail* is the most read national newspaper in print and online, with a monthly reach of almost 29 million people. The *Guardian*, which has the lowest print sales of the nine major national titles, was estimated to have a monthly audience reach of 25 million.

In terms of television news, the power of the major broadcasters has also been disrupted, although one in five adults in the UK use only TV for the news they access and the BBC remains the top news source, with 48 per cent of adults citing it as the place they get their news.[14]

Back in 1989, the arrival of Sky News in the UK heralded an era in which 24-hour news was able to hold audiences in its grip with its rolling coverage of major news stories, perhaps most memorably two Gulf wars and the events of 9/11. But now it is social media which beats the rolling news channel machinery to coverage of major events, and without the multi-million pound costs which come with running output centred around an expensive studio with anchors, contributors, behind-the-scenes production staff and correspondents in the field. The notion of anchors poised in a studio waiting for something to happen is at odds with the need to provide on-demand and more personalised services. Richard Sambrook, former director of BBC Global News, and Sean McGuire, former BBC News head of strategy, have argued in favour of: 'Returning newsgathering to what it says on the tin – a service that goes out to speak to people, investigates, considers and then files packages as need, with updates and commentary, freed of the need to fill empty space.'[15]

Journalism professor George Brock is clear about the challenge posed by consumers who know how to find what they want, at speed in a 'river of endlessly renewed material' which they can dip in and out of at will, conditions which mean they are likely to find the 'conventional pattern of mainstream television reporting to be slow, mannered and ritualistic'.[16]

Sambrook cites the shrinking audience share as the core issue – with the major news programmes costing £50–60 million a year but securing only a 2 per cent share of the available audience. Sambrook does see a future for the main evening bulletins 'as the Harrods shop window for the digital services that lie behind'. Sky's John Ryley sees things slightly differently, with television leading a multi-media service, with social media and mobile giving television news an additional impetus.[17]

From gatekeeping to gatewatching

A key element of legacy news production was the role of the journalist as gatekeeper – or rather the role of everyone in the newsroom as a form of gatekeeper.

Before the internet came to dominate the news media, the relationship between journalists and their sources was closed to the outside world. A source could pass on information, a journalist could ask questions about it, try to negotiate access to further detail, decide to ignore the information or even agree to delay or suppress publication of certain details. All this trading was done out of sight of the audience and without their knowledge, input or even influence.

The gatekeeping function might have filtered and brought some orderly decision-making to information which fed into the news agenda, but it can also be argued that this very process allowed journalists to serve their own interests and the commercial interests of the organisation they worked for over and above the needs and interests of the audience.

The internet has changed that balance of power 'by allowing sources (to) communicate direct to the public and by facilitating collaborative journalism', a shift that led reporter Alex Bruns to develop the notion of journalists 'gatewatching' an audience with the power to produce and be involved in disseminating news.[18]

Author Ken Doctor called 2016 the 'year of the platform', with Facebook, Google and Apple all striving to win at getting audiences to spend maximum time on their products. But, he argued, 'As platforms gain even more centrality in our lives, there are fewer gatekeepers for the digital news readers receive.' While these platforms might have offered new opportunities for publishers, they remain prey to the whims of the decisions, strategies and algorithms of those platforms. So, as much as the shift from gatekeeping to gatewatching was seen as a positive for news, Doctor outlined concerns that readers are now subject to the judgements platforms make about what is news, a shift away from diversity in judgement, with the platforms as a 'narrowing filter funnel'.[19]

The collaborative nature of online production and audience involvement in news has led to a rankings-style approach to journalism – professional journalists were seen as being at the top of the tree, able to bring a level of skill to coverage that the audience lacked; citizen journalists were seen as being in second place, able to contribute but lacking the required authority.

Ignoring this journalistic 'snobbery', it is possible to consider the ways in which audience contribution can 'challenge, complement and extend' its 'industrial counterpart' rather than replacing it, by:

- extending the breadth of coverage by reporting from areas where traditional reporters are not present;
- bringing depth to coverage through a greater variety of views and voices and
- extending coverage of stories over time by operating outside of normal news production cycles and making use of technology.[20]

The changing relationship with the audience

The news media was founded on the premise that only a handful of organisations could muster the financial capital and investment in the physical resources required to produce and distribute news products.

Prior to the internet, the economics of newspapers were simple. Readers paid for a copy of the paper and a huge range of organisations and people paid for advertising space by way of getting out their particular message.

The internet and the technology which followed 'broke' that system. It gave consumers access to news for free and afforded all with the means to record, film and distribute content, thereby opening up access to the news market to an array of start-ups. It gave advertisers the chance to take their business to new organisations or even set up their own advertising platforms. As newspapers started to lose core business – advertising from motor dealers, estate agents, recruiters and even individuals – they had to figure out how to make the same money they made out of print advertising through their online businesses.

It is a nut they have yet to properly crack. Money earned from advertising in print products is still hugely important to newspapers, totalling around £800 million a year, around four times the size of digital income for UK national newspapers.[21]

As well as losing security about their revenue-earning capacity, news organisations no longer have control over content, a combination of pressures which led former *Guardian* editor Alan Rusbridger to refer to journalism as operating 'in the teeth of a force-12 digital hurricane'.[22]

News organisations still produce content within traditional cycles – print deadlines and broadcast slots – while trying to serve their new masters – websites and social media platforms. They do this in the full knowledge that not all of this activity will earn the organisations they work for any money and in the knowledge that their audience is likely to have known about stories hours before via social media or, in the case of major breaking news, may possibly have contributed pictures, eye-witness accounts and shared with their own circle of family and friends.

What's trending?

Monitoring and tracking the chatter on social media is now a key part of any reporter's role. Industry is using increasingly sophisticated tools to support this work – to both stay in tune with what people are talking about, to help them direct resources and integrate content from social platforms into their own websites.

Tools, such as Dataminr, NewsWhip and Crowdtangle, allow reporters to find a breaking story faster than they would otherwise have been able to, helping them wade through millions of pieces of content, and getting over the problem that working without technology, a journalist would be unlikely to spot a breaking story until it has been tweeted many times. Social listening tools allow journalists to cut through the 'noise' rather than getting lost among millions of posts. As Alexis

Sobel Fitts, from the *Columbia Journalism Review*, states: 'They stop the one random tweet among millions and predict whether it will be big news.'[23]

'Managing' the audience – or working with the audience

Where once journalists were able to carefully manage their relationship and inter-action with the audience through the letters page, they now find themselves faced with an onslaught of interaction and difficult decisions how to manage that. A large part of the challenge lies in the fact that much of this interaction – comments on web stories, contacts on social media – is out in the public domain so demands time and careful attention.

Audience engagement editors, a role we explore in Chapter 7, are the norm in newsrooms now and are at the forefront of drawing in audiences and keeping them in a fiercely competitive environment with a huge amount of choice. They have to manage feedback from the audience, strive to develop relationships and loyalty, and use what audiences can contribute as part of their output.

Drawing in the expertise of readers, using them as a resource, can shape, unlock and enhance news. At Dutch news website *De Correspondent*, reporters have been key in drawing in the community, for example by asking for support with dealing with scientific research, with an appeal for help in this area resulting in more than 270 people responding with offers of expertise and their details being registered on a database.[24]

Inviting the audience to use their expertise in specialist areas is very different from taking footage from ordinary people on the ground at major stories.

Emily Bell, former director of digital content at the *Guardian* and now director of the Tow Centre for Digital Journalism, has been passionate about the power of the community as a resource for journalists – to help source, fact-check and enhance news – but has also echoed concerns about the status of ordinary people who contribute footage to major stories in sometimes dangerous circumstances and the industry's responsibility to them now they are part of 'our news ecosystem': 'we now have publishing systems which can amplify every act, alert the world to important events, but which also don't yet afford these new forms of journalist the same protections as the old', she said in her 2015 Hugh Cudlipp lecture.[25]

Who pays for news?

Technology has influenced news delivery in terms of speed, choice of format and audience interaction and, most fundamentally of all, it ripped away the once essen-tial need for an economic transaction – a payment – to take place in order for con-sumers to access news. And, as advertising revenues have continued to dwindle, the industry has been left asking: Who pays for the news?

In the struggle to grow revenues, publishers have put the blame for their diffi-culties on the shoulders of Facebook and Google. Facebook's 'Instant Articles' and Google's 'Accelerated Mobile Pages' (AMP) project might have helped publishers to extend their audience reach and monetise their content but the two giants have 'an iron grip on the digital display ad market'. For 2016, it was projected that £9 billion would be spent on digital advertising in the UK – and Facebook and Google were expected to take almost 53 per cent of that between them.[26]

Facebook Instant Articles was opened up to all publishers in April 2016, allowing them to give readers access to fast-loading versions of posts while also displaying some advertising and having the ability to measure page views. This brings a whole new dimension to Facebook but leaves news organisations shouldering the costs of producing the content which, 'for off-site environments they can't control, either commercially or editorially, comes with its own set of risks'.[27]

The *Guardian*'s John Naughton has questioned the power this gives to Facebook:

> while publishers can without difficulty shift their stuff to Instant Articles, they cannot control which ones Facebook users *actually get to see*. This is because users' news feeds are determined by Facebook's machine-learning algorithms that try to get what each user would like to see ... So once the content disappears into Facebook's algorithmic maw it becomes mere fodder for its calculations.[28]

The power Facebook has over content has prompted calls for it and Google to provide financial support for news organisations.

Think tank ResPublica suggested new media platforms pay a 1 per cent levy on revenue to support investigative, long-form and local journalism. Justin Schlosberg, author of ResPublica's *The Mission of Media in an Age of Monopoly*, has called for 'supporting a diverse ecology of "vehicles"' for endangered forms of journalism.[29]

He suggested that all organisations, no matter what size and no matter whether they were commercial or not-for-profit, should be able to bid for any form of cross-subsidy as a way of encouraging investment.

While cross-subsidies may be welcome, it is unlikely they would address the added pressure brought by consumers using ad blockers in response to being frustrated by online ads slowing down their browsing experience. Developers have been quick to capitalise on this frustration and there have been major rollouts of ad blocking technology, including via Apple's iOS 9 software.

Data from the Internet Advertising Bureau in March 2016 showed that 22 per cent of web users aged 18 or over used software to strip ads from digital content. More than 9 million British web users said they blocked ads, with consumers in the 18–24 age bracket most likely to use ad blocking software. Mike Colling, founder of media agency MC&C, claimed the digital advertising industry had lost sight of the value exchange – advertising in exchange for content – but pointed out that 'content is everywhere so less valuable to consumers – meaning the volume and nature of advertising must adjust'.[30]

While the industry works out how to make this adjustment, publishers have been forced to remind readers that the content they consume is supported by advertising, while trying to design ad models which are more acceptable to audiences.[31]

Are paywalls the answer?

The idea of putting up paywalls is something that news organisations have been slow to embrace but, with unprecedented falls in print advertising of up to 30 per cent during some weeks in 2015, it should be the business model to follow, according to Sir Martin Sorrell, chief executive of WPP, the world's biggest marketing services company and a huge spender on advertising. Sorrell believes that if publishers produce content that has value, consumers will pay, and he has urged publishers to understand that digital advertising will become less profitable in future.[32]

The experience of and approach to paywalls in the UK has been mixed. The *Guardian*, under former editor Alan Rusbridger, firmly rejected the paywall approach in favour of 'open journalism', but it is a decision which remains under question given that the company revealed in January 2016 that it had lost more than £100 million over 12 months. Since then, the company has said it aims to make its membership scheme account for a third of the overall revenues for Guardian News Media within three years.[33]

The fortunes of the *Guardian* are in stark contrast to those of *The Times* and the *Sunday Times*, which went behind a paywall in June 2010. By January 2016, *The Times* had 170,000 digital subscribers paying for website, smartphone and tablet access, and a further 400,000 who pay for a print and digital bundle.[34] During the course of its time behind a paywall, *The Times* has suffered a decline in print sales of 18.9 per cent, compared to a 42 per cent decline for the *Guardian*. *The Times* is also in profit.[35]

The *Sun*, however, scrapped its paywall in 2015 after two years and after attracting 225,000 subscribers. Most of them paid just £2 a week, yet the paper invested millions acquiring rights, including for Premier League goal highlights.[36]

Whatever decisions are taken, two things are clear. To survive, newspapers will have to find more ways to persuade consumers to pay for what they produce and, to do this, they will have to continue to try to strengthen their relationship with their audience if they are to succeed in such a challenging marketplace. Ways of addressing this will be investigated thoroughly throughout this book.

Case study: Reuters' *Digital News Report*, 2016

The Reuters Institute's *Digital News Report* aims to develop an understanding of the trends and themes at the heart of the transition to digital news. The study surveys around 50,000 people across 26 countries.

The five sets of data collected between 2012 and 2016 have shown a steady pattern of television and online news being the most frequently accessed, strong growth in social media and a decline in print newspapers. But there is a generational split. The 2016 report identified that social media (28 per cent) has overtaken television (24 per cent) as the main source of news for people aged between 18 and 24.

Smartphones

Of Brits surveyed, 46 per cent say they regularly use their smartphone to access digital news; this is up from 17 per cent three years ago (Figure 1.1).

Using your smartphone to access news is actually more common in some small European countries, rather than larger ones. More than two thirds of Swedes access news on their smartphone every week.

British audiences still rely heavily on the BBC. Of those online users who use online mainstream news sources, 70 per cent utilise the BBC as a primary source of information, against just 13 per cent who rely on Buzzfeed and the Huffington Post. These new, digital-first platforms are more commonly seen as secondary sources of news. This suggests that when hard news stories break smartphone users, who are short of time and task-focused, stick to traditional brands they believe they can trust. They visit newer publishers when they are casually browsing.

Value of news

The survey tracks the value of news and looks at four measures – accuracy and reliability; bringing new stories to audiences; analysis; and speed.

Television news is traditionally seen as the most important source of news in the majority of countries, although online is ahead in the US and Finland. It is also the most valued across the board.

Online news and social media are valued for alerting people to stories they didn't know about, but social media are considered least reliable. In the case of the under-35s, online news is considered best on all four value measures – although this group is still distrustful of social media.

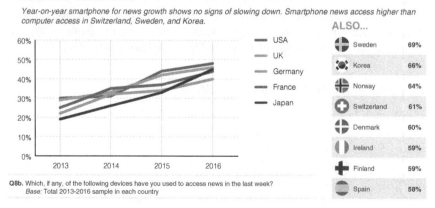

FIGURE 1.1 Growth of smartphone news use
Source: Image courtesy of Reuters Institute for the Study of Journalism, *Digital News Report 2016*.

Shift from desktop to social

The data showed a clear shift away from desktop access to news. Less than half of respondents – 46 per cent – considered their laptop or desktop computer their most important device for accessing online news, down from 80 per cent in 2012. The key shift here was not about people replacing one device with another – rather they are using two or three devices to access the news.

The power of Facebook is clear – 44 per cent of respondents use the network to find, read, watch, share or comment on the news each week, which is more than twice the usage of its nearest rival, YouTube. Japan is the only country where Facebook is not the largest network for news (Figure 1.2).

While Facebook has gained importance in terms of news consumption, communication with friends is still the primary driver on the platform; this is in contrast to Twitter, which is a platform where people go to seek news and the latest developments in it.

One of the interesting things about social media users is their propensity to access articles directly, rather than via a publisher's homepage. In the UK 59 per cent of people do this, up from 43 per cent in 2014. Strength of brand influences social media users when they are considering what link to use; in search results, the headline's relevance is the most important factor. What is also interesting about social news discovery is that it draws in females and younger groups.

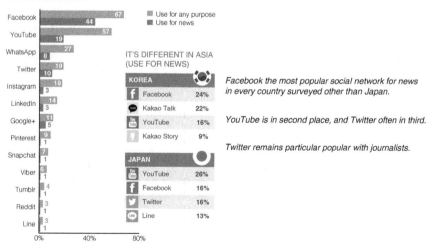

FIGURE 1.2 Top social networks for news (and for any purpose)
Source: Image courtesy of Reuters Institute for the Study of Journalism, *Digital News Report 2016*.

Battle for online audiences and revenues

The Reuters report says it is difficult to use the data to pinpoint groups who are more likely to pay for news, and it detected very little change in the absolute number of people paying for digital news in the year up to the publication of its 2016 report.

In most countries, around 10 per cent of online users pay for news – but in some countries it is much lower. In the US, Australia and the UK, digital or combined subscription packages are the norm, in contrast to Spain where smaller one-off payments dominate (Figure 1.3).

However there was some cheer for UK news organisations. The 7 per cent of Brits who do pay for access to news actually pay more than £80 a year on average, considerably more than people in most other countries (Figure 1.4).

What impact has all this had on the skillset of journalists?

Washington Post veteran and Politico co-founder Jim VandeHei has talked about 'journalists killing journalism' by 'stubbornly clinging to the old ways'.[37] The 'old ways' he refers to are about competing outlets producing hundreds of words and rival content on the same things when the better focus would be to work out what an audience wants, how they want it and how to produce that without huge costs.

That is where news start-ups have a huge advantage – they are framed within the skillset of the entrepreneur, by their very nature they have to work out how to operate with marginal costs, and from the very outset their resources can be mar-shalled towards delivering niche content to a defined audience.

If there is to be a shift from old ways to new ways in journalism it will be driven in a substantial way by the recruitment and training practices of news

PROPORTION WHO PAID FOR ONLINE NEWS IN THE LAST YEAR
ALL COUNTRIES

Highest in Norway and increases seen in many markets – Ireland, Austria, Poland, Japan, Italy, Portugal, Denmark and the Netherlands. Dip of 2% in the USA as some publishers abandon paywalls and free apps

% THAT HAVE PAID (ANYTHING) FOR ONLINE NEWS IN THE LAST YEAR

Q7a. Have you paid for ONLINE news content, or accessed a paid-for ONLINE news service in the last year? (This could be digital subscription, combined digital/print subscription or one-off payment for an article or app or e-edition). *Base:* Total sample in each country

FIGURE 1.3 Proportion who paid for online news in 2015
Source: Image courtesy of Reuters Institute for the Study of Journalism, *Digital News Report 2016.*

YEARLY MEDIAN PAYMENT FOR ONLINE NEWS
ALL COUNTRIES (IN POUNDS STERLING)

FIGURE 1.4 Yearly median payment for online news
Source: Image courtesy of Reuters Institute for the Study of Journalism, *Digital News Report 2016*.

organisations. But to what extent have the perceptions of the skills required for industry and recruitment practices shifted to really accommodate the shifting sands of the industry?

In the days before the iPhone and social media, shorthand, media law, a driving licence (and accompanying car), enthusiasm, a lust for exclusives and a little black book bursting with carefully collected contacts were the qualities and skills a newspaper editor sought when employing his newsroom staff.

Even amidst the turbulent impact that digital change has wrought upon newsrooms – with the introduction of websites, social media platforms, content management systems, video and audio packages, blogs and smartphones – until recently it seemed that the skills required of new recruits to the regional newspaper industry had changed very little.

Despite the new pressures, it was still more important to editors that reporters had a good grasp of legal issues, excellent interviewing skills and tight, bright writing styles over a sound knowledge of data coding, being au fait with Facebook and knowing how to make a decent video using a smartphone.

Studies have shown the difficulty the news industry has had with successfully unifying a traditional product with brand new digital technology. This is evidenced by the fact that employing editors, until relatively recently, sought traditional journalism skills over and above the multi-media skills and abilities.[38] One study examining job advertisements for journalists working in online media found traditional news journalism skills were given more prominence that technological skills.[39] Another study found the core skills required in the newsroom were traditional.[40]

These findings were echoed in research by the National Council for the Training of Journalists (NCTJ), which decided against changing its curriculum based on results that showed a preference by editors for traditional skills.[41]

It took more than a decade after newspapers started using the internet and digital innovation for newspaper editors to indicate that new digital skills were of comparable value to those traditionally possessed by journalists. One study concluded that older journalists were finding themselves overlooked for promotion in favour of younger staff who were perceived to think more digitally.[42] A 2015 view of industry found employing editors within the whole news industry valued traditional journalistic skills and digital skills equally.[43]

So, what makes a well rounded journalist in this current day and age? It seems that traditional qualities are becoming less significant as digital skills and knowledge become more of a focus in newsrooms up and down the country, as outlined in the case study below. The NCTJ qualification and having a driving licence still register as important, but their relevance is diluted in the face of video, websites and online demand. Ideas and writing skills are still making their mark, but only when combined with the ability to use social media and create captivating content for the web.

The constant evolution of digital technology and opportunity suggests that the list of affiliated skills will only increase. So perhaps today's most attractive journalism candidate is a person who can do it all and more; they can turn their hand to old-school skills whilst dazzling their potential new employer – and audiences – with a knowledge of all things digital – not only that which exists in the present, but demonstrating a grasp of and enthusiasm for the digital-yet-to-come.

Case study: What skills do newsrooms want?

A study of job advertisements for news positions at regional newspapers within the UK has seen, for the first time, digital skills being listed as a more desirable attribute over traditional skills.

Advertisements, placed on UK regional newspaper industry website holdthefrontpage.co.uk (from November to January 2014/15 and November to January 2015/16), were analysed using a set of traditional-skill keywords and a set of digital-skill keywords. The collection included all levels of employment ranging from editor, deputy editor, newsdesk, specialist reporter, reporter, online journalist and trainee reporter.

The traditional words were:

> deadline, pressure, contacts, driving licence, shorthand, print, copy, tight, writing, enthusiasm, self-starter, exclusive, energy, ideas, news sense and qualifications (NCE, NCTJ, NQJ).

The digital keywords were:

> digital, multi-media, platforms, website, social media, user generated content, breaking news, data, Twitter, Facebook, online, web skills, hits, unique user, visitor, likes, blog, code, video, podcast.

The aim of the study was to find whether traditional or digital skills were more highly valued by employers. It also aimed to find out which skills from both sets were most sought after and what kinds of jobs were being advertised.

After two years, with analysis of 188 advertisements, the results showed a much higher emphasis on digital over traditional skills. Editors were looking for people with a strong knowledge of social media and video skills. They wanted candidates who could break news online and write for the newspaper website.

Of the traditional skills required, editors still favoured qualifications like the NCTJ Diploma and National Qualification in Journalism (NQJ) and shorthand. However, the necessity of those skills appeared less in the second year of the study, when emphasis on digital keywords also increased.

Importantly, the job titles and places of work also displayed change over the study. In the first year the job titles barely strayed from traditional areas like specialist reporters, trainee reporters, editor and news editors – and only 5 of the 98 advertised roles were listed as being for online journalists. In the second year this changed dramatically, with 31 of the 90 advertised positions being for multimedia or online journalists. Positions for trainee reporters were the most advertised across both years of the study.

In the second year of the study newspapers were also seen to be advertising for reporters to work solely on online platforms linked to the printed titles.

There is an obvious imbalance between digital and traditional keyword language – indicating a desire for a newsroom driven by digital as much as the printed product, rather than a potentially different reality. This would back up the evidence found by Canter,[44] who found writing and digital skills to be of equal value to traditional skills by employing editors.

Of the digital keywords, many represent a skill or describe a knowledge required, rather than being a skill in their own right. The most popular keywords certainly suggest an environmental quality, with the words 'online', 'digital', 'social media' and 'website' making reference to the priorities and products of the employing newspaper. This contrasts with the traditional keyword list – where specific skills such as 'NCTJ', 'driving licence', 'qualification' and 'shorthand' all rate more highly than other, more generic or environmental qualities or subjects. This difference could be down to the fact that traditional journalism skills are easier to define. There are set qualifications which are either possessed or not possessed by a candidate, rather than criteria of more subjective 'desirabilities' as found in the digital list. It could also be down to the fact that while traditional skills have remained unchanged for years, digital skills are constantly evolving.[45,46]

Despite the results demonstrating a strong shift towards interest in digital abilities, the prevalence of traditional skills should not be overlooked. The NCTJ qualification came high up the list of skills mentioned in the advertisements, as did 'driving licence'.

The future

The technology, the ability to share and develop audience, is open to anyone but the knack of identifying a genuine audience which will gather around and stay loyal is another matter.

Facebook's success perhaps lies in founder Mark Zuckerberg's recognition that social networking itself is not an activity but a 'platform for various social activities expressed through different applications'.[47]

News organisations are adapting to the shifting balance of power. They know that rather than expecting the audience to find content, they have to find the audience and they have to be aware that the audience will come to their stories in a range of different ways and via a range of different devices.

This has led to a push towards the idea that journalists should only need to think about content and the best way to present it. That, as storytellers, journalists should use the vast array of tools at their disposal and be open to presenting on a range of platforms.[48]

In detailing his vision for a news organisation, *New York Times* editor Dean Baquet talked about the importance of video in storytelling and fewer stories being written just 'for the record', with reporters taking more responsibility for making sure their stories are read. 'Their editors, free from worrying about filling specific print pages, can say yes to a much wider range of story ideas that do not fit the old print architecture.'[49]

While news organisations have become increasingly open to experimenting and using an array of platforms, this does now quell the disquiet that publishing via platforms such as Facebook and Snapchat means the audience is consuming content away from publishers' own sites.

Dr Rasmus Kleis Nielsen, director of research at the Reuters Institute for the Study of Journalism, has outlined three ways news outlets approach relationships with platforms such as Facebook and Snapchat. The most common is 'coexistence', followed by confrontation and collaboration.[50]

Adam Singolda, who heads up content discovery platform Taboola, has sounded concerns about a collaborative environment which could see news outlets become so dependent on social platforms, Facebook in particular, that they lose all control over their brand identities, user experiences and reader relationships.[51]

What about start-up newsrooms?

The Pew Research Center found that in 2016, news start-ups and journalists tied to no news organisations were some of the most successful fundraisers using the Journalism category on Kickstarter. The amount raised is small – but significantly more people are now contributing to journalism projects, up from 792 in 2009 to 25,651 in 2015. According to report authors Nancy Vogt and Amy Mitchell, it 'represents a new niche segment of non-traditional journalism driven in large part by public interest and motivation. It is bringing voice and visibility to efforts that would likely otherwise go unnoticed or unfunded'.[52]

The news industry faces a dichotomy. Journalists can make a strong case for premium quality products but there is still a question mark over whether the industry can raise the necessary revenues to support the production and publication of such products in the right quantity and to serve diverse audiences. And even if news organisations do raise the revenue to support such a venture in the first instance, can it generate the sales and a big enough audience with enduring loyalty to justify keeping the product going in the long term?

Politico co-founder Jim VandeHei believes a content revolution – where platforms quickly replace one another – will pick up speed, but it promises a 'profitable future for companies that can lock down loyal audiences, especially those built around higher-quality content'.[53]

'From the rubble,' says VandeHei, 'will emerge a much better, more eclectic, more efficient way for all of us to watch, read and listen. It will be brimming with content we can be proud of – and happily pay for'.[54]

Further reading

Newman, N, Fletcher, R, Levy, D and Nielsen, R (2016) *Reuters Institute Digital News Report*. Oxford: Reuters Institute for the Study of Journalism. Available at digitalnewsreport.org

Notes

1 Shirky, C (2009) *Newspapers and Thinking the Unthinkable*. www.shirky.com
2 Rutenberg, J [2016] *For News Outlets Squeezed From the Middle, It's Bend or Bust*. New York Times.
3 Ibid.
4 Ibid.
5 Naughton, J (2016) *Here is the news – but only if Facebook thinks you need to know*. The Guardian.
6 Dawson, R (n.d.) *Newspaper Extinction Timeline*. RossDawson.com.
7 The Independent (2016) *The Independent becomes the first national newspaper to embrace a global, digital-only future*.
8 Chakelian, A (2016) *A new national daily newspaper without a website is launching today. Can it work?* New Statesman.
9 Sweney, M (2016) *The New Day newspaper to shut just two months after launch*. The Guardian.
10 Taylor, H (2014) *Newspaper circulation: How far it's fallen and how far it's got to fall*. themediabriefing.com.
11 Ponsford, D (2016) *National newspaper ABCs: i, Times and Telegraph titles all gain print sales after Independent closure*. Press Gazette.
12 Ponsford, D (2016) *National newspaper website ABCs: Sun fastest growing website in March*. Press Gazette.
13 Ponsford, D (2016) *NRS: Daily Mail most popular UK newspaper in print and online with 23m readers a month*. Press Gazette.
14 OFCOM (2015) *News Consumption in the UK – 2015 report*. OFCOM.
15 Sambrook, R and McGuire, S (2014) *Have 24-hour TV news channels had their day?* The Guardian.

16 Brock, G (2013) *Out of Print: Newspapers, Journalism and the Business of News in the Digital Age*. London: Kogan Page
17 Royal Television Society (2016) *The battle for news viewers*. Royal Television Society.
18 Jones, J and Salter, L (2012) *Digital Journalism*. London: Sage.
19 Doctor, K (2016) *Newsonomics: Facebook's Trending Topics and the growing power of the funnel filter*. NiemanLab.org
20 Meikle, G and Redden, G (2011) *News online: Transformations and continuities*. Basingstoke: Palgrave Macmillan.
21 Sweney, M (2016) *Silicon Valley's hoover leaves newspapers hunting for profit*. The Guardian.
22 Rao, P S and Chan, S (2016) *Alan Rusbridger, once Guardian's celebrated editor, severs ties with it*. New York Times.
23 Fitts, A S (2015) *The importance of 'social listening' tools*. Columbia Journalism Review.
24 Ciobanu, M (2015) *5 ways De Correspondent is building communities around its journalism*. Journalism.co.uk.
25 Bell, E (2016) *Emily Bell's 2015 Hugh Cudlipp lecture – full text*. The Guardian.
26 Sweney, M (2016) *Silicon Valley's hoover leaves newspapers hunting for profit*. The Guardian.
27 Davies, J (2016) *'Think monetization from day one': Facebook's tips for publishers using Instant Articles*. Digiday.com
28 Naughton, J (2016) *Here is the news – but only if Facebook thinks you need to know*. The Guardian.
29 Schlosberg, J (2016) *The mission of media in an age of monopoly*. Respublica.org.uk
30 Sweney, M (2016) *More than 9 million Britons now use adblockers*. The Guardian.
31 Wang, S (2015) *Anxiety is rising about the impact of ad blockers coming to iPhones and iPads with iOS next month*. NiemanLab.org
32 Sweney, M (2015) *Martin Sorrell on newspaper digital ad slowdown: 'Paywalls are the way to go'*. The Guardian.
33 Reynolds, J (2016) *Guardian chief exec: Aim is for membership fees to make up a third of revenue*. Press Gazette.
34 Davies, J (2016) *How The Times of London is driving digital subscriptions*. digiday.com.
35 Ponsford, D (2016) *While 'open' Guardian faces financial meltdown, paywalled Times is breaking even*. Press Gazette.
36 Sweney, M (2016) *News UK chief refuses to rule out scrapping Times paywall in future*. The Guardian.
37 Rutenberg, J (2016) *For news outlets squeezed from the middle, it's bend or bust*. New York Times.
38 Russial, J and Santana, A (2011) *Specialization still favoured in most newspaper jobs*. Newspaper Research Journal 32(91): 6–23.
39 Carpenter, S (2009) *An application of the theory of expertise: Teaching broad and skill knowledge areas to prepare journalists for change*. Journalism and Mass Communication Educator, 64.
40 Cleary, J and Cochie, M (2011) *Core skill set remains same in newspaper job ads*. Newspaper Research Journal 32(4): 68–82.
41 Gunter, J (2011) *Editors still prize traditional skills, finds NCE review*. Journalism.co.uk.
42 Nikunen, K (2014) *Losing my profession: Age, experience and expertise in the changing newsrooms*. Journalism 15(7): 868–888.
43 Canter, L (2015) *Chasing the accreditation dream: Do employers value accredited journalism courses?* jobs.ac.uk
44 Ibid.
45 Hogan, B and Quan-Haase, A (2010) *Persistence and change in social media*. Bulletin of Science, Technology and Society 30(5): 309–315.
46 Hodder, A (2012) *Change of pace*. benefitscanada.com.
47 Penenberg, Adam L (2009) *Viral loop: The power of pass-it-on*. London: Sceptre.
48 Nelson, L K (2016) *Building platform agnostic newsrooms and platform perfect content*. medium.com
49 Mullin, B (2016) *The New York Times of the future is beginning to take shape*. Poynter.org.

50 Ciobanu, M (2016) *Coexistence, confrontation or collaboration? Defining the relationship between publishers and platforms.* journalism.co.uk

51 Fiegerman, S (2016) *The new media startup pitch: Save journalism from Facebook's death grip.* mashable.com

52 Vogt, N and Mitchell, A (2016) *Crowdfunded journalism: A small but growing addition to publicly driven journalism.* journalism.org

53 VandeHei, J (2016) *Escaping the digital media 'crap trap'.* theinformation.com

54 Ibid.

2

THE BUSINESS OF JOURNALISM

With Andrew Youde

Publishing in the digital age may be easier than ever, but how can entrepreneurial journalists ensure they are building a business rather than maintaining a hobby? This chapter examines the many different strategies publishers are using in an attempt to achieve financial stability.

The way you view the business of journalism is likely to be coloured by where you fit into it. Technological disruption has been a bruising experience for legacy media, resulting in shrinking advertising income and hefty staff reductions, whereas for entrepreneurs and innovators it has provided an opportunity to get into the game. Newspaper bosses embraced the internet as a low-cost distribution method but failed to alter their business practices or produce content that served their digital audiences.[1]

For too long journalists have existed in ignorance of their company's financial position, a hangover of the Chinese wall between editorial and advertising.[2] A 2015 YouGov survey found UK adults are only willing to pay 92p a month to visit news websites, valuing news below search engines and email[3] – that is the reality publishers are wrestling with. It is why everyone, big or small, has to adapt to survive; entrepreneurial journalists are better placed than most to thrive.

Start-ups are lean, agile and inexpensive. If you can identify a successful revenue model you can grow. Media giants like the *New York Times* and the *Guardian* are under significantly more financial pressure to find an answer. While they generate healthy revenues they have huge costs to cover. In this chapter we will identify the financial planning you need to put in place and examine the different approaches publishers are adopting in a bid to develop sustainable, robust business models for journalism.

Writing a business plan

A business plan is an essential document to prepare for anyone who is considering forming their own start-up. The plan includes an overview of the business, the market in which it will operate, and crucially, how it will make money. A business plan is essential if you want to secure an investment or loan from a bank.

Example business plan templates can be found on the Prince's Trust website,[4] with further advice and guidance about how to develop one successfully. The plan should include business objectives, strategies, sales, marketing, and financial forecasts. They can help a start-up set its goals, identify costs and review over the short and medium term, measure its progress, and identify potential problems.

Costs and revenue implications for small business

Producing news costs money and there are a number of costs to consider as you embark on developing a start-up business. Chapter 5 suggests 'bootstrapping' your business, running it on limited finances, in the early days. However, you should be mindful of differing costs as your start-up grows and develops. Advertising revenue from your website is likely to be the main source of revenue in the early days but you should seek alternative income streams and be able to price them accordingly to meet those costs and generate profit. This section is a crash course in the financial side of the business, introducing notions of costing and revenue (or pricing), sourcing finance, business planning and taxation.

When looking at the aims and objectives of any small start-up, 'making a profit' should be on the list. In order to do this a business must ensure that it receives more in revenue than it spends in costs. Careful monitoring of both is needed. To help monitor costs, they are commonly split into:

- Fixed costs – These do not alter regardless of your level of output. They must be paid whether your start-up produces fifty stories a day or none at all. Examples of fixed costs are rent and insurance.
- Variable costs – These alter depending on your level of output. These costs are commonly the journalist's time to develop content but can also include travel or freelance support.

These costs are crucial to consider, as any work undertaken must cover all variable costs incurred, but also contribute to the fixed costs of the business. Over a period to time, usually a financial year, revenue must cover key fixed costs like rent and insurance. As your start-up expands you should be aware of the following potential fixed and variable costs:

- Premises costs – This could include rent or a mortgage to purchase a business property. There will be maintenance costs associated with this as well as connection of utilities including gas, electricity, telephone, wi-fi and water rates.

- Sales and marketing – This will include web hosting, the cost of designing your site, buying your web address and methods of promoting your content.
- Insurance – This could include professional indemnity insurance, car insurance, building and contents insurance and public liability insurance.
- Staffing – This could include paying for freelance support in areas where you lack expertise. Salaries of permanent employees, advertising and recruitment fees of staff, training, pensions and national insurance contributions also come under staffing, although these should be kept to a minimum initially.
- Finance – This means any form of loans, including interest repayments (see Sources of Finance section below).
- Professional fees – These may include the costs of accountants, solicitors, copyright protection or other expert professionals.
- General business costs – The total costs are hard to predict and are often more than anticipated. You may need to invest in office stationery, such as business cards to give to contacts. Other general costs can include office furniture, IT equipment (and repair costs), postage, travel/transport and coffee.

Controlling costs

There are several fixed expenses you should try to avoid at the outset. These include the cost of renting office space. One advantage a digital business has over a traditional one is that it doesn't need a physical office to get started. It may not be ideal to start a business from a spare bedroom but you should not squander this advantage easily.

Using remote-based software packages will also help you keep costs down. These store your content in the cloud, which means you can access it from anywhere you can get an internet connection. Whenever possible you want to avoid paying for expensive software packages that in many cases are available for free online. There are several software solutions that can help you run your business. These include the following:

- Microsoft Office Live and Google Docs perform similar functions. They allow you to word process, produce presentations and work on spreadsheets and store the documents online. Excel or Google Forms will help you track your finances receipts in a basic manner.
- Evernote and Trello help you organise your business workflow. They allow you to work collaboratively to pool your ideas, and offer the opportunity to structure them into topics. This is crucial when it comes to keeping on track with stories, marketing activity and scheduling.
- Dropbox allows you to collaborate with colleagues as you can share folders. This can be used by journalists as a virtual news basket.
- Skype allows you to conduct voice chat and video calls. The video calls can be used as content on your site, particularly if you edit them together with visuals of the topic.

These are just a few examples of the current office software available, but as technology evolves more tools will become available. The solutions you require will also change as your business grows. Larger newsrooms are increasingly uti-lising Slack, an initially free messaging tool that allows teams to communicate across a variety of topics. Matt Taylor, a production editor at *The Times*, believes it has removed the need for internal e-mails at the paper: "[It] helps alert every-one without the mess of mailing lists, and allows people to effectively catch up without having to be forwarded a long list, and then still remain included in the conversation."[5]

Calculating breakeven

Digital publishers' revenue typically comes from display advertising, measured in impressions, or through native advertising. Both involve fees being paid for cre-ating and displaying adverts that promote external companies. Careful pricing of advertising is essential; if your price is too high this will put customers off, and if priced too low, you may not cover your variable costs nor contribute at all to fixed costs.

Analysis of costs, in tandem with market research, which is covered in Chapter 5, is essential here, as you need to know how much potential customers will pay and how much other publishers charge for their services. By knowing your variable costs, primarily time, for an advert's production, and what your fixed costs are cur-rently running at, you can arrive at a 'breakeven' figure – where your price equals your costs. A percentage mark-up can be added to this figure to provide a price that will generate a healthy profit on the activity – this is known as cost-plus pricing. An alternative method of pricing is value-based pricing, which draws on the market research noted above and requires a detailed understanding of how much value cus-tomers attach to your services. Even with this pricing method, consideration needs to be given to the breakeven figure.

This all considers revenue-covering costs at an activity level, such as writing a piece of native content, but this should also be considered at the overall business level. If a publisher's business grows to include several areas, such as advertising, events, and training, then the business should consider these as individual cost-centres, and monitor the costs and revenues from each. It is often difficult to sep-arate the fixed costs between differing areas of a business, but analysis of differing cost-centres can help an entrepreneur to identify which areas are generating profits, and which may be operating at a loss. This can help you plan better for the future.

Sources of finance

Should you need to raise finance for your business, a range of sources could be available depending on the amount needed, required repayment time, and the purpose of the funds. This section outlines the range of options that you should be able to choose from.

Start-up funding is often split into the following three categories.[6]

- Seed funding – This is often a minimal amount of money that allows you to build a prototype. Seed money should be enough to get a basic news website launched.
- Early stage finance – Once your site builds up a sustained audience you could be eligible for early stage finance, which will be a larger sum of money. This will be easier to get if you have evidence of income from advertising or other sources.
- Growth finance – This is a significant investment in your business, which is often tied to achieving set goals or milestones. Achieving this level of funding will require clear evidence of your sustainability, and a detailed business plan for the future. Growth funding is targeted at helping you expand your start-up.

Other sources are commonly classified into internal sources, funds found within the business, and external funds outside the business. Further, sources are commonly labelled either short-term, to be paid back within a year, and long-term, where repayment can be over a number of years.

Internal sources of finance

- Retained profit – The use of existing profit built up within the business.
- Sale of assets – Selling personal assets, such as a computer, to fund other purchases.

Short-term external sources of finance

- Overdraft – A bank allows more money to be withdrawn from the account than is deposited.
- Trade credit – The time between the delivery of any supplies and payment.
- Personal credit card – If you go down this route identify a lender who will offer you a zero per cent interest credit card.
- Factoring – A journalist sells their invoices to a factor, a bank for example, who pay them straight away, at a cost, rather than waiting the normal 28 days for payment from customers.
- Leasing/hire purchase – Monthly payments are made for equipment, a printer for example.

Long-term external sources of finance

- Savings – The use of an individual's personal savings within the business.
- Loans – Typically from banks but can be from family and friends.
- Mortgage – For the purchase of property for the business, typically with repayments over a number of years.

- Grants – Often from government sources but also funding bodies that support journalistic projects or charities that assist business start-ups, commonly in areas of deprivation.
- Crowdfunding – Raising funds from many different backers, commonly through web platforms. This is outlined later in the chapter.

The legal structure of a business

You must select the most appropriate legal structure for your business. This decision will have implications regarding registering your business, taxation, how you can take profit from the business, and your responsibilities should it make a loss. The most common legal structure for start-up journalists is to become self-employed. The UK government advise[7] that you are classified as self-employed (a 'sole trader') if you:

- Run your business for yourself and take responsibility for its success or failure.
- Have several customers at the same time.
- Can decide how, where and when you do your work.
- Can hire other people at your own expense to help you or to do the work for you.
- Provide the main items of equipment to do your work.
- Are responsible for finishing any unsatisfactory work in your own time.
- Charge an agreed fixed price for your work.
- Sell goods or services to make a profit (including through websites).

This list encapsulates the business practices of most journalistic start-ups.

If two or more people combine to launch the business then it becomes a business partnership. Each partner shares the responsibility for the business and profits are distributed between partners. Income tax is paid on each partner's share of the profits and each is responsible for their share of any losses the business makes.

If the business grows and the financial responsibilities become too great for someone self-employed or in a partnership, then a private limited company can be formed. Here, the business is responsible for everything it does and the finances are separate from the director's own personal finances. Directors are responsible for running of the company but shareholders own it. A company limited by shares must have at least one shareholder; that person can also be a director. Any profits, after corporation tax has been paid, belong in the company.

Forming a private limited company puts extra demands on the business, which need to be considered in relation to the benefits of operating as a sole trader or as a partnership. If the business has relatively small liabilities, such as the low cost base of a 'bootstrapping' start-up, then structuring as a sole trader or partnership reduces the administration burden on the owners. Once the financial liabilities grow beyond what would be comfortable to be covered by the owners, then an analysis of the costs and benefits of forming a private limited company is needed. The administrative steps include:

- Registering the business with Companies House (incorporation).
- Formal agreement of all initial shareholders (memorandum of association).
- Details of company shares and the rights attached to them (statement of capital).
- Confirmed rules about how the company is run (articles of association).

The company will also have to register to pay corporation tax and file their accounts with Companies House.

As a result of these actions private limited companies are more expensive to set up than sole traders and partnerships, with owners having less personal control due to the compliance issues outlined in the above-mentioned documents. However, the company's finances are separate from those of the owners; there is protection from personal liability for the owners; lower taxes may be payable due to the differing rates of income and corporation tax; and there may be added credibility for a business, which can help with marketing or accessing finance.

Taxation

Should your business start to make profits then taxes will have to be paid. Even if a start-up business makes losses for a year or two, tax returns have to be submitted. This is important to know, as losses incurred can offset the tax paid on future profits. The legal structure of the business has implications for taxation, but for the purposes of this chapter the advice is focused on sole traders, the most common structure for a start-up.

If you have any concerns about taxes when running a business, visit the HM Revenue and Customs' (HMRC) comprehensive website for advice and guidance. They also provide a phone line to offer sole traders specific help and advice. The government advise[8] that to become a sole trader, you'll need to:

- Register as self-employed with HMRC to make sure you pay the correct income tax and national insurance.
- Keep records of your business incomes and outgoings.
- Pay your tax each year, usually in two payments, on 31 January and 31 July. You can use HMRC's calculator to help you budget for this.

We have already identified a variety of fixed and variable costs associated with running a business, and accurate records of these are important for tax purposes. All costs associated with the business can be offset against revenue to minimise the income tax payable. There are a variety of small business software packages to help keep accurate records of income and outgoings, and help to monitor the financial status of the business and prepare tax returns. Accurate records of income and expenditure must be kept, as HMRC can ask to see them.

To submit tax returns you must register with HMRC's online self-assessment, even if you prefer to submit paper returns. However, the online system is convenient and easy to complete, with extensive help features to guide your through the process.

Value added tax (VAT)

When registering yourself as self-employed you should also register the business for VAT purposes.[9] VAT is charged on business sales such as selling services and selling business assets. Businesses must charge VAT on their services but can reclaim any VAT paid on business-related goods or services – again, this necessitates accurate record keeping.

National insurance

All those in work pay national insurance contributions to qualify for certain benefits, including the state pension.[10] When self-employed, this is paid when making a profit of £5,965 or more a year.

Sources of income: advertising

Advertising has traditionally been a crucial income stream for news organisations. Prior to the internet, publishers and broadcasters were one of the few methods of reaching an audience, and so legacy media had a strong appeal for advertisers. But the new technologies have impacted on that in two ways: first, fewer people buy newspapers and watch television in a linear fashion, and second, cheaper alternative places to advertise have appeared online. The subsequent collapse of print advertising spend has been particularly hard for the newspaper industry as Facebook and Google have come to dominate the UK digital advertising market.

Despite this recalibration of the relationship between advertisers and news organisations, carrying display adverts on your site is still likely to be a key source of income – at least initially. Advertising networks, which act as middlemen between publishers and advertisers, are responsible for most online advertising. They take a percentage of the income for their role in the process. Google Adsense is the leading ad network and provides a quick and easy way to allow you to start the process of monetising your website. You can also use Adsense to generate income from your YouTube videos.

However, selling your advertising space directly to companies rather than relying on an ad network should generate higher returns. If you go down this route you should use an ad-serving platform to help you set up and track advertising on your site. Double Click for Publishers – Small Business, which is part of Google, and OpenX are two free platforms that you can use.[11] Comparing the cost of advertising with those of your competitors will allow you to set competitive ad rates.

Key terms

This is a brief glossary of advertising terms to help you get started. A full list is available on the website of the Internet Advertising Bureau UK.[12] Remember that advertisers will expect you to provide a detailed monthly breakdown of how their ads have performed on your site.

Above the fold   Derived from print media, the content immediately visible to a visitor without scrolling.

Ad creative   The format, design and content of a particular advert. Used in display advertising.

Classified advertising   Classifieds are traditionally short written ads, which are grouped under the service or product they are advertising.

Click-through rate (CTR)   The percentage of visitors who clicked on an ad; the CTR is used to determine an ad's success.

Impressions   The number of times a particular page has been seen. Advertising is usually sold based on the estimated cost of a thousand impressions; the advert being viewed a thousand times. This is referred to as the **Cost per mille** (CPM).

Ad blockers

Ad blockers allow visitors to view your website without seeing advertising. The reason many users download them is to speed up browsing and stop advertising eating into their data limits. A YouGov survey found almost 40 per cent of UK users have installed ad blocking on a digital device.[13] This rise in use has become a huge concern for news organisations in recent years, with fears expressed for the viability of digital publishing if large sections of the audience aren't seeing adverts.

After Apple launched iOS 9, which allows ad-blocking technology, ad blockers were quickly top of the iOS App store.[14] UK mobile carrier Three has gone a step further, announcing plans to roll out ad blocking for all users on its network.[15] Publishers are beginning to fight back against the ad blocking though. *Forbes*, the *Washington Post*, *City AM* and *Bild* in Germany are among the news organisations that have banned visitors who have ad blockers enabled.[16] The result of this battle between publishers and their audiences will have a big impact on the future viability of free access to news.

Native advertising

One tactic for avoiding ad blockers is to produce native advertising. This is advertising for a product which is produced in the format of your regular content. It is the digital equivalent of an advertorial. Although native advertising should be distinguished from regular content, by making clear it is paid for, the concept relies on maintaining the same house style and design. Buzzfeed has been a trailblazer of

Christian Payne is a specialist in creative technology, using tools for digital storytelling. He runs his own website, blogging as Documentally.

[In the future] I would really hope journalists are not only left to do good work through platforms and apps, but that we would be put into a position where we could self-host; so we're not just dropping stuff into the corporate channels for their personal money-making needs.

I also hope there is a lot more imagination around how revenue is created. There are a few developments happening now

FIGURE 2.1 Christian Payne

and advertising is just not cutting it anymore. We need to come up with new ways of funding what journalists are doing. Hopefully technological development will happen in those funding arenas.

native advertising, making it a crucial aspect of its business model. Its advertising team collaborates closely with sponsors to work out an approach that will resonate with Buzzfeed's audience. Four adverts were made for Purina before 'Dear Kitten', a viral smash that has been watched more than 26 million times on YouTube alone, was produced.[17]

Many leading publishers have adopted the native advertising model, including the *New York Times*. They produced a powerful investigation into female prisoners to promote the launch of the second season of Netflix's hit show *Orange Is the New Black*.[18] But research suggests UK audiences' opinion of news organisations would be damaged if native advertising spread to hard news topics.[19] Additionally, the UK's Advertising Standards Authority has issued guidance on product placement and advertorials to video bloggers following concerns that YouTube stars were being encouraged to keep their relationships with brands hidden from fans.[20]

Sponsored content

Sponsored content differs from native advertising because it is a conventional news story but with a named sponsor. This approach has appealed to legacy publishers in the UK with *MailOnline*'s Rugby World Cup stories and the *Guardian*'s Ashes cricket content being sponsored. This approach yields less financial return than native advertising but it avoids readers potentially confusing ads for news.

Pre-roll ads

If you plan on producing a considerable amount of video content on your site you should consider introducing your own pre-roll ads. These are the advertisements that play ahead of video footage on video sharing websites like YouTube. They are likely to gain popularity in future due to the expected increase in audiences viewing video online.[21] You can edit them onto the start of your footage before uploading it. Likewise, if you produce a considerable amount of audio you should consider introducing audio adverts; these appear in the *Guardian*'s popular 'Football Weekly' podcast.

All these various forms of advertising will generate substantially different rates of income, depending on the success of your site. You need to identify the advertising format most suited to your needs.

Case study: El Español

El Español was launched as a digital news website by Pedro J. Ramirez, one of Spain's most prominent journalists, in 2015. It followed Mr Ramirez being ousted as editor of *El Mundo*, Spain's second biggest newspaper.[22] Before the launch a staggering €3.6 million was raised to fund the project from more than 5,600 small shareholders, who invested between €100 – the price of one share – and €10,000 in the project. Mr Ramirez had already himself invested €5 million in El Español.[23] The site had 10,000 subscribers before a story had even been posted, while non-subscribers can read twenty-five free articles a month.

Clearly Mr Ramirez's fame was a crucial factor in El Español's crowdfunding venture, but its success demonstrates that if you can cultivate a community that is committed to a project then small donations can be a viable source of income. Social platforms were utilised to drive fundraising, with advertising on YouTube, Twitter and Facebook focused on followers of *El Mundo* and Mr Ramirez personally and delivering a call to action. Those who showed interest but did not invest were re-targeted in a second phase, and Mr Ramirez thanked each investor on Twitter.[24] It all contributed to creating a sense of a social movement, rather than launching a media organisation.

Crowdfunding

El Español is far from a unique example of audiences reaching into their wallets to fund valued journalism. Crowdfunding is proving popular in continental Europe with several start-ups receiving audience backing. Dutch start-up De Correspondent raised $1.7 million after engaging contributors with an alternative vision of funding high-value journalism. Krautreporter, based in Germany, raised $1.38 million to start an ad-free online magazine. Both sold their supporters the vision of joining a community, attending exclusive events and being part of a more inclusive reader–audience relationship.[25]

Their success inspired Direkt36, a Hungarian investigative news site, and The Blank Spot, a Swedish start-up that aimed to cover previously untold stories, to look to successfully appeal to audiences for funding.[26] Crowdfunding is also worth considering in a crisis; when AOL announced it was closing Massively, its gaming site, 1,300 readers stepped in to raise $62,000 in a fortnight to keep it going. $50,000 was raised within 48 hours of staff launching a Kickstarter campaign.[27]

Kickstarter is the best known of several well-established crowdfunding websites available. However Europe's start-ups have tended to build their own platforms, with De Correspondent using it as an opportunity to emphasise the number of contributors involved, rather than foregrounding the money raised. Before seeking crowdfunding you need to carefully consider whether you are aiming for philanthropic donations, are offering contributors equity or a shareholding in the company, or alternatively want to provide perks. You also need to be clear about whether you will keep all donations or return them if you fail to reach a specified target.

Membership

Asking your audience to become a member of your news platform could be viewed as a continual state of crowdfunding. But encouraging your readers to regularly part with money is more of a challenging task than a one-off. To be successful you will need to demonstrate your work to members on a continual basis, offer benefits of membership and help your readers feel part of a sustained movement or community. Legacy publishers in Britain are increasingly encouraging their readers to invest in their business models; the *Guardian* even has levels of membership on offer that tie in with events it organises.[28]

But membership is even more crucial for start-ups who can underpin the concept with a personalised touch. South Leeds Live, a hyperlocal publisher, asked its readers to become £1-a-week supporters with the incentive of having a print edition delivered to their home and their name displayed on its website. Crucially, they told readers it would allow them to keep serving 'your' local community, thus providing their audience with the biggest possible incentive to give.[29] It's also worth considering creative approaches, such as selling merchandise as per the *Telegraph* and the *Guardian*, to get your audience involved in your business model. Cultural start-up The Malcontent encouraged its readers to demonstrate their support by buying t-shirts.

A technology site, The Information, offered its annual subscribers access to 'people only the most well-known execs typically meet' during a visit to China. Subscribers had to pay their own way on the trip but would 'meet the right people'.[30] This demonstrates how your contacts can potentially drive membership, and therefore income, in a highly specialist field.

Events

Your ability to develop a substantial community of readers that regularly engages with your platform will be crucial to your initial survival. However, once your project has reached this level of maturity you can consider trying to physically draw this audience together for sponsored events. Although these can be demanding to put together, if you have the influence to attract speakers whom audiences want to listen to, events can bring a double benefit: opening up an additional revenue stream and raising the profile of your site.[31]

Wired magazine planned six events across 2016 in the UK alone, covering specialist topics as diverse as health, money, security and retail, promising attendees paying hundreds of pounds a ticket an insight into tomorrow's trends.[32] Although you are unlikely to start at such an advance level, this demonstrates how respected brands are able to exploit their name. There is currently more than one comic convention a week in Britain, which demonstrates that getting enthusiasts together to celebrate a shared passion can really spark audience interest.

You can tap into larger events too. The *Blizzard*, a quarterly football magazine, hosted an event during the first Manchester football writing festival, which ran for ten days in 2015. Hyperlocals like *Scarborough UK* and *AltReading* have placed themselves at the heart of their communities by running annual awards, which if turned into physical ceremonies could become sources of income. If you have a developed, engaged audience base then events can be an excellent way of moving your start-up to the next level in terms of both finance and exposure.

Non-profit journalism

Choosing to run a journalistic project as a non-profit may seem like an attractive option. Nevertheless, it doesn't remove the over-riding business concern of a start-up: you need to make enough money to survive. Turning a profit is likely to be a long way down the track anyway. Non-profits are normally established to serve a perceived public-interest need; to be successful they need to be underpinned by an even stronger sense of mission than commercial start-ups. This is because not only do you and your staff have to buy into your vision but funding bodies and donors do too.

ProPublica, a US non-profit, was established to produce journalism that 'shines a light on exploitation of the strong and the failures of those with power to vindicate the trust placed in them'.[33] It is a clear mission statement and ProPublica has won three Pulitzer prizes for its journalism in the last decade. Similarly, the Bureau of Investigative Journalism (BIJ), based in London, focuses on investigative journalism. If often collaborates with bigger news organisations to 'help educate the public about the realities of power in today's world'.[34] Both organisations rely on philanthropic donations and winning grant funding to support their work.

Surviving as a non-profit requires you to become as adept at writing grant applications as you are at producing powerful journalism. Working with a university can be helpful in this regard (see Chapter 5), as they regularly submit funding bids for research. Many universities also actively support the creation of social enterprises, particularly by students or recent graduates. In the UK you can also get support from UnLtd, Social Enterprise UK and Inspire2Enterprise, who help cultivate social enterprise. But be aware: social enterprises are not necessarily non-profit.

Gaining charitable status is extremely valuable, as it allows you to claim back the tax on income received. However the BIJ, which is based at City University, London, has twice been turned down for charity status, with the Charity Commission ruling that investigative journalism is not a 'charitable purpose'.[35] For this kind of reason, UK non-profits are increasingly becoming community interest companies (CICs) – these don't attract charitable status but legislation requires that their assets and profits prioritise the benefit of the community.[36] Non-profits can partner with educational institutions to utilise their charity status and, it's important to note, pursue other forms of additional income, like advertising or training, to fund their journalism.[37]

Case study: Blendle

Unless you possess the ability to produce content that is financially valuable to your audience, it is unlikely a hard paywall – such as those discussed in Chapter 1, operated by *The Times* and previously by the *Sun* – will work at the outset. But Blendle, a Dutch company, has developed a mechanism for getting audiences to pay for digital news in the same manner they pay for digital music – through micropayments. The premise of Blendle is similar to iTunes: the firm has created a platform where audiences can purchase individual pieces of journalism they are interested in from their digital wallet. They only pay for the journalism they read, with Blendle taking its cut, and getting a refund for poor reporting is easy.[38]

Blendle, which initially expanded into Germany before tackling the US market, has proved particularly attractive to the millennial audience. So far the best supported articles have been background pieces, analysis, long interviews and opinion; audiences have shown a desire to discover the 'why' aspect of news, rather than the 'what'.[39] Publishers can decide what price to put on their articles, with prices typically ranging from 10 cents to 80 cents depending on length.

The success of Blendle, which has received financial backing from the *New York Times* and from publisher Axel Springer, has become increasingly import to an industry that fears ad blocking. The next challenge facing the platform is replicating its initial success in continental Europe in the English-speaking news market.

Micropayments

Away from Blendle, alternative micropayment methods which may be more immediately useful to small newsrooms are springing up. Laterpay is a payment tool that offers you the chance to put your most valuable content behind a payment wall. Publishers set the price of accessing an article and readers get prompted to pay when their bill reaches €5. Newsrooms can vary prices from 5 cents upwards, operate the system through a Wordpress plugin, and charge for almost every type of content. Laterpay takes a 15 per cent fee for its services.[40]

There is optimism that micropayments can provide a vital source of income. The *Winnipeg Free Press* in Canada, which introduced a flat micropayments model for its website in 2015, generated $100,000 in revenue in its first year. Visitors, who are charged 27 cents an article, are spending on average $2 a month on the publisher's site. Among its readership, 4,300 have bought at least one article.[41]

Working in partnership with legacy media – case study: The City Talking

The City Talking started as a Facebook group in 2009 before becoming a website and then a free monthly newspaper that began publishing in Leeds four years later.[42] It has since launched similar city-specific editions in Sheffield, Manchester, York and Liverpool, with further plans to start-up in Taipei and London. The aim of the brand is to tell stories about those cities. Video projects are featured on The City Talking website.

Hebe Media, who publish The City Talking, have been successful in growing the brand by collaborating with legacy media organisations. In 2014 their newspaper starting being distributed with copies of the *Yorkshire Evening Post*, Leeds' historic daily newspaper, and The City Talking was named as one of fifty radical thinking individuals and organisations changing Britain for the better.[43] They have since produced feature documentaries on the Leeds music scene – in collaboration with the BBC – and Tech in Leeds, partnering with several organisations.[44]

Training

Digital skills are increasingly in demand across the economy, and as an online journalist you are well positioned to offer business training. It can help subsidise the journalism you are producing. The Next Web, which reports on developments in tech, offers a variety of online courses to visitors through TNW Deals, its sales portal.[45] The cost of running a physical training session should be worked out on a cost-plus pricing basis, taking into account the trainer's time and the hire of both the training space and any necessary equipment.

In order to be a successful trainer you need to give serious thought to the training cycle, which is likely to consider the following stages:

- Determining the training requirements.
- Designing the training approach.
- Developing the training materials.
- Conducting the training.
- Evaluating and updating the training.[46]

While the reason for training is invariably to improve performance, it is important that you determine what is needed from the training you have been asked to design and deliver. Is the need something that applies to the whole organisation, a particular group of employees or is it aimed at individual requirements? When designing your training make sure you devise learning objectives. What do you want people to be able to do by the end of the session?

You need to schedule the topics to be covered and develop an appropriate session plan. Give real thought to the activities you design and the materials you develop. You need to ensure you manage your presence when training. You need to think about your appearance, voice, pace and eye contact while delivering, as this can aid the way in which you convey your presence. Design your training area in a manner that best suits your participants – think about room layout – and talk to them and the organisation you were employed by at the end to evaluate the training. This will allow you to make necessary changes for the future.[47]

The hunt for a 'silver bullet' business model

Realistically, there is no quick-fix business model for journalism. There are pros and cons to every potential solution. The way publishers earn their money is becoming as diverse and fragmented as the types of content they are seeking to produce. Therefore your best route to sustainability is to develop a variety of income streams and monitor their success. It is only through this process that you will identify what works best for your start-up.

At the outset this mix is likely to include advertising, which still remains a vital source of income for publishers. Most of the audience would still rather put up with adverts than pay for the content they consume.[48] However, publishers, big and small, are finding the current advertising climate extremely difficult. The widespread adoption of ad blockers could kill off display advertising within the next few years. As a small publisher your best tactic is to offer your advertisers a service tailored closely to their needs and to regularly demonstrate the impact of their ad spend.

You will need to be creative about how you raise money, but there are benefits to this. Holding events, selling merchandise and encouraging crowdfunding offer opportunities to form a much deeper bond between individuals and the media they engage with than was ever possible when audiences passively got a daily newspaper delivered. It is more than just finance; it allows loyal readers to be a much bigger part of the process.

In summary, it is crucial to separate the collapse of mass media business models from journalism. Journalism is doing better than ever; now we just need to find a new way of paying for it.

Further reading

Briggs, M (2012) *Entrepreneurial journalism*. London: Sage.
Lessons from the local news lab – Part one. medium.com

Through the cracks: Crowdfunding in journalism. throughcracks.com
Starting your own business. gov.uk

Notes

1 Briggs, M (2012) *Entrepreneurial journalism.* London: Sage.
2 Williamson, D (2015) *Why journalists should care more about business models.* mediabriefing.com
3 Jackson, J (2015) *UK adults 'willing to pay only 92p a month to access news websites'.* The Guardian.
4 Prince's Trust (2016) *Business plans.* princes-trust.org.uk
5 Hazard Owen, L (2015) *How 7 news organisations are using Slack to work better and differently.* Nieman Journalism Lab.
6 Clawson, T (2014) *The funding escalator: How to raise finance and keep control.* Startups.co.uk
7 Gov.uk. *Working for yourself.*
8 Gov.uk. *Set up as a sole trader.*
9 Gov.uk. *Businesses and charging VAT.*
10 Gov.uk. *National Insurance.*
11 Briggs, *Entrepreneurial journalism.*
12 Internet Advertising Bureau (2016) *Jargon buster.* iabuk.net
13 Austin, S and Newman, N (2015) *Attitudes to sponsored and branded content (native advertising) – Digital News Report 2015.* Oxford: Reuters Institute.
14 Perez, S (2015) *A day after iOS 9's launch, Ad blocker top the App store.* TechCrunch.
15 Three (2016) *Three group plans to tackle excessive and irrelevant mobile ads.* threemediacentre.co.uk
16 Davies, J (2015) *Incisive Media becomes second UK publisher to ban ad blocker users.* Digiday.
17 Robischon, N (2016) *How Buzzfeed's Jonah Peretti is building a 100-year media company.* Fast Company.
18 Deziel, M (2014) *Women inmates: Why the male model doesn't work.* New York Times.
19 Austin and Newman, *Attitudes to sponsored and branded content.*
20 Sweney, M (2015) *New UK blogger guidance issued in wake of Kim Kardashian's banned selfie.* The Guardian.
21 Ericsson ConsumerLab (2015) *10 hot consumer trends for 2016.*
22 The Local/AFP (2015) *Rebel editor launches crowdfunded digital newspaper El Español.* thelocal.es
23 Wang, S (2015) *Spanish start-up El Español carves out a new digital space while competing with legacy media.* The Nieman Lab.
24 Nurra, M (2015) *Record crowdfunding for journalism supported by readers: the challenge of El Español.* journalismfestival.com
25 Johnson, K (2015) *What the most successful crowdfunding campaigns for journalism have in common.* throughcracks.com
26 Johnson, K (2015) *Krautreporter: Crowdfunding journalism is a movement and it's happening now.* throughcracks.com
27 Johnson, K (2015) *$50k in less than 48 hours to resurrect gaming website.* throughcracks.com
28 The Guardian (2016) *Become a Guardian member.* The Guardian.
29 Morton, J (2016) *Will you become a pound-a-week supporter?* South Leeds Life.
30 Lessin, J (2016) *Come to China with The Information.* The Information.
31 Briggs, *Entrepreneurial journalism.*
32 Wired (2016) *Wired events* Eventbrite
33 ProPublica (2016) *About us.* propublica.org
34 Bureau of Investigative Journalism (2016) *About the Bureau.* thebureauinvestigates.com
35 Ainsworth, D (2012) *Bureau of Investigative Journalism denied charitable status for second time.* thirdsector.co.uk

36 CIC Association (2016) *What is a CIC?* cicassociation.org.uk
37 Briggs, *Entrepreneurial journalism*.
38 Spence, A and Pompeo, J (2016) *The Dutch tech whiz who could save journalism*. Politico. eu
39 Klöpping, A (2015) *Blendle: A radical experiment with micropayments in journalism, 365 days later*. medium.com
40 Laterpay (2016) *I'm a content provider*. laterpay.net
41 Lichterman, J (2016) *The Winnipeg Free Press' bet on micropayments will generate about $100,000 in revenue this year*. Nieman Lab.
42 The City Talking (2016) *The City Talking: Leeds, Sheffield and Manchester*. thecitytalking. com
43 Nesta (2014) *Stop the press: A local newspaper that young people actually read*. nesta.org.uk
44 Hicken, L (2016) *The City Talking: Tech in Leeds*. thecitytalking.com
45 The Next Web (2016) *Online courses*. deals.thenextweb.com
46 Truelove, S (2006) *Training in practice*. London: Chartered Institute of Personnel and Development.
47 Ibid.
48 Whitman, R (2016) *People hate your ads but 85% would rather watch your ads than pay for content*. mediapost.com

3

INNOVATION

Standing out from the crowd: How innovative practice can help you rise above 'the noise' of the internet.

The internet has transformed our ability to tell stories. This is a positive – challenging the status quo should come naturally to any journalist. The desire to change the world around us is often a reason for joining the profession in the first place.

But far too often the way we tell stories online still revolves around what is the easiest format for us as journalists, rather than what suits our audience. We don't utilise the internet enough; too many newsrooms have transplanted journalism 1.0 onto a 2.0 platform.

Therefore when audiences see a new way of reporting it grabs their attention, it is different. This replicates entrepreneurship, as the best way to distinguish yourself in any market is to run away from established convention rather than towards it. If anyone can start a blog and write a story you should be looking for the opportunity to tell your stories in new, imaginative and creative ways in order to stand out. Positioning yourself as a distinctly different, innovative news organisation allows you to potentially nullify many of the advantages your larger competitors hold over you at the outset.

As journalist Michael Gladwell explains:

> When underdogs choose not to play by Goliath's rules they win ... even when everything we think we know about power says they shouldn't ... they will do what is 'socially horrifying' – they will challenge the conventions about how battles are supposed to be fought.[1]

This chapter will investigate the transformation that is happening in the industry in three distinct areas. The first is examining how digital-first news organisations, such as Buzzfeed and the Huffington Post, have challenged the traditional publisher–audience relationship. They engage readers in different ways and have become a platform for audience self-expression.

Then we will touch upon the new formats newsrooms are developing to provide audiences with a new perspective on their stories, such as games, data journalism and visualisations, before examining some of the big areas of potential innovation for the future.

A culture of experimentation

The need to adopt new approaches as a journalist has never been more pressing. Different formats and tools are being developed on a weekly basis to tell stories, each one offering the opportunity to deliver more value to the audience than had previously been imagined.

But for any form of innovation to be successful there has to be a degree of experimentation. Traditionally this has been frowned upon in journalistic circles. There is an inbuilt desire for the finished product to always be perfect. But having the courage to experiment, and dealing with the occasional failure that this brings, is necessary to create new reporting formats. Failing to adapt to changing times is simply not an option.

In 2000, video rental giant Blockbuster had the opportunity to buy the fledgling DVD-by-mail rental chain Netflix for $50 million. It turned this down, but customers decided they preferred receiving their films at home rather than driving to choose them, and fifteen years later Netflix was worth more than $30 billion while Blockbuster had been bankrupt.[2] The bosses at Blockbuster had failed to realise the sand was shifting beneath their feet.

Digital-savvy journalists are keen to avoid being caught out in a similar fashion. As visual storyteller Mariana Santos points out: 'Digital media changes at the speed of light [and] we need to be bold and not fear failure as that's part of the learning … we need to experiment and dare to do things in a way that hasn't been done before'.[3]

Publicly testing out new forms of content may be new to journalists but it isn't new to those who work in the technology sector. Testing better versions of software is a recognised stage of development, and as an entrepreneurial journalist straying into the world of tech you need to prepare yourself for the continuous learning curve of refining your content.

Case study: How Buzzfeed creates viral content

The growth of Buzzfeed from an outsider to a media giant is testament to the ability of its staff to understand the internet and turn that knowledge into a growth strategy. As Lefrance and Mayer observe, Buzzfeed is a 'rare example of a news organisation that changes the way the news industry works'.[4]

Although the site has a clear focus on a young, digital-savvy audience it aims to serve specific groups outside this demographic. They will be writing for 90s kids, nurses, short women and expectant fathers one day – with headlines that clearly identify those groups – and completely different people the next.

These 'identity posts' aim to trigger an aspect of the reader's background. This content could relate to the 'reader's hometown, generation, school, ethnic or religious origin, favourite band, TV show and so on'.[5] It is the opposite of the traditional mass market model. Buzzfeed is innovating by writing posts for individuals and estimating that there are enough of those individuals out there to find an audience.

With hundreds of new posts being written each day, ultimately it won't take too long before Buzzfeed is writing a story that is relatable to some aspect of your life. When you read it they hope it will spark an emotive response and you will first share the article on social media with friends, who will probably have a similar reaction, and then return regularly to the site to find more stories. The stories we choose to share with our friends and family help us define ourselves to them.[6]

As Jonah Peretti, the CEO of Buzzfeed, says: 'When people are sharing a BuzzFeed list or quiz, they're doing it partly for the content and partly to connect with someone else in their life.'[7]

Transforming your approach to audience

Some stories are so powerful they instantly capture the public's attention. The shocking picture of the body of Syrian toddler Aylan Kurdi washed up on the Turkish coastline in September 2015 put public pressure on Europe's political leaders to address a refugee crisis the continent was struggling to cope with.

More than 500,000 tweets about the picture were recorded within hours of the image becoming public. Campaigners gathered 240,000 signatures in less than a day, demanding that the UK government accept more refugees, which led to an almost immediate change in policy.[8]

Journalism can provide a unifying force, prompting those water cooler moments where people struggle to contain their desire to discuss the day's events and gauge the reaction of others. This passion for a topic requires people to feel attached to the hot button issues, which have driven debates on radio phone-ins and television opinion shows for many years.

All newsrooms want their stories to reach out as far as possible, and techniques are being utilised by reporters to encourage readers to engage with more of their content online. It is all aimed at going viral – the Holy Grail when it comes to digital storytelling.

As Penenberg says, virality 'takes advantage of our very human need to connect with one another … we are hard wired to socialise'.[9] Put simply, if readers view something that has an impact on them they are more likely to tell others about it. In 2012, Berger and Milkman[10] undertook a study to determine which *New York Times* articles got the widest audience. They found that the stories with the highest level of 'transmission' – that were shared the most online – were those that created an emotive response.

Stories that made people angry and anxious sparked high levels of sharing; likewise those which readers found practically valuable, interesting and awe inspiring. However, stories that made people sad didn't prompt vast sharing.

For stories to receive an emotive response they have to interact with the reader's identity.[11] This could be in a literal sense by taking place in their hometown or involving their favourite hobby, sports team or celebrity. Many football fans will happily spend hours discussing their team's form on social media or fan forums, which have become 'virtual terraces'.

Or it could be by reacting to their personal ideology – their sense of right or wrong – or by triggering personal memories. Buzzfeed identifies what its audience wants by analysing the data on what they previously shared. It helps it forecast what will work in the future.

Peretti explains:

> If they are sharing it a lot, why is that? Maybe they are sharing it because there are corgis in it, maybe it's because it's tied to a holiday like Fathers' Day … so you test that and make another piece of content that is about corgis but isn't about Fathers' Day.[12]

If a post is a hit with their audience they can then repackage it across a range of platforms. A series about the problems of being a short girl began with an article that was viewed more than 8 million times; it then became a scripted YouTube video, and subsequently inspired a cartoon on Facebook.[13] That initial success was fully exploited.

Community posts: utilising the enthusiasm of readers

Buzzfeed and the Huffington Post, founded a year earlier in 2005, are now aiming to consolidate their position as digital news giants. A key innovation in achieving this is by encouraging their audience to express themselves by contributing their content to the site, often for free.

Writers can apply to be part of the Buzzfeed community by signing up for an account, making a post for the site and suggesting their idea to Buzzfeed's community editors. Instructional posts advise contributors on creating content that fits the Buzzfeed model and committed writers are motivated by two sets of rankings – one, being among the top community posts, and two, looking at total views of their posts. Similarly, the Huffington Post encourages writers to pitch ideas to them and those posts are published in the Huffington Post's house style.

On both sites the posts supplement the content produced by paid staff writers. Jason Linkins, political reporter at the Huffington Post, believes the newsroom provides 'an architecture that enables thousands of other people to have a space to come and write and play and inform and start conversations. Those people are the Huffington Post bloggers – who flock to the site for a chance of being heard.'[14]

The real winners in this structure are the hosts. Buzzfeed and the Huffington Post share many of Penenberg's characteristics[15] of thriving viral internet companies such as Facebook, Google and eBay – they are web-based, often free and have built-in viral growth, as users provide some of the content. News websites often struggle because unlike Facebook, Google and eBay, they usually pay journalists to create the content their audience uses.

If contributors begin sharing the burden of writing stories for the website, it allows the news organisations at the centre to grow quicker, as it can provide more content to its audience. There will be hiccups, and contributions will need overseeing, but it is easier for newsrooms than having to produce it all themselves.

Buzzfeed's community, which has more than 500,000 members and produces more than 100 posts a day, has been carefully developed. As Bassan says, 'the way Buzzfeed … cuddles its members is attention worthy. Buzzfeed deems the community not just as a traffic source, but as a powerful asset of its website.'[16]

The benefits for those members are clear to see – they are effectively borrowing the platform of an established news organisation to publicise their writing and build a personal audience. However, mobilising this audience to another platform is likely to be difficult. To see the long-term benefits as an entrepreneurial journalist you need to build your own news platform from the ground up, otherwise you will always be helping to build someone else's news organisation.

Innovations in storytelling

Having the vision to identify the best way of telling a story to your target audience is crucial. For example, if you are reporting on students' exam results there are potentially several ways of tackling the story:

1   Taking pictures of people opening their results and interviewing students and teachers about their reactions.
2   Running a live blog using a hashtag on Twitter to discover those reactions and utilising user-generated content in your coverage.
3   Measuring the results of the school or college against previous years, nearby competitors and the national average.
4   Using the data to create a map of the locality indicating where students perform best and worst.

All these approaches are equally valid. Traditionally, news organisations would have adopted the first approach but different audiences often prefer different styles of coverage.

A younger audience would probably prefer to see the results through their peers' eyes (option 2), whereas residents interested in standards of schooling in the area might prefer option 3. Option 4 could appeal to parents seeking to identify the best place to live in the area with regard to school catchment. It is important to rationalise the best approach for your audience and then utilise analytics afterwards to determine your success. The ability to tailor your approach to your audience is crucial to providing a strong and sustainable news service.

Gamification: current affairs as the basis for online games

On the face of it news and games are unlikely bedfellows. The news presents real life, complete with all its failings, whereas gameplay offers a level of escapism from day-to-day drudgery. However, audience response has demonstrated that gameplay is increasingly becoming a new frontier for journalism.

In 2013 the *New York Times*' most popular piece of content was a dialogue quiz.[17] The most popular story in the *Slate*'s history was the Adele Dazeem name generator, created after John Travolta's mispronunciation of actress Idina Menzel's name at the Oscars.[18] Games are becoming increasingly big business for news organisations due to the huge audiences they can potentially draw in. Readers who find a game entertaining are likely to share it with their friends on social media, creating the opportunity for it to go viral.

In the digital age, storytelling is often best achieved by abandoning the approach of directly telling the audience and instead letting them discover it for themselves. Newsrooms are applying the same sense of experimentation utilised in their everyday storytelling to develop online games.

Brian Boyer, editor of National Public Radio in the USA, puts the target audience at the heart of his approach. He says: 'The question we ask ourselves is who are [our] users. And then we ask what are their needs and then we think, "What can be built?" We are always trying to create the most audience-serving experience.'[19]

This process of tailoring content to your audience is vital. If they aren't going to engage in the game, then as a publisher it isn't worth your time developing it. Even when the game is launched you need to examine analytical data to establish how successful it has been. This will inform your planning for the next project.

The increasing availability of low-cost and free game-building platforms which make the task relatively easy, offers the opportunity to experiment with a variety of different games. Riddle.com in particular is simple to use and allows you to create interactive content such as quizzes, polls and lists in minutes. Co-founder Mike Hawkins says the platform has been developed with busy journalists in mind:

> Our theory is that users today don't want to passively consume content – they want to engage and share their opinions. Journalists can use Riddle to quickly create and add sentiment widgets, polls, lists or quizzes to their content – for example, 'How much do you know about Brexit?' – as part of a piece on their referendum.

Here are a few pieces of advice when creating a game:

- Put your audience at the heart of it. Remember it will only be successful if they use it.
- Base the game on facts, not opinion.
- Prioritise clear design – users need to be able to read text clearly.
- Will your users be able to play it on their phones? If not, you are losing a big part of your audience.
- Test the end product. It shouldn't be too easy or too hard.
- Timing is important – Buzzfeed launched a quiz based on football teams' suffixes days before the new season started in August.

Certain topics are more likely to lend themselves to games than others. Hard news stories do present more of a challenge. As Joey Marburger, director of product at the *Washington Post*, says: 'The news is hard to gamify because it's the news. It is not fun to play something where you know people are dying'.[20] Despite this challenge, '1,000 Days of Syria', created by US journalist Mitch Swenson to highlight the conflict in that country, and 'Cutthroat Capitalism', developed by *Wired* magazine to inform readers about the business models of Somali pirates, have shown it is far from impossible.

Case study: How UsVsTh3m used games

In a similar vein UsVsTh3m blazed a trail through UK online journalism for two years with its ability to inform users about current affairs through games. The site was launched in 2013 with a newsroom of five journalists on short-term contracts, acting as an internal start-up within publisher Trinity Mirror. Within six months it was receiving 7 million unique visitors a month.[21]

In part this was due to ensuring UsVsTh3m would work on all devices – widening the audience to include both people at work on desktop computers and mobile phone users. It combined softer games with harder-hitting news ones, which challenged its readers. UsVsTh3m demonstrated that jokes could be just as effective as a news report in making a point.[22]

Here are a few examples:

- 'Where's Damascus?' (Figure 3.1) – This asked readers to identify Damascus on a map as the UK Parliament debated whether to bomb Syria. Journalism academic Emily Bell praised this as educational by 'immediately [confronting you with] … your own geographical brilliance or indeed ignorance'.[23]
- 'Jeremy Hunt's realistic A&E crisis simulator' – In this game (Figure 3.2) users have to direct a doctor through several tasks at once against the clock. Health Secretary Hunt was grappling with rising A&E waiting times at the time.
- 'How much are you hated by the *Daily Mail*?' – A quiz where readers answered a series of questions to identify how they match up to the conservative values of the *Daily Mail*. The *Mail* had just attacked the father of then-Labour leader Ed Miliband.

FIGURE 3.1 'Where's Damascus?' An interactive game devised by UsVsTh3m
Source: Image courtesy of Trinity Mirror.

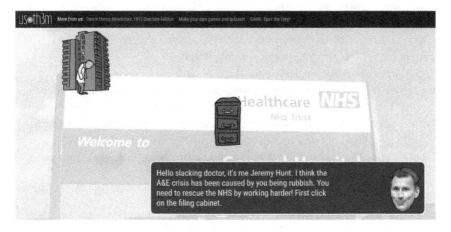

FIGURE 3.2 'Jeremy Hunt's realistic A&E crisis simulator'. An interactive game devised by UsVsTh3m
Source: Image courtesy of Trinity Mirror.

The speed with which UsVsTh3m reacted to current affairs was a key aspect of its success. This allowed it to capitalise on the emotive reactions of its audience to the latest news, which in turn drove engagement in a similar manner to Buzzfeed.

When Environment Secretary Owen Patterson blamed badgers for 'moving the goalposts' after marksmen failed to reach their culling target, UsVsTh3m turned the saga into a football game within the day. 'Four hours and 21 minutes to publish a fully playable game about a news event that happened that morning. Nobody else could come close to doing that then; nobody else has got anywhere close since,' recalls Tom Phillips, editorial director at Buzzfeed.[24]

Martin Belam was new format editor at the Daily Mirror *and is now social and new formats editor at the* Guardian.

I can't believe the best way to tell a story online is a 500-word article. In the internet we have got a two-way method of interaction. After 20 or 25 years of the web we are still not exploiting the platform in an inspirational way. News has decided to just do articles.

We need to accept games as a place where you can do serious stuff. If you call it games somehow you can't do it. Games make more than films but nobody takes games as seriously as an art form or an entertainment form. It's a very interesting way to tell stories.

FIGURE 3.3 Martin Belam

Games can make political points through satire. The badger penalty shoot-out was [about] a public figure saying something ridiculous in front of the press. You can also ask why a blonde 14-year-old girl going missing gets more press coverage than any other girl: The page can count down 30 seconds … 25 seconds until another child goes missing. It's something that leaps out at you. They go missing a lot; most children are absconding from care homes.

Also if you look around any urban space, every single person will be just fiddling on their phone. You have to get it on there.

Using data to tell eye-catching news stories

We now live in the age of big data. The amount of data is more than doubling every two years; government information – such as employment rates, hospital waiting times and pollution figures – is all now available online.[25] The rise in data being captured and the opportunity to gain access to it is a potential goldmine for journalists. It could provide endless opportunities for stories and offers the chance to produce more objective journalism, where the facts tell the story.

As an entrepreneurial journalist, a crucial aspect of this expansion in data is that public sector datasets should be freely available. But you should be aware that data journalism does require a good standard of numeracy and can initially be time-consuming – and therefore expensive to produce.

Step one: find the data

This is becoming easier as publicly funded bodies are being urged to become more transparent. In the UK, data is provided online by the government and the Office for National Statistics. Regional datasets are provided by local councils and Europe-wide ones by Eurostat. You may also submit a Freedom of Information Request (FOI) to access data from public bodies.

In addition to those sources, news organisations like the *Guardian*, Buzzfeed and The Huffington Post provide datasets they have used. Specialist data sites, such as Statto, which provides football statistics, are also online, so its worth searching them out. Pressure groups, like Greenpeace, and charities such as the National Society for the Prevention of Cruelty to Children (NSPCC) also compile figures in reports they produce.

If the figures you are looking for aren't available as a dataset you need to collate them yourself or scrape them from the site. When producing data journalism ensure the site you take the information from is reputable (and the source is attributed in the story). Otherwise you could end up producing a misleading article.

Step two: organise the information

This is where it's likely to get harder. The dataset of your dreams will be all laid out and easy to navigate. Most will need some work to get to that point. Things to address include:

- Checking spellings and ensuring they are consistent.
- Identifying bizarre bits of data. If it looks wrong, check it – it probably is.
- Ensure you use relative data. It needs to be a fair comparison. You can't compare straightforward totals of police numbers in Yorkshire (around 12,000 square miles) with those for Rutland (about 150 square miles). In this case you would need the number of officers per 100 square miles.

The data needs to be organised. This involves putting it into columns and rows. You can do this in either Microsoft Excel or a spreadsheet in Google Docs. Google Refine can also help you deal with messy data.

Step three: identify the story

By now you should be able to identify what stories the data is telling you.

To gain a broad perspective of a sector or issue you need to identify the average, particularly if you are seeking to put the figures into historical context. For example, the figure for the average house price only really makes sense when you are told if it is higher or lower than in previous months and years. Due to the imbalance of house prices across the UK you would be advised to begin looking at regions to discover whether an increase in property costs in London was driving the trend or if it was uniform growth across the nation.

Once you have done this, the next step is to find the best individual stories from that data. This is usually about identifying outliers. Who/what/where is the worst or the best? Are there any results that strike you as surprising or challenge preconceptions? Once you have done this you can try and find some of the reasons behind those results.

If you are working with spreadsheets you should use *pivot tables* to help you compare figures, especially when using large datasets. This can provide you with several completely different stories about the same data.

Step four: allow readers to interact with the data

Anna Leach, former editor of UK data blog Ampp3d, believes making data interactive allows stories to become much more personal to the audience. 'A general story about crime figures not catching your attention? How about knife attacks on your route home from work – you're more interested. Interactives are a natural tool for data journalists.'[26]

The ability to make a story relatable to individual members of the audience is a key driver in raising interest in a story. It works in a similar way to the identity posts Buzzfeed produce – it is what journalism professor Alberto Cairo calls the 'me' factor.[27] As data journalist Martha Kang points out, reporters need to 'Allow readers to go beyond the questions you asked in your piece to ask and answer their own.'[28]

Creating the ability to interact with the story and personalise it is a key consideration when it comes to visualising your data.

James Ball, who worked on the data behind the Snowden NSA files and the Wikileaks disclosures, says:

> You want to know what numbers are right. Are the reports credible? How do we split this up? What is the data actually telling us? You get into the habits of data journalism, which is 'do I believe the numbers in front of me?' […] Exclusives aren't just about if you know a source no one else does. They can be about thinking of a different angle or being bothered to dig through numbers in a way no one else has. And then checking that you are right.[29]

Simple and mobile-friendly data visualisation

There is an assumption that producing data journalism always has to be complex. However, it is crucial that the audience understands the story you are communicating to them. You must also be aware that audiences increasingly read stories on their mobile phones (more on this in Chapter 7), which aren't suited to complicated design. As an entrepreneurial journalist you should be keen to cater for the mobile audience, as this is likely to continue growing in the future. This often requires a creative approach to solving design concerns.

Here are three examples of stories where innovative solutions have been found:

- *China's stock market crash cost $1.5 million every single second (Vocativ).* This story has two simple but very effective visualisations. The first is a real-time counter totting up how quickly the losses in the stock market occurred, starting from $0 when you open the page. The second is a GIF, a looped video clip, that demonstrates how many average-price American houses would vanish if property disappeared as quickly as wealth during the Chinese stock market slump. The GIF continues playing as the counter mounts up.
- *More people may have died building venues for Qatar 2022 than will play in the 2014 World Cup (Ampp3d).* This article placed the death of 1,200 construction workers preparing for the Qatar 2022 World Cup into context. It put markers for 23 dead workers next to each of the 23-man squads for the 2014 tournament. Readers scroll through the 32 teams before realising at the end there are 464 more dead workers than players in the 2014 tournament. It is a hard-hitting visualisation that works on mobile and demonstrates the scale of the human loss.[30]
- *These Legos make it depressingly clear just how much money the 1% has (Brookings Institution).* This three-minute video, featuring veteran economics reporter David Wessel, demonstrates the impact taxes have on the gap between rich and poor. It involves representing $10,000 in income with one Lego brick and shows the level of inequality in America. This is a simple but highly effective way of visualising data.

Key tool: Datawrapper

Datawrapper is an online data visualisation tool that is utilised by news organisations around the world. Its interactive visualisations are ideal for mobile audiences and they can be embedded into your news website. It is simple to use and to alter graphs once they have been created. Datawrapper is an ideal platform if you want to produce an explanatory visualisation up against a tight deadline. Datawrapper is initially free but premium versions are charged for.

Creating a chart in four simple steps

1   First organise your data into rows and columns – giving those descriptive titles – and sign up to the site. Then you just need to copy this into the white box under the heading 'Upload your data'.
2   You are then asked to check the data and cite its sources, including, if possible, a web link.
3   On the Visualise tab you are asked to provide a title and a description of the data, and to choose the style of visualisation. You can also choose the colour and the size you want it to appear on your site.

4   Then you publish and are provided with a link to your chart and an embed code for your website.

More complex visualisations

More detailed visualisations obviously take more time to produce, which is a factor you need to be keenly aware of as an entrepreneurial journalist, but they can offer the opportunity to make more of an impact. They are often necessary when you want to analyse several factors at once. These visualisations need a clear structure, to match the story's narrative, and to be familiar to people.[31]

'Mapping the EU migrant crisis' by Matt Francis[32] is an excellent example of making a complex visualisation appear structured to the reader. It maps the flow of migrants across Europe from their country of origin to their eventual destination. It is based on figures provided by Eurostat. The initial chart looks complex as it includes all the routes of migration, complete with figures. However, its strength is the ability for readers to interact and click on countries to see how their populations have been affected.

Key tool: Tableau Public

The migration graphic was produced using Tableau, which is free data visualisation software. Tableau, which is downloadable, offers a variety of graphics from basic bar or line charts to more complex designs such as maps, bubbles and treemaps. If you are keen to produce eye-catching graphics for a primarily desktop-based audience, it is probably the tool for you. Tableau Public is free but more advanced versions are charged for.

Infographics

Infographics have become increasingly popular in both print and online news at a time when technology is making them less time-consuming to produce. Infographics offer the opportunity to provide readers with in-depth information in a more appealing manner than a lengthy written story can. As data journalist David McCandless points out: 'Design is about solving problems and providing elegant solutions, and information design is about solving information problems … visualising information can give us a very quick solution'.[33]

However, like any piece of content, these solutions rely on journalists being clear about what they are aiming to communicate and choosing information their target audience is interested in. It is a misguided entrepreneurial journalist who wastes hours producing an infographic their readers don't care about. As we have established, the topic needs to engage your audience if you want the content to find a wider audience. There is more chance of this happening if the information is memorable,[34] either because it is shocking or challenges perceived wisdom.

It is important to first sketch out an infographic. This will help you to identify what the key story is and creates clarity about what you are aiming to achieve. Including icons from the topic you are covering in your design bonds the content to the infographic.

Key tool: Piktochart

Picktochart is a web-based program that assists non-designers to produce high-quality infographics. The site offers templates to work within and offers a variety of stock icons, photographs, visualisations and fonts. There is also the opportunity to upload your own material.

'Distance to Mars',[35] a motion infographic that visualises the huge distance between Earth and Mars, was created using Piktochart. It demonstrates how graphics can provide visual context to our understanding of large numbers. Piktochart is free but its paid packages offer more resources.

The future of visualisations

News organisations are increasingly aiming to make their visualisations more interactive and personal to the audience. As we discussed above, this often encourages engagement and propels the content further across social media. That transmission is more likely to happen if the content makes the audience feel angry or surprised about a topic.

The *Guardian*'s interactive map, 'Where Can You Afford to Buy a House?' is potentially hard-hitting for its audience as it asks for your earnings and then tells you the regions in the UK where you could afford to buy an average-priced home. It comes at a time when young adults, particularly those living in London, are facing up to the fact that they may never earn enough to own their own property. Using a visualisation to cover hot-button issues like this can trigger social sharing, bringing it to the attention of a wider audience.

But data also has the power to challenge preconceived ideas and spark discussions about how we deal with problems as a society. 'Chicago's Million Dollar Blocks',[36] a project by American academics, challenges the practice of giving lengthy prison sentences to Chicagoans living in low-income households. It tells the reader there are more than 850 blocks in the city where $1 million or more is spent keeping residents in jail. Readers are encouraged to navigate a heat map of the city showing where the cash is spent. The project has two distinct audiences – people who live in Chicago, who can investigate their neighbourhood, and the wider community, who may wrestle with the larger societal issue.

The wow factor will always attract audiences. The *New York Times* produced 'One Race: Every Medalist Ever', following Usain Bolt's 100m win at the 2012 London Olympics. It is a 3D interactive graphic that places every 100m medalist since 1896 on the same track to show how far athletes have advanced in that time. You can produce similar graphics with Adobe's After Effects. The video originated from a written piece discussing how much faster sprinters could possibly go in future[37] and demonstrates how approaching topics creatively can establish new forms of digital storytelling.

Where do we experiment next?

The methods of storytelling detailed in this chapter demonstrate how journalists are increasingly experimenting to find new ways of engaging audiences and building communities of readers. Newsrooms are also telling stories in a wide variety of innovative ways. This chapter offers a snapshot of those methods and you should investigate them further if they interest you.

'Hearables' – wi-fi earbuds that allow audiences to better engage with audio on the move – could be part of the next wave of innovation. News organisations are already investigating how they can be used to serve audiences.

A thread running through this chapter is that the news is getting more personal. Audiences are fragmenting and it is much more about appealing to individuals rather than aiming at a mass market. As an entrepreneurial journalist it is vital you remember this when launching a digital project.

Metadata – information created as you use technology – is already playing an increasing role in personalising the content presented to us. The news organisations that can best present individual readers with the stories they want will thrive in the digital age. As Jonathan Stray, former editor of AP, puts it: 'I'm still holding my breath for an interaction design breakthrough, some elegant way to create the perfect personal channel.'[38]

Until that day arrives the task facing you as an entrepreneurial journalist is to regularly find innovations that engage your target audience. Being able to do this opens the door to building a community of readers and the creation of a sustainable news platform.

Notes

1 Gladwell, M (2009) *How David beats Goliath*. The New Yorker.
2 Graser, M (2013) *Epic fail: How Blockbuster could have owned Netflix*. Variety.com
3 Albeanu, C (2015) '*We need to be bold and not fear failure*' – *Q&A with Mariana Santos*. Journalism.co.uk
4 Lafrance, A and Mayer, R (2015) *The eternal return of Buzzfeed*. The Atlantic.
5 Bassan, V (2015) *13 things newspapers can learn from Buzzfeed*. European Journalism Observatory.
6 Rockey, A (2015) *Alison Rockey, Vox: Creating a social newsroom*. slideshare.net
7 Lafrance and Mayer, *The eternal return of Buzzfeed*.
8 BBC (2015) *Has one picture shifted our view of migrants?* BBC Trending.
9 Penenberg, A (2009) *Viral loop: The power of pass-it-on*. London: Hodder and Stoughton.
10 Berger, J and Milkman, K (2012) *What makes online content viral?* Journal of Marketing Research 49(2): 192–205.
11 Penenberg, *Viral loop*.
12 Ruhle, S (2014) *Buzzfeed CEO: How we find viral content*. Bloomberg.

13 Robischon, N (2016) *How Buzzfeed's Jonah Peretti is building a 100-year media company.* Fast Company.

14 Linkins, J (2011) *How the Huffington Post works (in case you were wondering).* Huffington Post.

15 Penenberg, *Viral loop.*

16 Bassan, *13 things newspapers can learn from Buzzfeed.*

17 Mayer, J (2014) *Why journalists shouldn't be threatened by the most-viewed NYT story of 2013.* joymayer.com

18 Lichterman, J (2015) *Riddle me this: How can news orgs better use games and quizzes?* Niemen Lab.

19 Foxman, M (2015) *Play the news: Fun and games in digital journalism.* Tow Centre for Digital Journalism.

20 Ibid.

21 Reid, A (2015) *What Trinity Mirror's new formats taught news about digital.* Journalism. co.uk

22 Ibid.

23 Bell, E (2015) *UsVsTh3m's demise shows challenge of making news for Facebook.* The Guardian.

24 Bradshaw, P (2015) *Ampp3d and UsVsTh3m: 9 of their best moments.* onlinejournalism-blog.com

25 Lohr, S (2012) *The age of big data.* The New York Times

26 Leach, A (2015) *9 things I learnt from doing mainstream data journalism.* annaleach.net

27 Cairo, A (@albertocairo) (2015) *The 'me' factor in #dataviz #infographics.* Tweet. 20 August, 1:09 p.m.

28 Kang, M (2015) *When asking data-driven stories, let readers ask questions, too.* Mediashift.org

29 Ball, J (2015) *Journalism week.* Leeds Trinity University.

30 Bradshaw, *Ampp3d and UsVsTh3m.*

31 Vital, A (2015) *How to think visually.* anna.vc

32 Francis, M (2015) *Mapping the EU migrant crisis in Tableau.* wannabedatarockstar.blogspot. com

33 McCandless, D (2010) *The beauty of data visualisation.* TED.

34 Lankow, J., Crooks, R and Ritchie, J (2012) *Infographics: The power of visual storytelling.* Hoboken, NJ: Wiley.

35 Paliwoda, D and Williams, J (2013) *Distance to Mars.* distancetomars.com

36 Cooper, D and Lugalia-Hollon, R (2015) *Chicago's million dollar blocks.* chicagosmillion-dollarblocks.com

37 Quealy, K (2012) *Sketches from One Race, Every Medalist Ever.* chartsnthings.tumblr.com

38 Stray, J (2015) *Annual report: The Tin.*

4

BUILDING YOUR IDEA

Starting a news website requires the ability to take an idea, develop it and build a business model around it. This chapter examines how the internet has changed journalism before identifying the best routes to success and the pitfalls to avoid.

Journalists rely on independent thought to break news. No-one told Wilfred Burchett to travel 500 miles on a train packed with Japanese soldiers to see Hiroshima in 1945.[1] He did it because as a war correspondent he knew the world needed a first-hand account of the horrors caused by a nuclear bomb.

The ability to develop a nose for news relies on a journalist's imagination, creativity and awareness of the world around them; knowing the impact of a national story will be felt locally, investigating public services and identifying past stories that need following up. All these qualities are also crucial when you are aiming to launch your own news start-up.

Being a journalistic entrepreneur is far from easy; you are aspiring to create a new product that will be valued by an audience enough for it to become sustainable. In order to foster ideas like this you need to adopt a positive mindset. You need to suspend logic for a minute, back your ability and believe you can succeed where others have failed. Journalistic entrepreneurs have an advantage over staff at legacy publishers in this situation – your idea doesn't need to be approved by your colleagues and managers, it doesn't need to fit into the company's vision, it is your idea and you are free to pursue it. In big companies, if one person figures out what's wrong with an idea that's often enough to kill it.[2]

It's not as simple as solely hoping for the best; you then need to apply rational thought to ensure your ideas stack up. This chapter will examine how you can begin rationalising your initial concept, give it legs, explore how you can best position yourself in a hectic journalistic marketplace and identify some of the challenges you'll need to overcome to build an audience. Taking the time to spot flaws in your logic at this stage will help significantly when it comes to launching your site.

Is my project a good idea?

Not all your ideas will make for a viable business. Once you're in a position to evaluate concepts you need to begin working out which one is going to be the best fit for yourself and your team. Below are four key aspects you should consider during that process. But remember: narrowing down your options like this doesn't mean jettisoning every aspect of a rejected idea. Maybe some of the suggestions will work well with a different concept.

Does it utilise your skills?

As an entrepreneur you need to focus on the areas where you and your team can excel from the outset. There is no point prioritising video if you can't use a camera, or wanting to produce data journalism if you hate numbers. Keep it simple and identify the areas where you can best showcase the skills of you and your team.

A study of thirty-five small-to-medium journalistic start-ups around the world found that the projects that succeeded were those that focused on the founder's particular strength. This was usually in journalism or technology.[3] Don't make the mistake of pursuing what you think you should be producing at the expense of something that fits your abilities. You need to focus on projects that you can realistically deliver.

Potential audience size

This is a key issue you need to ask from the outset. Do you think enough people will be sufficiently interested in your site to make it sustainable? Digital audiences have fragmented, but not to the point where a hyperlocal snowboarding site in Britain is likely to be financially viable. No idea should make it off the drawing board if you don't believe enough people will visit it, because it is a waste of your time. There is no point kidding yourself about this either, as it will only store up more problems for later on.

You are looking for a topic that is big enough to engage a monthly audience in the tens of thousands, but not so popular that you are going to face insurmountable competition. This is not the easiest market size to find and it will rule out many projects. When you've found one that fits, visit Chapter 5 to examine how to conduct market research.

Do you care enough about it?

Launching a start-up news website is demanding. Making it successful will consume huge amounts of your time and require you to overcome problems on a daily basis. So you really need to care about what you are doing. Being motivated by the challenge, valuing the content you produce and believing that the site will benefit future careers are all positive factors that will motivate you and your team.[4]

You need to care when you get to a story first, when a reader praises your article or when your analytics say your readership is growing, because otherwise you won't find this process rewarding. News is an industry that relies on intrinsic motivation. Journalism is never going to be a highly paid sector and the public's view of reporters is poor at best.

Once you have found a project, the next challenge as a founder is to instil a positive frame of mind in everyone else. Highlight the strides forward you are making, such as positive audience reaction, and offer a degree of autonomy by listening to ideas, rather than restricting people to producing the same type of content endlessly. This type of encouragement is crucial when start-up funding is in short supply and creating economic pressures for all involved. Research has found that as few as 20 per cent of employees are actively engaged with their work.[5] You need to ensure you and your team form part of this driven workforce.

Timing

Launching your business at the right time for your audience will provide you with momentum. Bill Gross, founder of Idealab, a business incubator, found timing to be the biggest reason behind success in 200 start-ups he analysed. Gross believes the recession was crucial in ensuring Airbnb and Uber thrived. 'The best way to assess timing is to really look at whether customers are really ready for what you have to offer them. And to be really, really honest about it.'[6]

The value of this research has been demonstrated in Scotland, where increasing support for independence has led to several digital start-ups taking audience share from traditional pro-unionist print media. Crowdfunded news site Common Space saw its traffic jump to 200,000 unique users in May 2015 when the Scottish National Party won fifty-six seats in an election landslide. Editor Angela Haggerty, who leads a team of activists turned journalists, believes the change has 'essentially come from activists that were unhappy with media coverage of events around the [2014 Independence referendum], but those people have then seen the wider problems around media, and they want to create a better media.'[7]

Likewise, if you live in an area that has just lost its regional newspaper now is probably an ideal time to launch a hyperlocal news site. The Lincolnite, a hyperlocal started by three graduates from the University of Lincoln in 2010, was ideally placed when the daily *Lincolnshire Echo* newspaper went weekly a year later. By 2013 the site had won a special award at the Online Media Awards.

Identifying a growing niche market and becoming a specialist in it

How niche markets became economical

The internet has dramatically shifted the economics of production, a fact high-lighted by Chris Anderson in *The Long Tail*. This has already had a significant impact on the world of journalism. Mainstream commercial publishers and broad-casters mainly aim to produce news for the largest possible audience. In producing these stories they use news values and their experience to gauge what the average person in the street is interested in.

The economics are simple: the more people you attract, the more advertising you can sell and the more money newspapers make from sales. This is particularly important when the methods of production are expensive, such as running a TV studio or publishing newspapers, and staffing costs are high.

But the internet means that what was previously unaffordable to produce is now cheap. This has lowered the barrier to entry; you need fewer staff and publishing costs are nominal, so you don't need to aim yourself at the mainstream to survive. It has suddenly become economical to write for specialist audiences. In turn this has provided individuals with more freedom to find material about particular topics they are interested in.[8]

Writing online about a mainstream topic such as Premiership football or celeb-rity gossip is fraught with difficulty because there is a lot of competition from well-financed legacy media at the top and amateur bloggers writing for free at the bottom. It is very difficult to establish yourself in this marketplace. If you choose a niche there will be less competition and more opportunity to establish yourself. It will also allow you to become an authority in this area.

Adopting a single-subject focus

Specialist sites are becoming an increasingly influential part of the digital news eco-system. As mainstream news providers struggle to produce comprehensive coverage that satisfies audiences they are being 'outmanoeuvred by the speedboats zipping around them, relatively small sites that have passionate audiences and sharply focused information'.[9] Digital readers are more adept at knowing where to find specialist content and are spending less time reading general interest news. The sites that spread themselves thinly over a wide range of subjects run the risk that their audience will leave to pursue a more in-depth understanding of a story. As Anderson points out, 'The act of vastly increasing choice seemed to unlock demand for that choice.'[10]

Starting a niche site requires a high level of interest in the topic and an awareness of its potential audience. As a founder you need to fuse journalistic ability with a degree of knowledge that will help you become a respected commentator on that subject.

For example, if you are already a motorsport fan it makes the process of launch-ing a site covering motorbike racing much easier. You have prior knowledge to be able to assess if the sport is under-represented in the media, such as how many people go to races and watch on TV. You can also reference bike modifications and past contests when you are interviewing drivers and demonstrate this expert knowledge in your coverage. You know about the talking points that fans feel passionate about. Some of this can be learnt on the job, but it is easier if that inherent interest already exists.

The focus provided by being specialist allows reporters to go into depth on issues and cover stories than would otherwise be ignored by the mainstream media. In 2013 InsideClimate News, which covers environmental issues, won a Pulitzer prize for the standard of its reporting on oil spills in America.[11] Political niches have also proved fertile, as demonstrated by Politico, another Pulitzer-winning site. This has become the essential source for Washington insiders by focusing on delivering key political news seconds after it happens. It has a loyal following among busy lobbyists and political staff, who rely on specialist news for their careers on Capitol Hill. The site's success has led to the development of a thriving subscription service called Politico Pro, and expansion to provide coverage in even greater depth.[12] In Britain, Guido Fawkes, a right-wing political blog that focuses on covering Westminster, has proved similarly popular and diversified into reporting on several further niche topics.

Successful niche sites tend to engender greater reader loyalty and audience engagement than mainstream sites. This also manifests itself in happy readers recommending others to the site, which – as we are about to discover – is a crucial factor in nurturing any digital start-up.

How to reach your target audience

Audience is a recurring theme in this book; this is because without an audience you don't have a business. You need to put your audience first. Focusing on this concept is how the MailOnline became the most read English news website in the world. It broke with the editorial views of its print version, the *Daily Mail*, because it became clear that different people were reading the two products.[13] As a result the MailOnline, which attracts a much younger audience, provides a daily diet of showbiz to attract its readers, whereas its print counterpart remains focused on the issues that concern ageing middle England.

If you can build something that even a small number of people want and are prepared to return to regularly then your site will grow through word of mouth and your promotion. As journalist Adam Penenberg puts it: 'If you make something people really want, your customers will make your business grow for you.'[14] Your best chance for growth revolves around converting the vast majority of first-time visitors to your site into returning readers.

As an entrepreneur you cannot afford to produce stories based solely on your own interests. You are the publisher, not the audience. You might be a twenty-something graduate with a busy social life, but it is likely the majority of your target audience is not. Therefore you need to conduct audience research, as discussed in

Chapter 5, and learn to use analytics to gain insights into your readers' behaviour, as outlined in Chapter 7. If you are a young journalist it is likely you will be writing for an audience older than yourself so you need to be aware of this fact. You need to be able to identify with the lifestyle of older readers. One of the reasons *Strictly Come Dancing* is such a ratings success for the BBC is that the average age of BBC1 viewers has crept up to 59.[15] The age, gender and geographical location of your audience will also have a sizable impact on the way you promote your content, which will be discussed in Chapter 9.

The internet is awash with all manner of content vying for audience attention at any one time. To succeed in such a complex marketplace your journalism has to be different from the rest. It has to offer a unique selling point (USP), something your site does better than anyone else in your field.

Prioritising speed

The most traditional way of beating the opposition is to be first. Exclusives have long adorned the front pages of newspapers and left rivals struggling to catch up. Being first is particularly attainable if you have developed expert knowledge and reliable contacts in your specialism. However, there are several factors you need to be aware of.

First, you need to be sure your story is right, otherwise going solo leaves you particularly exposed to legal problems. Digital exclusives don't tend to last very long so you need to post them at peak traffic times, heavily promote them on social platforms and protect your intellectual property by watermarking images and video to avoid your content being copied. But if your site relies on your ability to be first to big news you need to be realistic about achieving this regularly, especially if you are competing against better-financed competitors.

Adding value

An alternative approach is to focus on value. This relies on providing a higher standard of coverage, approaching issues in a different fashion, producing off-diary stories or having the authority and reputation to provide an expert viewpoint.

Providing a higher standard of coverage can be achieved in several ways. Many news outlets, particularly legacy media, are still adapting to the internet as a platform. As a result posts are often primarily text-based and usually offer limited multimedia for the reader to engage with. Therefore there are myriad options when it comes to producing stronger content that can play to your newsroom's strengths. The most obvious is including either video or audio in your coverage, alongside several images. Utilising your mobile phone as a reporting tool can now quickly produce this coverage, as you'll discover in Chapter 8.

Focusing on the figures, either as an initial or supplementary article, is a widely used method when identifying a different angle to a story. You could include a basic data visualisation or infographic. Be aware that finding the data can be time consuming, so if you want to produce a complex piece of work you need to be sure you will get the necessary rewards in terms of traffic. Quizzes or listicles can spark interest if promoted correctly, and often represent a more time-efficient method of creating supplementary content.

Finding off-diary stories relies heavily on your imagination and ability to make them relevant to the audience. Pursuing interviews with notable figures in your field/area, reflecting on big events at significant anniversaries and finding residents affected by national or international stories are among the techniques that can provide a rich seam of stories. It is unlikely you will be able to afford to launch long-running investigations at the outset, but the Freedom of Information Act (FOI) has allowed journalists in the UK to better uncover juicy stories about public authorities.

Having a recognised reputation as an expert in a field is a privileged and advantageous position to be in as a journalist. The regard that specialist reporters are held in by niche audiences is giving them increasing clout in the digital age, a situation we examine in depth in Chapter 5. Allied with cost-effective platforms, it is resulting in an increasing number of specialists pursuing their own projects, either as a full-time occupation or a part-time sideline.

Mic Wright, who forged a reputation as a technology and culture writer, co-founded a media company and launched The Malcontent, a site that focused on politics, media and culture.[16] Jonathan Wilson, the highly regarded *Guardian* football writer and author, founded the *Blizzard*, a print and digital publication that features in-depth analytical pieces. Wilson wanted it to become a platform for eclecticism, where writers could write about the football-related issues important to them.[17]

The USP of these projects is tied to the journalists themselves; they come with a pre-supposed audience in a similar manner to broadcasters like Jeremy Clarkson or Chris Moyles, who themselves have moved away from the mainstream media. The audience value their opinion because they are seen as established sources. Additionally this influence model is attractive to advertisers, who want to be associated with high-quality content and have their ads seen by a loyal audience.[18]

If you focus on being an added-value news platform you will need to be pragmatic. Ignoring the news agenda in your field completely because your primary focus is elsewhere is a high-risk strategy, as your site's success will be solely reliant on traffic from in-depth posts that you hope will catch on with your audience.

Your audience will expect you to respond to the news agenda, and even if you aren't aiming for exclusives you should aim to provide some form of timely coverage, for example a responsive opinion, which we will examine in Chapter 6. Ultimately you will need to find a balance between prioritising speed and adding value that suits your readership.

Hyperlocal journalism

Hyperlocal websites are an increasingly influential force within the news ecosystem. These sites, which are visited every month by around 15 per cent of people in the UK,[19] are tied to a specific geographical area such as a district, village or small town. Delivering news for that community is their USP. This is the type of news British regional newspapers are finding increasingly difficult to produce with reduced numbers of staff reporters.

Around 650 active hyperlocal websites exist in the UK, although the true figure could be higher.[20] On average this army of grassroots news providers produces a story every two minutes for twelve hours every day.[21] Hyperlocals report on a multitude of issues, but common topics across two thirds of sites are events, local government affairs, history, business, and transport.[22] These staples, along with the weather, are proving popular with audiences and engagement with these sites is growing, particularly among mobile readers, which replicates the general trend in this area. London is home to eighty-five hyperlocals and a further twenty operate in Birmingham, demonstrating a trend towards big cities splintering off into community silos.[23]

However, despite appearing to be thriving, hyperlocals often prove to be financially unsustainable as businesses. The sector as a whole is heavily reliant on part-time founders, two thirds of whom fund the costs of hyperlocal sites themselves,[24] in addition to often being the sole reporter writing on the site. Hyperlocals struggle for visibility and recognition in the cultural landscape and too many struggle to make ends meet financially.[25]

Building influence as a hyperlocal

Hyperlocals are grassroots journalism at its finest. They exist because residents are naturally curious about the events happening in the areas they spend their lives in. They want to know why a housing development is being proposed at the back of their house, why the council is digging up the main road again and why the local school has failed its latest inspection.

When launching a hyperlocal news site, targeting a self-defined community is a better idea than trying to amalgamate areas together to create a patch you feel is manageable.[26] Self-defined communities have a much stronger emotional appeal for a resident, which creates a stronger pull for your site. This makes it more likely your audience will identify with it and makes it easier to attract advertisers.

You need to become a visible presence within the community, both online and offline, to raise awareness of the site and build a reputation as a trustworthy news provider. Online this means launching your site, posting content and becoming extremely active on social media – see Chapters 7 and 9 for more information. It also means tracking your area on sites like FixMyStreet, which encourages residents to publicly report problems in their community. Offline it means getting to know local councillors and officials, immersing yourself in community groups and building relationships with local businesspeople, historians and other notable people. The *West Leeds Dispatch* hosts regular meetings at a coffee shop to allow its readers to talk about issues, offer tip-offs or discuss writing for the site.[27] Building trust with key individuals is extremely important to local news; losing access to the privileged information they hold will make your job a lot harder.

One way to serve the community and raise your own profile as a hyperlocal is to lead or support a community campaign. Campaigns usually arise out of events, but if you ingrain yourself within your community you will become aware of opportunities to get involved. Almost three quarters of hyperlocals have actively campaigned to change things within their community,[28] a figure that demonstrates how the internet has enabled social activism among communities.

The *Brixton Blog* succeeded in saving the Lambeth County Show – a free event that attracts around 200,000 people every year – after launching an online petition.[29] The *Upper Calder Valley Plain Speaker* campaigned, along with the

Daniel Ionescu is managing editor of The Lincolnite, and one of its three founders in 2010. The Lincolnite now has a staff of twelve and more than 500,000 visitors to its website every month.

We finished our dissertation in April and had May free. We did it on a daily basis and were able to beat the local newspaper to stories. We had 5,000 readers in the first three months and decided to give it a real go.

FIGURE 4.1 Daniel Ionescu

We got regional development agency funding and won through a *Dragon's Den* style competition to get £1,500 over three months to buy a couple of computers, a camera and rent a small office space. In the first two years we had part-time jobs that helped us keep it going.

The first year was about having consistent, reliable content. People wanted to see if we would still be there. By the end of the second year people were becoming friendlier. We won a lot of mindshare when the local newspaper went weekly: everything they covered was old.

A couple of years ago we opened a digital business magazine in Lincoln. This gave us a very sure foothold in the business area. We organized the Lincolnshire Digital Awards, with 250 guests, and the Lincolnshire Business Expo, a business-to-business trade event, with 750 people coming.

We met the editor of the *Lincolnshire Echo* and BBC Lincolnshire to discuss having a 2015 general election debate. We had an EU referendum debate with BBC Lincolnshire. We are big enough for that, we have enough reach. We are now launching a county-wide daily news website because Lincolnshire is getting a devolution deal and getting a single mayor and no-one covers that particular area.

established *Huddersfield Examiner* newspaper, to save A&E services in Huddersfield and Halifax,[30] a fight that gained momentum when plans were announced to close the A&E department at Huddersfield Royal Infirmary. The Yorkshire town has fewer than 150,000 residents but within two weeks a Facebook group calling for the service to be retained had 44,000 members and a similar number of people had signed a government petition. A meeting to discuss the plans was packed out and more than 1,100 people watched a livestream feed of it.[31] Being involved in similar popular grassroots campaigns builds public trust, engagement and awareness of your news platform.

Case study: Hyperlocals and the 2015 general election

The 2015 UK general election provided a platform for hyperlocals to demonstrate their value to their audiences. They became more integral to the constituency campaigns by providing a range of in-depth analysis, demanding more access to candidates than five years earlier and involving readers in their coverage.

During the campaign The Lincolnite took the bold step of jointly broadcasting a public debate with candidates in Lincoln's marginal constituency seat, alongside running separate livestream one-on-one interviews that involved readers' crowdsourced questions.[32] Meanwhile The Richmond Noticeboard ran profiles of each of the candidates for the North Yorkshire seat but bared its teeth by publishing the fact the Conservative candidate initially failed to respond to a request for information.[33]

On election day hyperlocals used a variety of innovative tools and techniques to keep voters informed. Inside Croydon ran a 15-hour live blog covering voting in Croydon's three parliamentary seats, providing a mix of local and national coverage until 7 a.m.[34] OntheWight, a hyperlocal covering the Isle of Wight, livestreamed the seat's declaration before using data visualisation to put the constituency's vote in context.[35]

Following the results, The Edinburgh Reporter uploaded election night audio interviews with the city's successful Scottish National Party candidates to allow readers to get to know their new MPs,[36] while Wrexham.com included an analysis of the reporting of other media outlets in its take on the night's events.[37] The standard of overall coverage received praise from the traditional media, with David Higgerson, digital publishing director at Trinity Mirror Regionals, noting that hyperlocals had a 'very good general election'.[38]

Hyperlocals and the BBC

The BBC's renewal of its current royal charter in 2016 has led to increasing calls for the corporation to develop a closer working relationship with the regional media, including hyperlocals. In order to be granted a new charter the corporation has outlined plans to employ up to 100 public service reporters who will produce impartial coverage of council and public services in an attempt to scrutinise decision making at a local level.[39] But although this coverage will be shared with the local media, the proposal has the potential to be a double-edged sword for hyperlocals. They should receive access to the stories, freeing them to cover other stories, but they could potentially lose their USP.

The creation of a 'news bank' of regional video and audio content that local newsrooms could access[40] is also being proposed. In theory this would allow hyperlocals to pull in stories relevant to their area, although it is unclear how audiences would react to generic local content. A potentially more exciting development is that community journalists may soon have access to the BBC's archive, which would allow them to reuse past material to create a variety of new broadcasting focusing on their area.[41]

Since 2015 BBC Online has offered increased visibility to hyperlocal platforms by including their news coverage in its 'local live' newsfeeds, alongside traditional regional media sources, with links to the full story.[42] The BBC's *Inside Out North East*, a regional news programme, even broadcast an investigation of a series of allegations by citizen journalists at Real Whitby, an influential hyperlocal in North Yorkshire.[43] However, there is now increasing pressure on the corporation to offer financial assistance. This has included calls for BBC Online to buy credited content from hyperlocals as a way of bolstering the sector.[44] Just how much the world's oldest and largest public service broadcaster is prepared to support the hyperlocal sector will have a big bearing on its long-term future, alongside encouraging local authorities to redirect some of the £50 million spent on statutory public notices with the regional press.[45]

Google has vowed to help local news providers by highlighting the original source of news stories that then become national or international talking points. This increase in visibility gives a significant boost to the coverage hyperlocals provide.[46] You can monitor the performance of your stories on Google News by downloading the Trisolute news dashboard.[47]

Regional specialisms

An alternative option when starting a project focusing on a niche audience is to focus on a regional specialism: this is a third way between specialist and hyperlocal sites that combines elements of a focused topic with a clearly defined geographical patch.

The advantage of this option is it allows you to thrive while still covering a popular or wide-ranging topic, one that may ordinarily have too much competition or be too demanding for a small newsroom to provide daily coverage. Restricting yourself to an area means you can get a foothold in the market by becoming a regional expert. This allows you to build up stronger contacts than your competitors who are covering the same specialism for national or international news outlets.

Cultural sites in Britain's biggest cities are becoming particularly popular. In Bristol, Drunken Werewolf has been providing readers with the latest about the music scene for a decade, while 24/7 Bristol focuses on events and community interest pieces, as well as publishing a free monthly magazine.[48] We Are Cardiff is an award-winning site that shares stories about culture, arts and people living in the Welsh capital. Similarly, Created In Birmingham has been promoting and discussing Birmingham's vibrant creative community since 2006, hosting several offline events in the process.

Both Edinburgh Foody and Eating Edinburgh critique eateries in Edinburgh, while Manchester's Finest keeps that city's residents updated with the latest places to go. I Love Manchester was even born out of a viral campaign to restore Mancunian civic pride following the city's 2011 riots.

Ground your plans in reality

Finding a part of journalism's complex ecosystem to inhabit is far from a straightforward prospect. But it is achievable. There are concrete aspects you should plan to achieve such as ensuring you play to your strengths, creating a driven newsroom culture, identifying a USP that can allow you to dominate your niche – be it geographical or specialist – and being realistic about the type of journalism you produce.

Addressing these issues will help you negotiate the range of unquantifiable unknowns you will encounter along the way. The overriding one is your audience. Your journalism is now on the clock, you've got to produce content that your audience wants, not what you want to produce or pure high quality journalism. There needs to be a balance.

As Gawker writer Hamilton Nolan states: 'Many writers believe that our brilliant writing will naturally create its own audience … The problem is that nobody ever bothers to inform the audience'.[49] The MailOnline receives lots of criticism in journalistic circles but it remains the market leader, demonstrating that for all its detractors it undoubtedly knows its audience inside out. Huge traffic figures have allowed it to enact its business plan.

Economics is also the reason specialist sites dedicated to large cities are well positioned to thrive. Large numbers of young adults with disposable income live in our cities, the kind of people advertisers fall over themselves to market to. If you develop a niche that attracts this kind of audience you give yourself an excellent chance of survival. The era of the hard headed, business-focused journalist is upon us.

Notes

1 Pilger, J (ed.) (2011) *Tell me no lies: Investigative journalism and its triumphs*. London: Vintage Books.
2 Horowitz, B (2014) *Can-do vs. can't-do culture*. Recode.net
3 Robinson, J J; Grennan, K and Schiffrin, A (2015) *Publishing for peanuts: Innovation and the journalism start-up*. Open Society Foundation's Programme for Independent Journalism.

4 McGregor, L and Doshi, N (2015) *How company culture shapes employee motivation.* Harvard Business Review.

5 Birkinshaw, J (2012) *Reinventing management: Smarter choices for getting work done.* Chichester: Wiley.

6 Gross, B (2015) *The single biggest reasons why start-ups succeed.* TED.com

7 Turvill, W (2015) *Scotland sees 'flowering' of news websites as national press wilts north of the border.* Press Gazette.

8 Anderson, C (2009) *The longer long tail.* London: Random House.

9 Carr, D (2011) *News trends tilt towards niche sites.* New York Times.

10 Anderson, *The longer long tail.*

11 Nolan, K and Setrakian, L (2013) *Seeking the single-subject news model.* Tow Centre for Digital Journalism.

12 Batsell, J (2015) *Engaged Journalism: Connecting with digitally empowered news audiences.* Chichester: Columbia University Press.

13 Bateman, T (2012) *How MailOnline took over the world.* BBC.

14 Penenberg, A (2009) *Viral Loop: The power of pass-it-on.* London: Hodder and Stoughton.

15 BBC (2014) *BBC Television's performance remains very strong overall, but there are challenges to be tackled, Trust review finds.* BBC Trust.

16 Wright, M (2015) *About.* The Malcontent.

17 Wilson, J (2016) *About.* The Blizzard.

18 Briggs, M (2012) *Entrepreneurial journalism.* London: Sage.

19 Journalism News (2015) *BBC and hyperlocals: A winning collaboration?* Soundcloud.

20 Ofcom (2015) *Internet citizens 2015 Executive summary.* Ofcom.

21 Harte, D (2013) *'One every two minutes': Assessing the scale of hyperlocal publishing in the UK.* Birmingham: Jomec Journal, Birmingham City University.

22 Radcliffe, D (2015) *Where are we now? UK hyperlocal media and community journalism in 2015.* Cardiff: Centre for Community Journalism.

23 Harte, D (2014) *Hyperlocal news websites: Some 2014 stats.* daveharte.com

24 Williams, A, Barnett, S, Harte, D and Townend, J (2014) *The state of hyperlocal community news in the UK: Findings from a survey of practitioners.* hyperlocalsurvey.wordpress.com

25 Radcliffe, *Where are we now?*

26 Briggs, *Entrepreneurial journalism.*

27 West Leeds Dispatch (2015) *Join us at West Leeds Dispatch community news café!*

28 Williams et al., *The state of hyperlocal community news in the UK.*

29 Dickens, T (2012) *Lambeth County Show confirmed with 400k budget.* Brixton Blog.

30 Upper Calder Valley Plain Speaker (2015) *Two towns, one fight: Why we have to keep both A&Es open 24/7.*

31 Source: Popham, J (2016) Twitter.

32 Lambourne, H (2015) *Weekly joins forces with hyperlocal site for live election debate.* Hold The Front Page.

33 The Richmond Noticeboard (2015) *What election candidate Rishi Sunak (Conservative) says to constituents.*

34 Inside Croydon (2015) *Vote 2015: Live coverage of Croydon's general election.*

35 Perry, S (2015) *Andrew Turner returned as Isle of Wight MP: The detail.* onthewight.com

36 Stephen, P (2015) *Political representation across the capital features new faces* The Edinburgh Reporter.

37 Wrexham.com (2015) *Wrexham's general election: Media roundup.*

38 Higgerson, D (2015) *General election 2015: Learning from hyperlocal sites across the UK.* davidhiggerson.wordpress.com

39 Linford, P (2015) *BBC to share 'public service content' with local press.* Hold The Front Page.

40 Ibid.

41 Community Journalism (@c4cj) *What's the latest on the BBC's #hyperlocal plan? @emma-meese reports back.* 15 January 2015, 4:28 p.m. Tweet.

42 Prior, D (2015) *BBC launches hyperlocal forum and reaffirms ambition to use more content from hyperlocal publishers.* Prolific North.

43 Real Whitby Webmaster (2015) *Real Whitby, the BBC and faceless public servants.* Real Whitby.

44 Radcliffe, *Where are we now?*

45 Radcliffe, *Where are we now?*

46 Sawers, P (2016) *Google News gets local source tag to highlight local coverage of major news stories.* venturebeat.com

47 News Dashboard (2016) *Maximise your coverage in Google News.* newsdashboard.net

48 Bristol 24/7 (2016) *About us.* Bristol 24/7.

49 Nolan, H (2016) *The problem with journalism is you need an audience.* Gawker.

5

BEING AN ENTREPRENEURIAL JOURNALIST

With Wayne Bailey

What is entrepreneurial journalism? How to begin thinking of news production as a business.

Entrepreneurship is on the rise – and journalism is one of many professions where this is increasingly evident. The combination of an economic downturn and a digital revolution has led to the number of new businesses registered in the UK surging to more than 580,000 a year, with more than half of people aged between 18–30 wanting to start their own company.[1]

Technological disruption and young creative minds joining the ranks of existing journalists is resulting in the news industry fragmenting. While this disruption is predominately portrayed as hastening the death of newspapers, it is also offering entrepreneurs the chance to compete. As author Stephen Johnson observes:

> It has never been easier to start making money from creative work, for your passion to undertake that critical leap from pure hobby to part-time income source … Widening the pool means that more people are earning income by doing what they love.[2]

The availability of online platforms is a democratising force; it is allowing journalists to wrestle power back from publishers and broadcasters. They are becoming emboldened and increasingly freeing themselves from strict editorial lines. This offers more choice for audiences, as instead of working in large teams channelled towards producing a single cohesive product, reporters are stepping away to find niche digital audiences.

Journalists can do this because they are becoming more skilled generally. The sharp decline in reporter numbers across the industry means they no longer have a sub-editor to check their copy or a producer to put together their package.

Reporters are being encouraged to be work across several different platforms on a daily basis. This is making newsrooms more efficient; journalists can now perform far more tasks because they are more highly trained. But the question many are asking themselves is: If you increasingly have to do it all yourself anyway, why hold on to the publisher who dictates how you work and what you cover?

For many journalists employment has always been a fluid business. There has always been the opportunity to work shifts and freelance, so becoming an entrepreneur is an extension of this. Many combine work with jobs inside and outside

---

Matt Cooke is Google News Lab lead for the UK, Ireland and the Nordics. He was previously a BBC presenter and producer.

The Google News Lab aims to provide training and support to individual journalists, those who are freelance or are working in small, medium or global sized newsrooms. We're trying to scale our training and development programmes to online audiences; in fact our website provides some 45 self-paced lessons and guides on a range of tools.

FIGURE 5.1 Matt Cooke

Another area we focus on is empowering the new voices in the media – from citizen journalism, to eyewitness media to the start-up community. In the US we've worked extensively with Matter VC to supercharge their training efforts to support media startups in the US and further field. We're actively looking at how we can replicate that approach elsewhere in the world too.

In the UK, the Campus London site offers a place for entrepreneurs and start-ups to work and create – it's part of the area often referred to as Silicon Roundabout near Old Street.

Away from London we run a range of workshops to help stimulate and inspire – the Digital News Roadshow events are a partnership with Trinity Mirror Regionals that bring an afternoon bitesize training workshop to a regional audience. In the last few months we've welcomed over 250 journalists to attend the free sessions in Manchester, Leeds, Birmingham, Belfast and Cardiff. On top of this we're also expanding our workshops and free training opportunities with organisations like the NUJ and NCTJ.

journalism, providing a sense of freedom and less dependence on news organisations undergoing huge change.

As the number of digital entrepreneurs increases, grassroots communities, such as Hacks/Hackers, are being formed to provide a support network for these new journalistic projects. This is being replicated regionally, and all this divergence is encouraging support from technology giants such as Google, who want to remain at the forefront of digital news.

Journalists as personal brands

Building a reputation has always been vitally important for reporters. Beating the competition, producing high-quality stories and developing a strong set of contacts have always been the way to get hired. Now, instead of using those skills to get a job, journalists are directing them at building their own news platforms.

In the digital age it is far easier for reporters to identify their own success. Working for a newspaper you know how many people bought a copy and the position of your stories in the paper tells you what your editor thinks about them. When material is published online, analytics tell you how many people actually read your individual article. If readers share the story on social media it can take on a life of its own, which often has little to do with the news platform it originated from. For an entrepreneur this clarity about your audience reach is vitally important.

The journalists who thrive in this environment are the innovative ones who can produce eye-catching material on a regular basis. They are specialists, who can attract an audience with their expert knowledge. Two high-profile journalists who demonstrate this trend are Nate Silver and Glenn Greenwald. They both have huge personal followings on social media and both left traditional publishers – the *New York Times* and the *Guardian* respectively – to launch digital projects built around their niche.

Developing a specialism is crucial for any journalist as it offers a degree of security in an evolving industry. If you're yet to develop your specialism, building your own digital project will provide an exploratory platform away from editorial oversight.

Finding your niche

If you are going to write about a topic exclusively you need to feel passionate about it. Investigate the range of coverage already produced and if you feel you can better it, you've found a potential specialism.

Once you've chosen a niche it is time to start getting comfortable with the idea of running a small business. This will probably be the first time you've been your own boss so you have to be aware that the buck now stops with you. This involves responsibility for everything and making all the big decisions, decisions that will impact on your family and any investors and employees. If you are going to take on this challenge you need to be clear from the outset why you want to build your project. You should ground your project in things that really matter to you; this will provide motivation to overcome challenges that come your way as you aim to bring your vision to life.[3]

The biggest challenge of being an entrepreneurial journalist is the need to become financially aware (see Chapter 2). Producing news costs money, most crucially in man-hours, and if you don't have any income you will eventually become one of the increasing number of failed digital start-ups.

Key marketing principles and practices

For many journalists, running their own start-up can be an attractive prospect. But it is imperative that, as an entrepreneurial journalist, you ensure that marketing is integral to your start-up. Here are some pivotal principles and practices that you need to address to develop your audience. You need to ensure that you understand your audience's needs and provide the right service, at the right time, in the right manner.

To ensure that your business is a success, being marketing orientated is an important ingredient. Having this type of attitude will help you to develop a loyal audience. You need to adopt an approach to marketing that focuses on the needs and wants of readers.[4]

There are three key areas that you need to take account of in order to do this. First, you need to analyse your current position within your market and undertake an audit; second, you need to undertake market research to gather vital information about your sector; and finally, you need to develop the correct mix of tools to attract a new audience who will engage with your content. The mix will change depending on the differing needs and wants of your potential and existing readers.

Market analysis

A market can be analysed in a number of different ways. Analytics can help you to identify key competitors, as well as any sociocultural, technological, economic/competitive and political and regulatory factors (STEP) that could influence how a particular market behaves.[5]

To make a success of your start-up, you need to meet the needs and wants of your target audience more effectively than your competition; to do this, carrying out a competitor analysis is paramount. Whilst getting overly distracted by your competitors could have a detrimental effect, profiling major competitors is prudent if you are to gain an understanding of their strengths and weaknesses.

Undertaking a marketing audit can also be a useful way to aid the understanding of a market. A marketing audit is defined as 'the systematic collection, analysis and evaluation of information relating to the internal and external environments that answer the question "Where are we now?"[6] By carrying out an audit you will be able to gain a greater understanding of the environment in which you have to operate, external issues that are largely beyond your control, and internal issues over which you have a direct influence.

To audit your external environment a STEP analysis should be carried out. Whilst each element should not be considered in isolation, when conducting a STEP analysis you should consider each of the four headings in Table 5.1 below.

Once an external audit has been undertaken, a list of key variables will be identifiable. The variables will either pose a threat to your business, which could lead to you not meeting your objectives, or to potential opportunities that you could then try to exploit.[7]

Whilst external influences are important, by analysing internal issues you will begin to understand the weaknesses of your project. These could lead to you failing to meet your objectives, which in turn, could help your competitors. An internal audit will allow you to ascertain the strengths of your business, such as a unique selling point (USP) that may give you an advantage over your competition.

Once the audit has been completed, you will begin to gain a clearer picture of the strengths and weaknesses of your business, as well as any opportunities that need to be exploited, or threats that need to be overcome. It is useful to summarise

TABLE 5.1 Conducting a STEP analysis

Sociocultural environment	*Technological environment*
You need to try to understand what drives your audience, and in doing so, pay attention to your market in terms of its demographics. You also need to give some thought to the attitudes and opinions of your target audience and culture more widely.	You need to be aware of any technological advancements and innovations that might influence your start-up.
Economic environment	*Political and regulatory environment*
You need to have an awareness of both micro and macroeconomic issues as they can have an impact on the behaviour of your readers and impact on the decision making of potential readers.	You need to understand how external forces (international, national and local governments, regulatory bodies/laws) impact on your start-up.

TABLE 5.2 Conducting a SWOT analysis

	Positive	*Negative*
Internal	Strengths: Passion for topic; specialist knowledge; highly trained journalist	Weaknesses: Lack of experience of managing your own start-up
External	Opportunities: To build reputation and audience	Threats: Competition

these issues by carrying out a SWOT analysis, a useful tool that can be utilised to aid decision-making.

Your SWOT should be a team effort and you need to make sure that you are client focused and that you take account of issues that are important to your readers. You also need to make sure that you are honest.[8]

Market research

Market research predicts whether or not there is room in the marketplace for another competitor or if there is a gap in the niche market that needs filling. It involves the design, collection, analysis and reporting of data that is relevant to your particular marketing situation.[9] Research your competition before launching your start-up; if you produce a site that is too similar to an existing one it will diminish your impact.

When undertaking market research you need to decide on what information is needed and you need to set some objectives. You also need to develop a plan and consider how you intend to gather your data and interpret what you find.[10]

Market research will help you identify gaps in your current plans and ways that you can produce better content than your competitors. You could do this by reacting to news faster, producing a wider range of stories, raising the standard of coverage or delivering more innovative content. To make your site sustainable you need to build an audience. Getting this audience will involve competing against a variety of existing news sources.

If you are launching a hyperlocal site you will probably have competition from existing regional newspapers in the area. If you are focusing on a specialism you need to get to know what content is already produced in this area, even if it appears to be aimed at a slightly different market.

You should use a web traffic service to find out how much traffic competing websites receive.[11] SimilarWeb is a site that provides crucial information on your competitors' audience size, engagement time and bounce rate. It also tells you where your competitors gain traffic from, informs you about their social media per-formance and allows you to compare the performance of different sites. Finding out the scale and nature of your competitors' audience will help you plot realistic goals for your project's growth. You should also look at their social media presence to see how many people follow them, how well they interact with their community of readers and who their key journalists are. Obviously if they are already familiar to you this is an advantage. Continuous monitoring of this information is essential for your market awareness.

Planning

Getting your project off the ground initially requires you to assess the strengths you and any co-founders bring to the table. You are going to be the engine driving the success of this project so you need to ensure you are maximising your abilities.

Work together to draw up a comprehensive list or a mind map of these. If you are flying solo you should find a trusted confidant or mentor who can provide a sounding board for ideas.

Then you need to start identifying the tasks you need to complete in order to get your business off the ground. This project planning should be split into three areas, which we will refer to as your advancement framework.

1   Content – This should be the motivating factor for you: what do you want this website to produce? Remember the web rewards start-up specialists rather than generalists, so once you've identified your journalistic strengths, focus on them at the outset.
2   Development – How are you going to take this idea from the drawing board onto the web? Identify the most crucial things you need to do and how you are going to address them. Your financial resources and available manpower are crucial to business planning.
3   Finances – How are you going to make this into a sustainable venture? You need to investigate your expenditures and find ways to minimise these. In terms of your income, how are you planning on generating it? Initially this is likely to be from advertising. So how will you attract advertisers? (see Chapter 2).

Naming the site

When it comes to naming your project you will need to plan carefully. Here are a few things to bear in mind:

•   Choose a name that reflects your site, so hyperlocals should include the name of the patch and specialist sites should reference the specialism. This will increase the chances of it being found in web searches.
•   Consider the availability of .com and .co.uk (or other national) suffixes for your web address.
•   Don't make the name too long or difficult to spell, it makes it harder for you audience to find you.
•   If possible make it memorable.[12]

If you have a selection of strong contenders and you are still unsure, survey members of your potential audience to get their view. You could use social media as an effective method of receiving feedback or poll opinion on Twitter.

Building your site

The best way to establish whether your project will be successful is to build it – but on a budget. It makes no financial sense to chuck everything but the kitchen sink at a news start-up until you are certain that it has a good chance of success. Eric Ries' 'lean startup' methodology refers to this as producing the minimum viable product

(MVP),[13] a process designed to provide the opportunity for a high return without incurring significant risk. In layman's terms it offers the chance to be successful without losing your shirt.

In the digital age you can launch a website either for free or a nominal outlay, and this is where you should begin. Bootstrapping your project, running it on limited finances, in the early days will allow you to build up an audience without significant financial pressure and give you time to assess how successful your site can be. It requires you to strip your concept down to its most crucial aspects to prove the audience wants what you're building.[14]

Set initial goals

When you get ready to launch you should set yourself some initial milestones to reach. These should be informed by the competition research you have undertaken and should act as a motivating force. They should centre on your initial advancement framework.

- Content – How many stories are you expecting to produce a day/week? How many of these will feature multimedia?
- Development – How many people can you get to visit your site? How many followers do you think you can attract on Twitter? How many people can you engage with on Facebook?
- Finances – How much income can you raise? Try to be realistic. If you are relying on advertising, how many companies can you attract to advertise with you? What will they pay?

All these targets are quantifiable goals. They rely on figures rather than feelings to give you the answers, which should drive you on to achieve them. Try to be realistic when you set them; they should be reviewed on a regular basis to keep your enterprise growing.

Building and developing a reputation

It is difficult to build up audience trust as a start-up for one simple reason – you have no track record for them to judge you on. This is a key area where your competitors and legacy media as a whole have a significant advantage. The audience has used these news organisations before and already judged if they are trustworthy.

Trust in British journalists generally hit historically low levels in 2012 following the phone-hacking scandal and crisis at the BBC. Pollsters YouGov revealed that for the first time ever, more people distrusted BBC news reporters (47 per cent) than trusted them (44 per cent) and only 10 per cent trusted tabloid journalists.[15] For your news platform to be a success you need to address this trust issue.

Initially you can do this by crafting a mission statement and making it visible on your website. As well as addressing trust issues, this gives your audience an indication of the journalism you intend to produce and provides a motivational reminder to yourself and your colleagues when times get tough. You should use it as a guide for content. Before publishing any story, check it against your mission statement.

When The Intercept launched in 2014 it announced its dedication to producing 'fearless, adversarial journalism',[16] setting itself up for its first article by founding editor Glen Greenwald, a piece that attacked America's security services. Identifying the purpose driving your enterprise is key to it beating its competitors. Author Simon Sinek suggests asking yourself: 'What's your purpose? What's your cause? What's your belief? Why does your organisation exist? Why do you get out of bed in the morning? And why should anyone care?'[17]

Joanna Abeyie is a multi-award winning journalist, entrepreneur and founder of Shine Media, which promotes diversity in journalism.

Online now you might see the same story covered everywhere but what you've got to think about is, how are you going to cover it differently? What are you going to tell me that's new about it? Can you shock me? Can you interest me? Are you going to spark a conversation? Are you going to spark a debate? What emotions will I provoke that will make them react to it? That's what you always need to think about when you are doing anything.

FIGURE 5.2 Joanna Abeyie

Keep people engaged with you because if you are trying to build up your own website you can say to advertisers, these are the people who come and visit our site. This is how long they stay there, once they've read that they move over here. You can prove to someone why it was worth putting adverts on your site.

Getting access to people and getting your own stories is what is going to separate you from other reporters. If you have had a conversation you have gained the authority on that story straight away. It also builds trust and loyalty. Your audience will know you have your finger on the pulse. It enhances your profile.

When you've answered these questions your mission statement should be posted on an 'About' page on your site which includes ways of contacting you and clear information about how you will proceed with any complaints. You should be able to build a long-term strategy from your mission statement, with key targets for the future.

Before launching it is also important to consider your personal reputation online. If you want to be taken seriously as a journalist you need to make sure your profile on social media platforms and online forums represents the image you want to convey to your audience. There is room for elements of your personality to come through, and some reporters have separate personal and professional social media platforms. But you need to critically examine material you have posted online to see if it is detrimental to your career. For example, publicly backing a political party is unlikely to go down well if you are expected to report balanced political news.

Planning to drive growth and maintain momentum in the first year

So once you've launched you can devote all your time to producing high-quality journalism? Well, not quite. This is now the start of the huge battle to make your start-up sustainable. Central to this is creating engaging content, attracting people to your site, ensuring those readers return and then attracting even more people. This should be the beginning of your never-ending tussle for audience-share.

As we've already discussed, you will be working to quantifiable goals. Your biggest weapon in this fight is analytical data. Your analytics will be able to tell you how many pages have been accessed on your site, how many visitors have been on it, when they did so and what content they engaged with. We will go into depth about analytics in Chapter 7.

It is very tempting to let this information drive all the decisions about content on your site. It certainly should drive many – ultimately you have to attract an audience to survive and pragmatism dictates that lofty journalistic ideals may have to take a back seat when you have to make the books balance. However, you need to ensure that you don't lose your overall focus. Iconic BBC war correspondent Martin Bell warned of the dangers of losing your integrity as a journalist when he asked: 'What do we believe in? If it is only making money we are clearly in the wrong business as money can deflect, if not corrupt, us. But if we have standards and values and principles, then we should stand by them because they are what we believe in and what sustain us.'[18]

Balancing chasing audience share against sticking to the standards that underpin your journalism is a high-wire act that you will have to manage on a daily basis. Even if your start-up gets traffic at the start, appealing to the lowest common denominator is unlikely to be a long-term strategy for success. Many digital newsrooms have found an uneasy compromise by targeting audience penetration with soft news, which then allows them time to write weightier investigative pieces, which typically attract smaller audiences.

However you decide to do it, your key challenge as an entrepreneur is to keep the numbers rising in your first year. Plateau too early and it is likely you will not have a large enough audience to make your site sustainable. Whatever your business plan looks like – Chapter 2 should help you shape this – it will require you to have a regular engaged audience to bring in enough income.

Initially you will have to seek out feedback from your audience. Getting information from your readers will quickly highlight issues you don't even know exist. The longer you wait for it, the longer these problems will fester. Tech entrepreneur Sam Altman believes founders should put nothing in between themselves and their users. Altman recommends listening to a small group of your audience and acting on their advice (see Figure 5.3). He advises: 'You should make this feedback loop as tight as possible. If your product gets 10 percent better every week, that compounds quickly.'[19]

One digital newsroom that has embraced this tight feedback link is ProPublica. This non-profit investigative site invites readers via social media and mailing lists to remotely test their new products. Users are then asked to complete tasks and the recordings are reviewed by the team to aid development, providing a 'gateway drug to empathy with the audience'.[20]

Sorting the wheat from the chaff is vitally important, as you can work out which are the experiments to persist with and which are the ones to dump. Remember, your time is precious so identify the valuable lessons so you can avoid making similar mistakes in the future. Physically meeting with your audience also allows

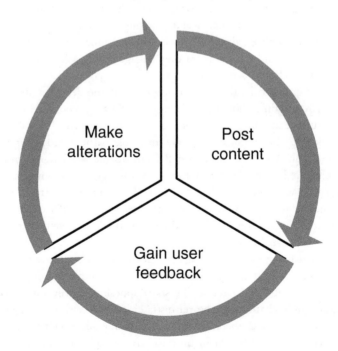

FIGURE 5.3 The feedback cycle you should follow in the early stage of your site

you to conduct grassroots marketing. Pinterest CEO Ben Silbermann organised meet-ups with his audience three months after launching in 2010, when the site had only 3,000 users.[21] Visitors were incentivised to spread the word about the site and it went on to become a runaway success.

Building your team

Launching a news site will involve learning many different skills on the job. But it's likely you will come to a point where you need specialist expertise that either you or your colleagues don't possess. There are two responses to this – either finding short-term freelance support or adding a permanent extra member to your team.

If the short-term need is a creative or technical skill that can be produced remotely then your first port of call should be an online marketplace like Fiverr, 99 Designs, or Guru. These sites offer 'e-lancing' services where employers can commission freelances to complete a wide variety of tasks online. If you use these sites check the previous feedback left about the freelancer. Fiverr works on the premise that most gigs posted cost $5, although more complex ones cost more, making it a cost effective way of finding support.

You can find additional contributors by announcing on social media that you are looking for writers, approaching community groups and message boards and e-mailing nearby universities that teach journalism to offer work experience. Independent Media, a South African start-up, has launched an extensive internship programme to teach journalism graduates how to be mobile journalists, and then encouraged them to develop as reporters in the field.[22]

Your financial position may not allow it, but be aware that offering even a small amount of money for writing articles will increase the chances of contributors being interested. If your contributors are new to the profession, remember to give them constructive feedback to aid their development.

If you identify a long-term skills gap you probably need to add to your team. An alternative to the costly option of paying this new member a salary is to offer them equity in your start-up. This means they will own part of the business with you and any other founders. It allows you to conserve your precious cash reserves, and your new staff member will be invested in the future of the project. This will require you to be more transparent, particularly about the company's finances.[23]

If you are a hyperlocal or regional platform, having staff who live in the communities they cover is extremely beneficial. Technological improvements allow you to decentralise your newsroom and use journalists' homes as regional hubs. This can improve storytelling by heightening awareness of local issues and reducing the time spent commuting.[24] When Speigler Online wanted to investigate how Germany was adjusting to the large-scale influx of refugees in 2015 it sent fifteen mobile journalists to different parts of the country to broadcast what they found.[25] This wouldn't have been possible prior to the widespread adoption of smartphones.

Don't burn out

Digital start-ups are notoriously hard on entrepreneurs who invest everything into making them a success. You need to work smarter, not harder, and avoid falling into what author Oliver Burkeman coined the 'effort trap': 'We chronically confuse the feeling of effort with the reality of results ... to reach creativity heaven, though, you'll need a different approach – one that prioritises doing the right things, not just lots of things'.[26]

With a journalistic venture you need to remember it is a marathon not a sprint, prioritise longevity and sustainability over short-term gain. Aim to stick around to serve your audience in five years' time.

Journalism start-ups in Western Europe are notoriously slow burners compared to their American competitors. The US retains significant advantages in terms of technology, advertising spend, a narrow legacy media structure and big potential audiences, both at home and abroad.[27] It is no coincidence that the biggest players in the digital news playground are American. As the Reuters Institute, based in Oxford, states, survival is success for European start-ups.

Your personal circumstances will dictate the amount of time you can spend on your start-up. Working elsewhere to pay the bills while building up a business is not uncommon. Entrepreneurs on Kickstarter spend an average of 25 hours a week on their projects, most in addition to working.[28] You need to work out how much time you and any co-founders can regularly commit to ensure your workloads are realistic.

We often believe working harder and harder will resolve problems and result in better outcomes, but this has often been disproved. Henry Ford went against convention and adopted a reduced five-day, forty-hour week in his factories back in 1926. The result was an increase in productivity. Likewise Facebook co-founder Dustin Moskovitz believes more rest would have increased the quality of his contribution to the company. He says: 'The research is clear: beyond 40–50 hours a week, the marginal returns from additional work decrease rapidly and quickly become negative.'[29] Creativity is diminished when you are tired.

If you find yourself working an ever-increasing number of hours you need to structure your workload better to ensure you are prioritising the most important issues. Spend your time on areas where you can make a significant difference rather than getting side-tracked performing menial tasks.

Marketing your start-up

Use social media to tell your audience that your readership is growing. You should announce when you reach milestone numbers in terms of page views, followers on Twitter and likes on Facebook. This creates a momentum behind your start-up and encourages your audience to think of themselves as a community.

As your audience grows you need to keep on top of your sales marketing. Your advertisers want to know how you can help them reach their target market, you need to provide them with an answer. Analytics increasingly provide you with a more detailed picture of your audience, so alongside where they live you can often identify their age demographic, gender and hobbies. This information is vitally important to your advertisers.

You should make this information available in an advertising section on your website. It should include information about the specialism and mission of your site, reference the style of coverage you produce, include examples of your best work (including awards and nominations) and supply detailed audience data. As time goes on add testimonials from satisfied clients. You may even want to produce a short video that allows you to insert updated figures. There should also be several ways for interested businesses to contact you.

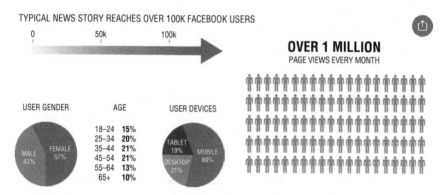

FIGURE 5.4 Breaking down your audience in terms of age, gender and ways they access your site helps potential advertisers
Source: Image courtesy of The Lincolnite.

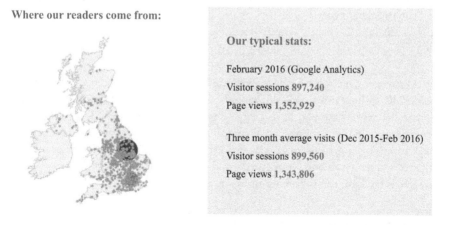

FIGURE 5.5 Making your headline audience figures available, especially if they are broken down geographically, is also extremely important
Source: Image courtesy of The Lincolnite.

Graham Poucher is an award-winning senior press officer and PR manager for Welcome to Yorkshire and Yorkshire's Grand Depart of the Tour de France. He is now a director of Poucher PR.

FIGURE 5.6 Graham Poucher

Make a plan and stick to it. Get the core essence of your business nailed down – basically what do you offer and what do you stand for. Who do you want to target and why. Find a need or gap in the market and start working your way into filling it.

Honesty and being open builds your reputation. The hardest thing in the world is to say no, to turn down business when someone wants to pay you to do something. But if you know deep down that they don't need you or you can't help, it doesn't make for long-term relationships. Hopefully they'll remember when you said no to save them needless cost when they next really do need someone to help.

When pitching your services be honest, do your research so you know your stuff and understand the client, their audience, their needs or problems. Then offer them a solution or service so appealing it's hard for them to say no. They need to be excited and you need to be memorable. You need to be the person they remember as 'the one who …'

It's vital you choose the right staff. Your business is your baby, so you need to trust people who'll look after it, nurture it, protect it and grow it. Trust and commitment are vital.

Once you have gained detailed knowledge of your audience you can also plan sales calls to businesses your site would be particularly valuable to. For example if you become aware you have a large regional audience aged 18–30 you should be making sales calls to pubs, clubs, gyms, restaurants, takeaways and taxi firms in that area. You should produce a regular e-mail newsletter with the latest audience figures and send it to both your current and prospective advertisers. This sales activity needs tracking and following-up regularly.

Customer relations

When you are looking for advertisers the question you should ask yourself is: How will the companies I'm approaching benefit by advertising with me? You need to sell the sizzle, not the sausage. Spend your time explaining the benefits you can bring them, not explaining your product. Outline your USP – which we identified in Chapter 4 – and make this clear in your discussions. Adapt your pitch for every business to let them know how many of their potential customers visit your news site. Identify the most relevant analytical data to them and make this the centre of your pitch.

Training as a journalist should help when you attempt to encourage clients to advertise with you. Forget the hard sell – you want to be polite to engage your advertisers in a conversation. It is similar to winning round the trust of an interviewee. It will probably take more than one conversation to get an advertiser on board so at the outset you just want to raise their awareness.

Before you call, try to find out who the head of marketing is and ask for them by name. If that proves elusive at the beginning of a call, first ensure you are talking to the person who manages the budget. Then get permission to speak by asking if now is a good time, and if it's not call back when they suggest. Personalise the call by tailoring your service to their needs and tell them you are calling to establish if they might be interested in advertising with you in the future.[30]

If the first call goes well follow it up at a later date with your new audience figures and the stories you are covering that are attracting this demographic. You want to build up a strong relationship so avoid sending e-mails, as their tone can be ambiguous. Communication is central to providing a high level of customer service; respond to advertisers quickly and 'trump' their contact, if they e-mail you, ring them back or visit them.[31]

Altering course

Finding solutions to problems you are facing is an ongoing part of running a start-up. If the site is failing to meet the targets being set then you need to quickly diagnose what the problem is and set about solving it.

The first step is to investigate where you stand as a business by producing a new SWOT analysis. This involves demonstrating a degree of detachment and focusing primarily on figures to determine your audience size, income and outgoings. Forbes recommends conducting an internal and external audit to get a clear understanding of the marketplace and your competition, and give a realistic appraisal of your competencies.[32]

Internal

1   Use analytics to determine if the journalism being produced is finding an audience. If not you should look to alter it and experiment with alternative formats.
2   Reinvestigate your competition. If you are several months into the project revisit the research you conducted prior to launch to determine if your competition has grown in recent months.
3   Assess your income. If you are not attracting enough advertisers you should

ask those who are rejecting your services for feedback. You may need to offer different advertising options, alter your rates or devise a new business model reliant on other income streams.

4   Assess your expenditure. If you are running out of capital you need to identify where savings can be made.

You can carry out a content audit by downloading Screaming Frog, software that identifies all the links on your site. This information can then be combined with analytical data and social media interaction figures, available from sharedcount.com, to determine audience interaction with each individual post. A video explaining 'How to do a content audit of your hyperlocal website' is available on the Nesta website.

External

There are different ways of conducting an external audit. One would be to identify three independent, trustworthy figures well placed to conduct a review of your news site. Experienced journalists and academics would be ideal reviewers but avoid direct competitors. Ask them to compile an analysis of your site, which includes your content, social media presence and audience figures. Their findings will build on your internal audit and allow you to make decisions about the future of your site.

Alternatively you could hold a focus group of members of your target audience. This is a more detailed version of the audience feedback discussed above. It can be organised by putting a call out for volunteers on social media, by directly contacting audience members or contacting the organisers of a relevant community group; for example you could get feedback on your hyperlocal blog at a nearby coffee morning. Ideally you want between eight and ten people in your focus group to give a variety of views. Use Skype to conduct a video conversation if you can't speak to people face-to-face.

If you are hosting a focus group you need to ask open-ended questions to determine what its members think about your news site, so ensure you host the session in a room where there is computer access, and see if they have any interests that you are currently not covering. Investigate issues such as their preferred manner of accessing content (desktop, mobile or tablet), social network usage, type of content they engage with and time of day they are online. Record the sessions and pick out the key points made by the contributors.

Avoid using surveys to gain audience feedback, unless there is no other option available to you. Getting feedback face-to-face means you can ask follow-up questions to determine why a reader doesn't like a story, while a survey doesn't allow that option. Additionally, having too many disparate opinions makes it harder to build a cohesive response to a problem.

Findings and action

Once you have both an internal and external view of your start-up you can make decisions about its future. These should be filtered into the three categories of your advancement framework.

- Content – Which types of stories deliver the highest return in terms of audience engagement? Are there topics or forms of content you should avoid producing in future due to low engagement? When you are struggling, time-consuming stories need to deliver larger audience figures.
- Development – Can you tap into fresh online communities to drive interest in your site? Is your engagement with social media platforms sufficient? You may find your niche is too specialist to reach the audience figures you were expecting.
- Finances – Do you need to alter your advertising fees or marketing approach to attract advertisers? What alternative forms of income can you generate? Are there unnecessary expenses that be can cut? You need to balance the books to make your business sustainable.

All organisations have to adjust to suit their audiences' needs and meet their expectations, and even if you are initially successful it is likely you will have to adapt your business model at a later stage. To advance your start-up you should target aspects that require improvement, propose a solution and then test it. Then evaluate it to see if it was successful, and if it wasn't then begin the process again.

This development is continual and applies to the stories you cover, your target audience, your strategy for growth and your finances. Don't tinker with several things at once as you may confuse your audience and make it difficult to establish which changes were successful. Stage changes to happen gradually over a timed period and inform your audience of the reason behind them.

Students as ideal entrepreneurs

The technological disruption in journalism has occurred at an ideal time for young reporters. The old certainties, that audiences buy newspapers and watch daily broadcasts from a select group of news organisations, have fallen away. Many of the structures built by legacy publishers to support that business model, such as buildings and large staffs, are becoming potential liabilities.

This is occurring while the digital sector is booming, with almost 1.5 million British people employed in it. Although heavily weighted towards the southeast, almost two thirds of newly advertised digital jobs are based outside inner London, Britain's traditional power base. Digital clusters are becoming established in cities across the country and a northern start-up hub is being created in Manchester to assist small businesses, which make up 98 per cent of all British digital firms.[33]

These clusters are receiving increasing levels of support. In 2015 Google launched a 'digital garage' in Leeds to help entrepreneurs grow their companies, with plans to expand into other UK cities. This project coincided with the launch of the Google News Lab, which features best-practice tutorials to help journalists use new tools to produce innovative content.

This kind of support is invaluable to enterprising young reporters, who have a more instinctive grasp of the technologies driving the future of journalism and the audiences who use them. Many legacy news organisations are keenly aware of this and have begun tapping into the experiences of digitally savvy trainees to identify how they should be producing and distributing their content. Legacy newsrooms are entering an age of experimentation, and as the *New York Times* reports, 'to help change the culture we need better digital talent'.[34]

Enterprising journalists will prefer to go it alone, and the university is often a fertile ground to meet suitable co-founders and develop a start-up. Finding one or two partners who are committed to making a project successful is vitally important as it allows you to share the load, particularly if you have different skill sets. Entrepreneur Sam Altman recommends prioritising drive and commitment, saying: 'You're looking for co-founders that are unflappable, tough and know what to do in every situation ... you need someone that behaves like James Bond more than you need someone who is an expert'.[35]

How enterprise hubs at universities can help you succeed

There is an increasing amount of support within universities to help develop start-ups, which students should tap into. Enterprise centres are becoming increasingly common on UK campuses at a time when the government is encouraging entrepreneurs to grow the economy. These centres often offer three key resources to students – initial funding, accommodation and mentorship.

You are more likely to be able to access seed funding or early-stage finance from a university, although this differs depending on the size of the institution (see Chapter 2). As your business develops you are more likely to lose equity when you seek investment. If you are not a student the UK government offers start-up loan funding, which has to be repaid with interest over a fixed term.

Rent-free or low-cost office space is another crucial benefit of enterprise centres. As a digital business it makes little sense to pay for an office, but it may not be convenient to work from home. Having access to a workspace you can use when you require it, a landline phone number and a postal address can be extremely handy.

Furthermore, working alongside other entrepreneurs, business mentors and lecturers offers a community of support. Having contemporaries and experts on hand to discuss problems with can help keep you motivated and avoid running your own company becoming a lonely experience.

Picking the pieces out of failing start-ups

The reality of launching an online news platform in an explosive era of change is that not every project can succeed. This is why you have to bootstrap your site at the outset. The harsh reality is that it may never become a sustainable business, and it is better to find that out before you have invested significant amounts of money and time into the venture.

There is no set point at which you have to concede a venture is no longer viable. You may be so invested in your subject that you are content to run your site as a hobby, despite knowing it will always have a small audience. But for a venture to be entrepreneurial it needs to generate income and be sustainable. If it becomes apparent that this is never going to happen you should pull the plug, learn lessons from it and move on.

In 2015, Autopsy.io was launched to identify lessons learnt from American start-up failures. Founders post reasons for their companies' failure in the hope that it will help others to learn from their mistakes. Europe is slowly adapting to this reflective approach to initial failure. The continent, which has traditionally been tougher on failing entrepreneurs, has placed enterprise at the heart of its plans for growth, with European Commission vice-president Antonio Tajani declaring that 'Entrepreneurs are the heroes of our time … We want to make entrepreneurship an attractive and accessible prospect for European citizen[s]'.[36]

Despite this welcome cultural shift, it remains true that European journalistic start-ups rarely thrive unless they produce a higher quality product with lean newsrooms while maintaining diverse revenue streams.[37]

Notes

1 UnLtd (2015) *Apprenticeships for entrepreneurs reflects new economic reality.* unltd.org.uk
2 Johnson, S (2015) *The creative apocalypse that wasn't.* New York Times.
3 Schumacher-Hodge, M (2015) *6 things no-one tells you (but really should) about starting a company.* Medium.
4 Brassington, F and Pettitt, S (2006) *Principles of marketing.* 4th edn. Harlow: Pearson.
5 Brassington, F and Pettitt, S (2013) *Essentials of marketing.* 3rd edn. Harlow: Pearson.
6 Brassington and Pettitt, *Principles of marketing.*
7 Brassington and Pettitt, *Essentials of marketing.*
8 Dibb, S, Simkin, L, Pride, W M and Ferrell, O C (2012) *Marketing: concepts and strategies.* 6th edn. London: Cengage.
9 Kotler, P and Armstrong, G (2015) *Marketing: An introduction.* 12th edn. Harlow: Pearson.
10 Ibid.
11 Briggs, M (2012) *Entrepreneurial journalism: How to build what's next for news.* London: Sage.
12 Briggs (2012).
13 Ries, E (2011) *The lean startup.* St Ives: Penguin.
14 Cho, M (2015) *Start small: In search of the minimum viable product.* The Next Web.
15 Kellner, P (2012) *The problem of trust.* YouGov.
16 The Intercept (2014) *Editorial mission and Staff.* The Intercept.
17 Sinek, S (2010) *How great leaders inspire action.* TED.

18 Cited in Barnett (1998) *Dumbing down or reaching out: Is it tabloidisation wot done it?* The Political Quarterly 69(B): 75–90.
19 Altman, S (2014) *Lecture 1: How to start a start-up.* Stamford University and Y Combinator.
20 Hazard Owen, L (2015) *Two out of two news organizations recommend user research.* Nieman Journalism Lab.
21 Gannes, L (2012) *The secret behind Pinterest's growth was marketing, not engineering, says CEO Ben Silbermann.* AllThingsD.
22 Soobramoney, V (2016) *Mojocon.* Dublin.
23 Akalp, N (2015) *The pros and cons of offering equity to employees.* Mashable.
24 Roth, G (2016) *Mojocon.* Dublin.
25 Spertser, S (2016) *Mojocon.* Dublin.
26 Burkeman, O (2015) *Nobody cares how hard you work.* 99u.com
27 Bruno, N and Nielsen, R (2012) *Survival is success: Journalistic online start-ups in Western Europe.* Oxford: Reuters Institute for the Study of Journalism.
28 Briggman, S (2015) *Hours per week spent on a Kickstarter project.* Crowdcrux.
29 Moskovitz, D (2015) *Work hard, live well.* Medium.
30 Stears, A (2015) MADE Entrepreneur Festival, Sheffield.
31 Ramm, G (2015) MADE Entrepreneur Festival, Sheffield.
32 Aileron. *Five steps to a strategic plan.* Forbes.
33 Source: Tech City UK (2015) *Powering the digital economy.*
34 New York Times (2014) *Innovation Report.*
35 Altman, S (2014) *Lecture 2: Ideas, products, teams and execution, Part II.* Stamford University and Y Combinator.
36 European Commission (2013) *Unleashing Europe's entrepreneurial potential to bring back growth.* Press release.
37 Bruno and Nielsen, *Survival is success.*

6

STARTING YOUR WEBSITE AND WRITING ONLINE

Now you need to get your web platform off the ground and begin populating it with stories. This chapter will help you set up your site, begin managing it and help you plan a content strategy that suits your audience.

Once you have researched your market, plotted a business model that suits your project and put a basic workflow in place you are in a healthy position to launch your news site. The costs involved with the set-up and operation of websites are relatively low, which is advantageous for any entrepreneur looking to launch a new product in a challenging marketplace. However, your reputation as a news outlet can be badly affected by the appearance and navigation of your site, so you need to ensure that as many technical issues as possible are ironed out before your audience arrives.

On paper your newsroom production line will always work like a dream, but how will it fare in the real-world environment where huge stories can break at the most inconvenient times? Producing a high standard of scheduled multimedia content is one thing, but you need to develop a journalistic reflex in order to adapt your approach to react to news events. As a result we will examine how to repurpose content under pressure, run an engaging live blog, and ethically aggregate and curate material from social media platforms.

Journalistic start-ups operate a variety of content strategies, which has led to significant debate over the merits of producing short, snackable news against the draw of long-read journalism. Both approaches can be successful, but you need to find the mixture that best suits your project. You also require a strategy when dealing with readers' comments to ensure your audience feels they are being heard and listened to; especially when you find yourself in the wrong. This chapter will take you through the nuts and bolts involved in getting your news site off the ground.

Launching your website

The process of launching a website has got considerably easier in recent years. It has now reached a point where most tech savvy individuals should be able to follow a series of steps to get your site up and functioning. Below is a short glossary of terms which may help you navigate this chapter, before we start investigating how to set up your new platform.

Configuration files   In computing, these configure the parameters and settings for programs. The Wordpress configuration file connects the website to the database. This needs to be set up prior to launching a self-hosting site.

Content management system   A computer system to organise the material you want to publish. Wordpress is a CMS. It allows you to decide what you want to publish, when and how, and then performs this task as directed.

Embed   When you embed content into your website you use a code or text to tell the CMS to include material hosted elsewhere. Sharing platforms such as YouTube and Twitter make content on their sites embeddable.

Host   Hosts store information, such as a website, so it can be accessed online. In this chapter, self-hosting relates to finding your own web host rather than relying on free hosting from Wordpress or Bloggr.

Permalink   This is a permanent hyperlink to a post. Depending on settings they can include the post's title, the date of the post or other data.

Plugin   These are add-on programs that are compatible with Wordpress' CMS. They can make a significant difference to the functionality of your website. There are thousands of plugins available that will allow you to report in different ways or manage your site better.

Theme   These are templates you can upload to your CMS to give your site an initial appearance. This can be changed by altering design parameters, adding plugins and managing your menus.

Key tool: Wordpress

Wordpress has become the web's dominant CMS – it runs a quarter of the internet[1] – by promoting its own unique selling points, its ease of use and the fact it is free. The widespead adoption of Wordpress' CMS means its community of users is on hand to offer support if something goes wrong with your site.

Wordpress offers its users two options when using its content management system, to host the site on Wordpress.com for free or alternatively to download its CMS for use on your own self-hosted website. The Wordpress-based version can be set up in minutes, which is ideal for prototypes, but there are some limitations that can make long-term use problematic. Wordpress-hosted sites come with a 30MB data limit,[2] a web address with a .wordpress.com suffix and limited scope for personalisation. All of these issues can be addressed by upgrading your account, but it is often easier to opt to self-host from the outset.

You can download Wordpress' CMS for free from Wordpress.org. If you pursue this option you need to invest in a hosting package. Ideally you should choose one that is Linux-based, offers a significant amount of web space (around 500MB), a control panel to allow easy administration and an installation wizard to make set-up relatively painless.[3] Just Host, 1&1, and UK2 are among the providers who offer this service at a reasonable monthly price. You will also need to buy a web address containing your project's name.

Your web host will provide a step-by-step guide to help you set up your site on their platform. The process has five stages:

- Creating a database with your web host.
- Installing Wordpress in your webspace.
- Ensuring your domain (web address) points to the Wordpress folder.
- Creating a configuration file.
- Naming your site. Consider your site's security when choosing usernames and passwords.

If you self-host a Wordpress site or pay for an upgraded Wordpress.com site you can customise and develop your site by installing a multitude of plugins. Due to Wordpress' open source nature there is an extensive range of options open to you to enhance your reporting and the appearance of your site. Your inventive use of these tools is important in distinguishing your site from the competition.

Design

Once your site is set up you need to choose a Wordpress design theme that will provide the basis for its design. There is a huge range of themes available from various providers, who usually charge relatively low fees for the licence to use them. Ideally you want to find a supplier who offers a user's guide, technical support or ideally both to help you address any problems and access theme updates. Study the theme previews closely before purchasing to ensure it fits your requirements.

You should begin your search by examining magazine themes, as these are the ones aimed at news sites. If you choose a theme that is heavily reliant on images, remember you will have to take pictures or rely on Creative Commons images to fill those spaces, which could look less impressive than the preview.

Selecting a theme that will form the basis for your site's appearance will be one of the biggest decisions facing you prior to launch. Before choosing you should sketch out a plan of how you want your homepage to look. These is also no point choosing a design that goes against your core priorities for your content. The opportunity to vary the site's appearance, through colour or arrangement of site furniture, is also a positive as this introduces scope to freshen up your site in future, without losing its identity.

Pictures

Don't underestimate the importance of pictures in your design. For many print journalists images are often an afterthought, a throwback to when pictures were literally someone else's problem, historically the photographer and the sub. You should use display pictures in a big and bold fashion if possible, although obviously don't risk low resolution pictures becoming pixilated by stretching them too far. If your site becomes slow to load due to images you should compress them using Photoshop or Pixlr. Space on your site is still a valuable commodity online, but it doesn't need to be carefully rationed like a print product, so give images plenty of room.

SEO

When writing headlines for your site you also need to be mindful of the importance of Search Engine Optimisation (SEO). SEO is the art of making your content findable by internet search engines by making it clear to them what is on your site. Although promotion through social media should be your priority when it comes to attracting audiences, search engines are still a key route of access for audiences. Ensuring your permalink structure is set to display post names, rather than numeric or date-related information, will assist with this process.

Using an SEO plugin like Yoast and a Google sitemap plugin also helps improve your site's visibility. Including hyperlinks to external content and receiving traffic from hyperlinked content on other sites will improve your standing in the eyes of a search engine, although you don't want to provide too many opportunities for visitors to leave your site.

When writing posts, avoid being vague and ensure the story contains key words audiences are likely to search for throughout. Prioritise locations and notable people or organisations. These should be in the headline, main body of the story, captions for the story and the post's tags. Any audio or video you including on site will be unsearchable, so you may want to consider including an excerpt of the transcript containing keywords in the post.[4]

However don't let keywords ruin your stories. You need to make your headlines interesting enough to attract your audience, not just satisfy search engine algorithms. Your headlines need to focus on how the story affects people; don't be afraid to be direct or controversial because you need people to care enough to click on the article.[5] One way of testing the performance of your website is to conduct an A/B test (or split test). To do this you compare two versions of a web page – altering the aspects you want to investigate – in order to work out which performs better.[6]

Writing online

In the UK, legacy broadcasters and publishers still set the daily news agenda, as demonstrated by the 2015 general election campaign. However, as an entrepreneurial journalist you should be focusing on reflecting your news agenda in a way that is relevant to your target audience; you want to specifically engage them, not turn your news site into a mass audience product. As Kevin Sutcliffe, head of news programming at Vice, explains, the election campaign demonstrated why their site exists:

> News and current affairs [is] increasingly spoken to an older audience … the opportunity for others like Vice is to engage people in a different way. Looking at issues that we think are important but are just not being talked about like housing and rent costs.[7]

You need to plan to start conversations your audience will engage with, be prepared to investigate stories that will spark an emotive reaction and provide the articles readers will be discussing on social media or chat apps. Even if that audience is initially small, the transmission that comes with pursuing a news agenda that really speaks to your audience will drive up interest in your content.

Planned content

Keeping an up-to-date newsroom diary is crucially important when forward planning content; it always has been. This needs to be a key responsibility in your newsroom and updating it needs to be prioritised on a daily basis. Without it you are working with one hand tied behind your back. Annual anniversaries of historic stories need to be rolled forward, particularly when covering a geographical community that has lived through them; planned events, such as carnivals, parades and conferences, should be included to allow pre- and post-event pieces to be pulled together and thought needs to be given to how you will reflect feast days across the calendar. For example if you are writing about tech you probably want to begin writing a piece titled '10 things you'll definitely want to receive for Christmas' around October or produce your pre-season guide by mid-July if you're a football site. For hyperlocals make sure you post your 'Five places you can spend New Years' Eve' after Boxing Day and ensure your 'Great local toppings for your pancakes' article is ready at least a week before Shrove Tuesday.

But it's not just annual events that need to be scheduled. If you are keeping track of a court case, the defendant's next appearance needs to go in the diary, preferably with a clipping of previous coverage. The date a VIP is due to be making an appearance needs noting or when a key business, the council or the government is due to make a major announcement. Basically if you can see yourself writing about it, you need to know about it in advance as this gives you a major advantage in ensuring you produce the best coverage. Evernote, which is available online or as an app, can help you run a cloud-stored collaborative diary and remind you of key events.

Potential pre-pieces could include repurposing coverage of a community event from a previous year as a nostalgic look back, informing your audience of the importance of an upcoming announcement or explaining the stage a particular court case has reached, while obviously observing legal restrictions.

Planning ahead also allows you to plot a strategy for the medium of your coverage. If your coverage will include multimedia you can decide if you want to livestream video, produce a video package, record audio or take enough images to create a picture slideshow. If you were reflecting on a historic positive event, such as the London Olympics or the Grand Depart in Yorkshire, you could create a quiz to ask readers what they remember about it or include a visualisation or infographic to show how many people attended.

Learn the lesson from Buzzfeed, ask yourself *How do I expect my audience to react to this?* This has to be at the heart of your decision-making process when scheduling stories. Be realistic when you are forecasting, otherwise you will end up pouring valuable resources into coverage that people are largely indifferent to. You should also involve your audience in the planning process to build their engagement, a tactic that is outlined in Chapter 7. That isn't to say you shouldn't cover mundane stories, but you need to find a way of it landing an impact. Research by NPR Digital Services in America identified nine types of stories that drove engagement and sharing online: eight of these are listed below and can be pre-planned[8]:

1   Place explainers – These explain the background behind landmarks or elements specific to a geographic area. This can be expanded to explain assumed knowledge to new members of a specialist audience. They provide knowledge.
2   Crowd pleasers – These promote the positive aspect of a community. This encourages a feeling of pride amongst its members.
3   Curiosity stimulators – Weird and quirky news that grabs the audience's attention. The audience want to find out why and how this has happened.
4   News explainers – Provide context to developing or ongoing news stories. Relay the background for audiences that skim the news.
5   Feelgood smilers – Heart-warming, soft news tales, often involving animals and children. Can spark intense audience interest on social media.
6   Topical buzzer – The story people are talking about. Needs to be timed right to ride the coat-tails of that story.[9] If you want to know what people are currently searching for online across a range of topics visit Google Trends.[10]
7   Provocative controversy – An issue that angers the community. Likely to trigger intense discussion on social platforms.
8   Awe-inspiring visuals – Items of multimedia journalism the audience are particularly drawn to. Images that feature members of a community at an event often encourage people to attempt to spot themselves.

Each of these story types serves a specific purpose for your audience. They either provide information that readers are otherwise likely to use an internet search engine to find, grab their attention or encourage an emotive response. They are targeted to engage your audience in addition to providing them with the news.

The most controversial of these story groupings in a news context are 'feelgood smilers'. These provide audiences with instant gratification but little enduring value; although not clickbait, as readers are not misled by their headlines, they are sweet human-interest stories that would struggle to be classed by most journalists as news.[11] The reason they often co-exist with news is because audiences tend to read and share them widely, often at the expense of weightier news. Bingeing on this type of disposable journalism has been compared by Joshua Topolsky, a founder of The Verge, to indulging in a whole bag of Doritos: 'You look up and think "'What am I doing?"'.[12] One of the decisions you need to make at the outset of establishing a content plan is to decide where you stand on the type of material. Populist content can drive traffic to your website but if it is ill-suited to your target audience it can impact negatively on the mission underpinning your start-up and the morale of your staff. It can stifle creativity in a similar manner to churning out blockbuster movies for mass cinema audiences.[13]

However you plan, as a newsroom you should always have enough content scheduled to maximise your audience – depending on the analytical and dimensional targets you have chosen to define this – on a daily basis. But you will need to identify the weakest elements of that content quickly when events run ahead of you.

Evergreen content

Building evergreen place explainers into your news site can attract traffic repeatedly. Place explainers can be particularly valuable for hyperlocal sites or ones with a geographical patch. For example, writing about the backstory of a historic landmark would get initial views from members of your audience who are unaware of it; but in addition it will attract views for people who want to find out in the future. Similarly if you produce a feature about places to take children to for a day out in your area at the start of a school holiday period, you will attract initial traffic but then pick up additional visits from parents thereafter. Then all you have to do in future is update the story every major holiday. You just have to ensure your stories are optimised for search engines.

News explainers, giving the background to a story, can be particularly useful if you are covering long-running stories. The US presidential race, for example, lasts longer than a year so if you put together an explainer at the outset which outlines the candidates, their pledges, their donors and fundraising sources, and their chances of ending up in the White House, you can refer readers to it throughout your campaign coverage. It should be updated but the original would also provide a useful article to reflect back on at the end of the race.

If you are writing for a specialist audience, explainers can be valuable as a way of explaining terminology or assumed knowledge within that specialism to new members of that community. Internal linking to longstanding explainers within new content also has the advantage of keeping readers on your site, rather than in a new tab looking for the backstory. The *Washington Post* has gone a step beyond this by introducing a 'knowledge map' feature that provides highlighted links in stories that readers can click on. This opens a supplements tap on the right of the page that contains a brief overview of that highlighted section to provide context.[14] The 'knowledge map' is another example of personalising news, as it aims to solve the problem of readers with different levels of prior knowledge of a topic. The *Post* has also introduced a bookmark tool to help readers keep their place during long features.[15]

Reactive content

A significant proportion of any newsroom's content is going to be unforeseen. As Harold Macmillan once famously remarked, the hardest challenge is responding to events as they unfold. You should not respond to breaking news in a blind panic – you need to follow a clear plan of action to provide your audience with effective coverage.

First, you need to verify the news. With most stories this is relatively straight-forward but you need to be especially careful with information on social media, an issue outlined in more detail in Chapter 10. If a reputable news provider is running the story one approach is to include a line in your coverage detailing this, although it means you are relying on them being correct.

Next you need to get as much information as you can stand up on your website as soon as possible. It doesn't matter if this is minimal at the outset; many initial breaking news reports are only one or two lines. If you wait until you have the whole story you will have lost most of the potential traffic. If possible include a stock image and then immediately promote your story across your social media channels. If you have an app this is also the point you would send a push notification. Then you should return to your story and update it with new information as it comes in, posting new updates across your social media platforms when significant new information becomes available.

At this point you should consider multimedia content in more depth. You need to create an adequate library system to allow you to quickly repurpose previous content. In addition to raiding these internal resources you need to search for readily available external content; this involves searching social and content sharing platforms such as Twitter and YouTube to find embeddable content. Images marked for reuse under Creative Commons legislation and GIFs (short sections of looping video) are additional potential sources of content. Ensure any material you use is correctly credited to the copyright owner.

When David Bowie died suddenly in January 2016, this style of curation aided the creation of a vast array of multimedia obituaries on news websites world-wide. Journalism lecturer Paul Bradshaw identified sixteen different ways news-rooms had curated a huge archive of Bowie's songs, videos and iconic images alongside reactions to his death in their coverage. He reflected: '[Curation] has become the web native version of the obituary'.[16] If you find yourself using cura-tion as a regular tactic when reacting to breaking news you may want to consider using Storify, a Wordpress-compatible platform that specialises in this style of journalism.

Heavyweight breaking news

Being well established in a specialism or geographic location puts you in the driving seat when news breaks on your patch. You should make full use of the relationships you've built up covering everyday stories to position yourself ahead of media outlets who only appear during a crisis. Don't be afraid to remind officials you are the person they deal with every day. Engage with your audience to get their response to the events[17] and remember that as a patch audience, your readers will be expecting more detail than will appear in the broad-brush mainstream media.

Depending on the gravity of a breaking news story, you may decide to splinter off angles within the story into separate posts to offer this detail. This compartmentalising enables your audience to choose which aspects of the story they are most interested in. At the foot of each of these intertwined stories should be a hyperlink or tab guiding your reader to articles covering further aspects of the story. 'Flooding the zone' during a major news event[18] by pulling out all the stops to produce a range of content that delves deep into the story can drive a high level of traffic, but you need to monitor audience engagement levels to ensure this plays out as expected. If it doesn't you need to redeploy your resources back to planned content.

When a big story breaks now, everyone has the potential to produce media and these platforms become a library of potential resources. If you are adept at identifying the best ones then you can provide coverage to your audience, despite not being present. During the November 2015 terrorist attacks in Paris the emerging story was relayed to people in visual content posted across social platforms. A clip showing France playing an international football match against Germany as a loud bang goes off near the stadium formed a key part of coverage, not just for broadcasters but on social media via Vine. Stephane Hannache, a Twitter user, become a citizen journalist for the night, hosting more than 10,000 viewers on his Periscope livestream as shots rang out at the Balaclan theatre.[19] However, before embedding coverage into your site you should check it out thoroughly and if it is an external livestream make it explicitly clear to your audience that you have no control over the content on it.

Potential potency of speedy reactive content

Breaking news stories and opinionated follow-ups are driving audience engagement on Facebook for nearly every publisher.[20] Getting reporters to prioritise quick-hit news stories with an original angle and crisp headline has been successful for digital newsrooms in driving up page views and unique visitor numbers.[21]

This tactic relies upon attracting readers by offering a variety of content and keeping them hooked by providing enough material to keep them engaged, almost a light version of the MailOnline traffic model. However, this approach carries many of the hallmarks of the production line reporting or 'churnalism' approach derided by many journalists, who often feel it lacks the insight of original reporting. This is one of the areas where as a publisher, in addition to being a journalist you will have to make a clear judgement on your approach to sustainability. There is a strong argument that news organisations have always produced short, quick responsive coverage,[22] and all that is different now is the technology that aids instant publication.

Instant opinion

In the digital age almost instant opinionated follow-ups have their own term: the 'hot take'. However, the quality of a hot take relies almost exclusively on the journalist producing it. Opinion is the easiest thing to do in online journalism, but one of the hardest to do right. To give a valuable instant judgement on an event you should have prior knowledge of the facts involved, an important point missed by many people who daily pour out their opinions on blogs.

Hot takes originated in American sports coverage in the early 2000s before spreading to the political arena. But they have an increasingly poor reputation in journalism as they over-represent the views of disgruntled, old, white men, often lack a basis in fact and are seen as primarily a tool to drive traffic.[23] Manufacturing provocative opinionated reaction for the sake of it is unlikely to help you establish your site as a credible news outlet; if you produce a hot take you should ensure it will remain a credible piece of commentary once the heat has died down.

You should consider whether the subject is suitable before writing a hot take: opinion on hard news requires careful consideration, not haste. A basis in fact, an ability to put the news in context, and keeping your judgement short and sweet when details are still emerging should enable it to be a relevant and realistic appraisal of the situation.

Liveblogging

Liveblogging is used in both news and sports to provide rolling coverage; in fact BBC Sport Online and BBC local regions run full-day liveblogs on their sites. But it is particularly effective when focused on a particular event, like a breaking news story or a sports match. Although the tone of a liveblog is heavily affected by the seriousness of the story being reported on, it often allows the journalist to inject a sense of their personality into the coverage, making it more conversational and encouraging audience participation.

A liveblog brings the audience the latest information as it becomes available, rather than packaging it as a news story with a clear-cut intro, so including a short, regularly updated summary of events at the top of the page is crucial to aid understanding. Audiences are increasingly used to live coverage so they understand it is more disjointed and navigate the page to find crucial information they have missed. Liveblogs are easy to set up through Wordpress and, on a business note, provide an additional opportunity to include advertising on your site.

If you are running a liveblog you need to put considerable thought into planning it, as they tend to devour content. It helps considerably if you have already produced relevant content on your site, which you can signpost readers to within your liveblog to keep them engaged. If you are producing a reactive liveblog you will probably rely on external content much more, but you need to ensure there aren't too many links off-site where you can leak readers. In this situation involving your audience by getting them to post their reaction on social media can drive engagement and provide you with material to maintain momentum in your coverage.

Tom Rostance is a broadcast jour-nalist at BBC Sport Online. BBC Football's live pages had 141 million global page views during the 2014 Brazil World Cup.

Our live text commentary pages are always the busiest we have, but live text is now expanding beyond sport. Regardless of where you work as an online journalist live texts will be something you will do a lot of. We've introduced interactivity within our pages so now you can vote within a page.

FIGURE 6.1 Tom Rostance

Before doing a live text you need to do your research, you need to have at least a basic understanding of the topic you are writing about. When you are covering news you need to be aware of procedures too.

During a game your entries need to be at least one a minute, often more. It is more than a one man operation, while I'm typing someone will be putting pictures from the game in, some tweets or reaction from reporters in the ground so you have to be aware you are not just the author; you are an editor as well. You also need to remember with live reporting there is no filter between you and potentially two million people so once you hit publish it's gone. It's not like you send a story to the subs' desk and someone checks it for spellings and makes sure it all makes sense.

You need to be very wary of that but don't think about it too much because you'd be too scared to write anything. Don't make too many mistakes is my best advice. Don't get the score wrong, I've done that before and got all sorts of grief. When a goal is scored we aim to flash that up with the scorer's name within about ten seconds and then about a minute later to put up a more detailed entry with an image. Within about two minutes of the ball going in the net that would all be online. It has got to be up straight away.

Sometimes you'll get a moment in your career when you'll think, this is crazy. After 29 minutes of the World Cup semi-final, the hosts Brazil were getting beaten 5–0 by Germany. It was ridiculous; no one in the office could speak. But by the time it was 3–0 someone was already digging out the World Cup's biggest victories, the record win in a semi-final and what's the worst every performance by a Brazilian team, all those kind of figures. Sometimes all the planning goes out of the window; when Brazil are losing 5–0 after half an hour no-one has planned for that. The beauty of sport is that what is going to happen is not set in stone. That's why it's such a good job to do; you never know what is going to happen.

You have to keep it simple and be accurate when a lot is going on; it's very easy to go into meltdown and fall further and further behind the action. During that game our traffic went through the roof, people will be out not watching the game and suddenly find out the score. So everyone is piling onto our website. It's like they can't believe it really, they need to find out why? What is going on?

Everyone has their own style of doing live texts; just describing what happens quickly becomes boring so you need to add colour and humour to your report when appropriate. If it is also on television and people are second-screening the best way to do that is by telling them things they can't see. Try and involve reaction in your coverage, that is where having others working with you helps. Even though the World Cup was on terrestrial television our audience figures showed the people still wanted to interact with us and tweet in.

Aggregation

The business of aggregating news content has become extremely contentious. When you aggregate news you publish content initially produced by another news organisation. It differs from curation by nature of a post relying on one or two specific sources for the crux of the story, rather than a wide variety of content adding value to original reporting. Aggregation is not new; it has gone on for decades, particularly in newspapers.[24] But traditionally you had to wait for the next print run whereas in the digital era aggregation is almost instant, driving traffic away from the original source of the story. This can also cause problems if your business model revolves around charging for access to your content when your opposition operates a free-access platform.

The Huffington Post received criticism for its approach to aggregation as it attempted to grow its audience during the period of establishing itself as a major news platform. Writer Michael Shapiro alleges: 'Pieces appeared at ever greater length on the site, diminishing the likelihood that readers would follow a link back to the source ... while it never stopped supplying links, it made them just a little harder to find'.[25]

Guidelines are emerging around ethical aggregation, and if your site is to feature aggregated content it is important to follow these. Digital journalism professor Mindy McAdams recommends including clear attribution and a link to the original story and quotation marks around text you have copied. You should always aim to add value – such as an update, additional quotes or multimedia – to the original story or compare reports from additional sources.[26] Attributing information helps readers evaluate its reliability, so choosing the right ones provides a judgement on your news sense.[27]

Length of stories

As we've already discussed with regard to planned and reactive content, you need to develop a strategy when it comes to written content. You should be aiming to either be the first onto a story or the best, as the stories that are neither will find their audience squeezed.[28] A key part of this is identifying whether you are prioritising short written pieces, longer written pieces or, as is more likely, a mixture of the two. If everyone in the newsroom understands what is required from a story it makes the editorial process quicker and provides consistency across the site for readers.

As with most aspects of your start-up though, you need to continually monitor audience engagement.[29] If your analytics demonstrate your audience is unwilling to spend any more time on your long form content than your shorter stories, then you should consider publishing more short stories. They are usually quicker to produce and by sacrificing length you should be able to produce more stories.

Producing snackable news is consistent with a mobile-first strategy, which is outlined in more depth in Chapter 7. Producing stories in lists is an established snackable format, which has provided journalism with the now familiar term: the listicle. This approach, which often includes using many more images and GIFs (short looped visual clips), appeals to a young demographic. There are fewer words, which makes the stories quicker to read, and listicles are also likely to benefit publishers who aim to maximise page views and visits as key performance indicators (KPIs), as they encourage readers to click on more stories.

This approach mirrors social media, where users are presented with a series of short snippets of information that they can either digest or use as a starting point to find out more about an issue. If you are aiming to provide news that readers can digest while they are commuting or waiting in a queue this is likely to be a key format for you. However, it is unlikely that you will want all your coverage to be so tightly constrained.

Long form

If your audience is prepared to devote a considerable amount of time to reading long form content then you should endeavour to produce more of it. This demonstrates your readers are really engaging with the site and by producing less content, but making it more in-depth, you should keep them on your site longer. This deeper engagement is typically what well established news websites, that prioritise reader time on site, are aiming to promote.

The inbuilt danger of writing solely long form content is that every post needs to be a hit, otherwise you've lost your audience until the next post. This means you need to communicate with your readers regularly and use analytics to accurately determine the content your audience will engage with. Most long form content is produced to deliver a wow factor amongst readers, which encourages them to share it with social media contacts and return for the next instalment. It is primarily published for desktop consumers – a substantial though shrinking section of the audience – which involves targeting office staff during the daytime and evening surfers.

Case study: Wait but Why

Wait but Why is an informative, explainer website which challenges the convention that modern audiences want quick, short form stories. The site's founders, Tim Urban and Andrew Finn, didn't believe that online articles should be short, and to make their site viable banked on a unique selling point (USP) that enough readers had the attention span to read high quality articles that usually surpass 2,000 words.

This bold approach in a light news environment has turned out to be extremely successful. In little over 18 months the site had 1.6 million unique visitors a month, 4.6 million page views and more than 100,000 subscribers to their newsletter, which was translated into several different languages. A story examining the psychosocial reasons why Generation Y is so unhappy was shared more than 2 million times.[30]

The site posts an average of one explainer a week. Its strapline 'new posts, every sometimes' indicates the site will only produce a high-quality article when it is ready rather than to a set deadline. This challenges the traditional newsroom structure that news is produced consistently, regardless of events. In this regard Wait but Why has joined Buzzfeed in challenging the conventions of publishing for the digital age, albeit using a completely different approach.[31]

Stories from Wait but Why, like Buzzfeed and the Huffington Post, are very successful on social media; the site has more than 310,000 likes on its Facebook page.[32] But it is for a specific reason: their accessible stories, which have the advantage of being evergreen, pique the curiosity of their audience to the point where readers are moved to share them with their friends so they too can find out about something new.

As writer Michael Grothaus observes, there are several reasons why Wait but Why's format has been successful. Its founders have developed a reputation for research and hard work but their explainers are written in a layperson's style and they focus on a topic they are genuinely interested in. Despite the length of the stories, design is considered and text is broken into blocks and images are used to support the words, rather than the other way around. Additionally the site's readers have become a valued and engaged community, discussing the topic independently at length in the comments section.[33]

How adaptable the Wait but Why model is to other long form websites is difficult to gauge. A significant amount of the site's appeal is tied in with Urban, who monopolises the writing duties on the site. But the site emphasises why you should always keep experimenting and innovating in the digital era, because going against perceived wisdom has the advantage of making your platform stand out.

Building a community of readers

If you want to develop a passionate community of readers, similar to Wait but Why, distribution is almost as important as the quality of your content. In Chapter 9 we will discover how social media can help you attract your target audience, but how can you hook readers once they have discovered you? The answer is a slightly older technology: e-mail.

Distribution though an e-mail newsletter may seem an odd step to take for a forward-thinking news website but publishers have discovered that it attracts loyal readers, who are prepared to read the e-mails and click through to stories they are interested in. The *New York Times* adopted the approach of breaking its broad coverage into thirty-three niche sections and was rewarded with an open rate of up to 70 per cent from its readers.[34]

The message is clear: If you personalise the news to suit the interests of individual readers there is a better chance they will engage with your stories. Therefore you should have a visible e-mail newsletter sign-up box on your website and consider breaking up the content on your site into even smaller niches because doing so may result in even higher open rates. A provider like Mail Chimp, which is compatible with Wordpress, will offer you a free service initially, allowing you to scale up your operations when you have more readers and income to play with.

Selling ad space in your newsletters is another form of income, although this needs to be done sparingly to avoid the newsletter being judged as spam. A few newsrooms, such as Quartz, Ozy, and The Briefing, are even using e-mail as its own self-contained platform, offering readers the full story in their inbox, therefore avoiding the risk they won't click through.[35]

Reacting to comments

Responding to readers' comments about a story has increasingly become an important aspect of a journalist's job, particularly when you are aiming to promote reader loyalty. A study by the Engaging News Project found when reporters replied to statements about the stories, the tone of the comments sections usually remained civil. Adopting an objective stance, including links to further information, answering questions and highlighting helpful comments were all seen to be helpful in promoting a higher level of discussion.[36]

However, many news websites have been finding it harder to manage comments, particularly when there are so many competing demands for journalists. The Verge and The Daily Dot closed their comment sections in 2015 because they became too difficult to manage.[37] As a start-up you should aim to encourage readers' comments; if you designate an audience engagement editor, a role that is examined in more detail in Chapter 7, then moderating comments should be part of their role.

You should ensure that you have a brief policy statement that outlines your expectation of your readers' comments and how they will be managed. In addition you should also install a Wordpress plugin, such as Akismet or Antispam Bee, to stop comment spam appearing on your site.

When stories go wrong

If you thought you'd never make a mistake as a reporter, tough luck, you will. But it is how you respond to an error that demonstrates your worth as a journalist in the digital age. Transparency and honesty with your audience are key watchwords.

A Glamour's listicle titled '13 little things that can make a man fall hard for you' went viral for all the wrong reasons in July 2015. It provoked a storm of criticism for encouraging women to engage in a series of man-pleasing activities and prompted a witty takedown by Vice.[38] Glamour heeded the advice of its audience and replaced the post with a response to the furore, agreeing the article was misplaced and apologising for slipping off message.[39] Although it got its original post wrong, Glamour had responded in the best way possible, holding its hands up and making light of the original article. In the digital age we all make mistakes; accepting that fact and meeting those errors head-on is usually the best solution.

Entrepreneurial journalists are often flying solo or in small teams so often lack the support of experienced colleagues who can catch almost every mistake before your work is transmitted to the audience. Rolling online news has softened the harshness of meeting deadlines for physical print newspapers, allowing stories to be swiftly updated. But you should let your audience know this has happened.

Put a clear structure in place

As Sarah Marshall of the *Wall Street Journal* says: 'No news organisation has all the answers when it comes to digital'.[40] Plans you put in place prior to launching will need to be adapted once you've road tested them in the real world as you find a way of working that suits yourself, colleagues and contributors.

Having a clear structure for the types of content you aim to produce, when covering both planned and reactive stories, is crucial to ensuring your news site works. All your contributors need to know how long their posts should be and what style of reporting and multimedia coverage you are expecting before they start writing it, otherwise you are wasting time and resources. You must also ensure you listen and react to your readers, an issue that the next chapter – which focuses on analytics – can help you address in greater depth.

Notes

1 Gelbmann, M (2015) *Wordpress powers 25% of all websites*. w3techs.com
2 Wordpress (2016) *Support: Adding storage space*. Wordpress.com
3 Sugden, M, cited in Marsden, P (2015) *How to build a budget news website*. Leanpub.
4 Unitt, C (2015) *SEO tips for hyperlocal publishers*. Nesta.
5 Briggs, M (2013) *Journalism next*. London: Sage.
6 VWO (2016) *The complete guide to A/B testing*. vwo.com/ab-testing
7 Sutcliffe, K, cited in Byrne, C (2015) *Getting engaged? The relationship between traditional, new media and the electorate during the 2015 UK general election*. Oxford: Reuters Institute.
8 Athas, E and Gorman, T (2013) *9 types of local stories that cause engagement*. NPR Digital Services.
9 Ibid.
10 Unitt, *SEO tips for hyperlocal publishers*.
11 Klinger, L and McBride, K (2016) *Stop calling every news article clickbait*. Poynter Institute.
12 Somaiya, R (2015) *When clicks reign, audience is king*. New York Times.
13 Ibid.
14 Wang, S (2015) *How the Washington Post built – and will be building on – its 'knowledge map' feature*. Nieman Lab.
15 Lichterman, J (2016) *The Washington Post is trying to make it easier to read long features*. Nieman Lab.
16 Bradshaw, P (2016) *Curation is the new obituary: 16 ways media outlets marked Bowie's life and death*. onlinejournalismblog.com
17 Gerson, D (2015) *4 tips for engaging your audience during breaking news events*. Poynter Institute.
18 Briggs, M (2012) *Entrepreneurial journalism*. London: Sage.
19 Newman, N (2016) *Journalism, media and technology predictions 2016*. Oxford: Reuters Institute for the Study of Journalism.
20 Dahl, K (2016) *Why hard news is thriving on Facebook*. Medium.
21 Batsell, J (2015) *Engaged journalism: Connecting with digitally empowered news audiences*. Chichester: Columbia University Press.
22 Yemma, J, cited in Batsell, *Engaged journalism*.
23 Reeve, E (2015) *A history of the hot take*. New Republic.
24 Buttry, S (2012) *Aggregation guidelines: Link, attribute and add value*. The Buttry Diary, stevebuttry.wordpress.com
25 Shapiro, M (2012) *How the Huffington Post ate the internet*. Columbia Journalism Review.
26 McAdams, M (2013) *Aggregation and curation in journalism*. Teaching Online Journalism, mindymcadams.com
27 Buttry, *Aggregation guidelines*.
28 Gutjahr, R (2015) *The future of journalism: Make it snackable!* Medium.
29 Shishkin, D (2015) *3 components of the digital transformation of newsrooms*. World News Publishing Focus.
30 Grothaus, M (2015) *The secret of writing smart, long form articles that go absolutely viral*. Fast Company.
31 Weigert, M (2015) *Wait but why: You do not need $100 million to create a successful online publishing brand*. Meshedsociety.com
32 Wait but Why (2016) *Homepage*. waitbutwhy.com
33 Grothaus, *The secret of writing smart, long form articles*.
34 Moses, L (2015) *How the New York Times gets a 70 per cent open rate on its newsletters*. Digiday.

35 Moses, L (2015) *Publishers are treating email newsletters as a platform of its own.* Digiday.

36 Muddiman, A, cited in Ciobanu, M (2015) *Watch: How journalists should engage with readers in the comments.* News:rewired.

37 BBC Trending (2015) *Is it the beginning of the end for online comments?* BBC.

38 Golby, J (2015) *How to make men love you: Taking apart the ridiculous 'glamour' article everyone's getting made about.* Vice.

39 Glamour (2015) *13 little things that can make a man fall hard for you.* Glamour.

40 Ciobanu, M (2015) *'No news organisation has all the answers': Q&A with Sarah Marshall.* journalism.co.uk

7

ENGAGING, MEASURING AND REACTING TO YOUR AUDIENCE

Web metrics can help journalists to identify successful content, measure growth and plan their future coverage. So how can you build and relate to your audience? And which analytics should you be focusing on?

The availability of instant audience feedback is increasingly impacting on the content journalists produce online. There are myriad metrics to analyse – page views, site visits, time on page – and identifying the ones that matter will be crucial to driving the growth of your digital project.

Start-up newsrooms need to excel from the outset when it comes to traffic to drive much-needed growth. It is no longer enough to produce top-quality journalism and publish it. As an entrepreneur you need to publish it, assess how your audience is responding to it, react to that response and then continue to track the audience's level of engagement. It is a demanding process but following it through will result in your content travelling further. And if your content is strong enough, this will drive an increase in your audience.

You need to use the metrics and dimensions at your disposal to establish several key things. These include how many people are visiting your site, what time they are visiting, what content they are engaging with and how long they are engaging with it for. Once you have the answers to these questions you can start the process of identifying what you need to adapt in order to trigger more traffic in the future. It is a constant game of seeking improvement.

Building your audience and measuring growth

Monitoring the performance of your content should be at the heart of your day-to-day operations. In large newsrooms this is often the role of a team of analysts; in others it falls to one audience engagement editor, a role we'll look at in this chapter. Even if it is only part of someone's role in your newsroom, it is still absolutely vital. Without it you will struggle to maximise your audience.

Although analytics should be scrutinised throughout the day, a daily debrief to everyone in the team will help you to assess the data. You need to point out your successes, discuss pieces that struggled and encourage the newsroom to resolve these issues. As Chris Moran, the *Guardian*'s audience editor, suggests, the approach to adopt is 'there's probably a reason why something didn't do well, so let's try to find out why and let's change it'.[1]

The pressure of producing news, especially with a small team, often results in similar mistakes being replicated over time, so it's important to step back from the daily grind to identify formats and topics that perform well with your target audience. You need to discover what made that content successful, and reproduce it. If was a short form piece about David Cameron which included video, you'll need to experiment to determine if your audience is really interested in politics, your multimedia or the fact it was bite-sized story.

Alongside analytics that monitor your website's traffic, you need to keep track of the reach of your stories on social media. In Chapter 9 we will discuss how promoting your content on social platforms should be your primary tactic when it comes to attracting traffic. To monitor how many times a story has been shared across social media platforms, visit Shared Count or Buzzsumo and type in the story's URL. The site can tell you the most shared stories on your site and your competitors' sites. You can also search for the most shared content by topic.[2]

Key tools: web analytics – Google Analytics/Chartbeat

You need to ensure you have access to analytical data which will give you the required level of insight into the behaviour of your audience.

Wordpress-hosted blogs will give you basic information around page views, visitors, comments and which country your visitors are based in. They will also tell you the day and time when your blog receives the most traffic. If you self-host a Wordpress site, which is recommended, your host will provide you with its own analytical data. You need to assess if this meets your requirements.

Alternatively, Google Analytics is a freemium analytics platform that will provide you with a vast array of data. This includes crucial information such as bounce rate, average visit duration and pages visited per visit. You should be aware that the platform refers to visits as 'sessions'. Google Analytics also offers a range of insights into your audience, which can be useful when looking to pitch your site to advertisers.

The most advanced real-time analytical data is provided by Chartbeat, which is available for a nominal monthly fee. Chartbeat is increasingly used across the industry, including by the BBC, to offer instant feedback to newsrooms on their site's performance. It includes a wealth of instant in-depth information about your audience's behaviour. This helps inform decisions about the positioning of content and promotion on social media, and tells you which stories are engaging your audience. Both Chartbeat and Google Analytics integrate with self-hosted Wordpress sites.

Setting targets

As a digital newsroom you need to set weekly or monthly quantitative targets based around your chosen Key Performance Indicator (KPI) to motivate your start-up to grow. These should be achievable and be reviewed on a regular basis to determine if you are demonstrating the growth required to make your project sustainable. What 'sustainable' looks like will depend on your ambitions, the size of your team and the income you can generate. That is why you need to keep your outgoings nominal at the outset, to give yourself enough time to build an audience and implement your business model.

Competition has powered the growth of many digital-first news outlets. In the past at Gawker, a big board in reception told everyone the most visited posts on their network. A separate leaderboard, containing the name of the writers who have attracted the most visits, was stationed nearby complete with ascending or descending arrows.[3] It may appear extreme but it demonstrated how Gawker put metrics at the heart of its organisational culture. The message was clear: our writers are expected to attract an audience with everything they post.

Similarly, you should aim to reach your targets by sharing your newsroom KPIs among individual reporters. These individual targets will need to vary depending on their experience, the number of hours they work per week and the area they write about. For example, writing about sport will usually attract more traffic to a hyperlocal blog than writing about politics.

UK publisher Trinity Mirror proposed introducing personalised traffic targets to their regional newsrooms in 2015 in a memo stating: 'Every employee will need to consistently generate and deliver story ideas which reflect an inherent knowledge of their audience and what engages them.'[4] Putting the emphasis on reporters to cultivate their personal audience in this manner encourages them to produce populist and engaging content, to self-publicise on social media and develop their own specialisms within your news site.

However, there are inherent dangers in adopting a totally traffic-driven approach that measures KPIs which fail to recognise quality control and high standards. As journalism professor Roy Greenslade points out, targets relying on high page views and visitors alone suggest: 'labour-intensive journalism is not required. Just bang it out as quickly as possible, stick it up and move on to the next "story" about a cat with two tails.'[5] If you want to build a long-standing news brand you need to weigh up the financial imperative of building an audience with the long-term aim of developing a reputation as a trustworthy news source. This is a debate we will investigate further in this chapter.

Using analytics to strengthen your journalism

Start-ups generally find it hard to focus at the outset. One of the most common ways they fail is by trying to do too much.[6] As an entrepreneur you need to find the thing you do better than everyone else and exploit it.

Using analytics to pinpoint the successes in your journalism will enable you to identify areas of strength. You should use metrics to give you an indication of the content your audience want to read and then reflect on how you can meet that need. This can be a difficult process as audience demand might suggest you move away from your preferred style of reporting. However you need to be pragmatic in adopting a business-minded approach to the demands of your readers.

Here are a few key questions to ask yourself on a regular basis:

- Are readers returning to the site?
- Are they remaining on the site for a while or leaving quickly?
- Which topics on your site are proving the most popular? Which only attract nominal interest?
- Which format/styles of content are proving the most popular? Does the time spent developing them equate to their readership?
- Are readers accessing the site through social media? If so, is any one platform working best? If not, how are they being referred to your content?

Finding out the answers to these questions will help you to identify your strengths. The process of focusing them is referred to as 'weeding the garden' by MTV co-founder Bob Pittman. Pittman, a media executive, suggests 'being honest with yourself. What really is a winner?'[7] When reviewing your output, avoid mediocre content being funded through an unwillingness to cut your losses. Operating a lean newsroom with a sharply-defined focus reduces the burden of content production and identifies a clear modus operandi. It also creates time for further experimentation in the future.

Key terms

Here is a brief glossary of analytical terms to give you an insight into the metrics and dimensions you will be dealing with. It is by no means exhaustive and is intentionally written in an accessible manner.

Active visits   This is a real-time metric telling you the number of people currently visiting your site.

Bounce rate   Visitors who 'bounce' leave your site after viewing one page. You want your bounce rate, which is expressed as a percentage, to be as low as possible.

Direct traffic   Visits where readers have accessed your site by typing the URL into their browser or clicked on a bookmark.

Engagement   The level of engagement users have with your content can be identified by analysing the time they spend on a page and your bounce rate. You should, alongside this, identify users' landing and exit pages and the number of repeat visitors.

Inbound link   The link a user clicked on to visit your site. Most of these will probably be social traffic. You should monitor which links have the highest response rate and replicate them.

Landing page/exit page   The page a visitor arrives at on your site is their landing page; the page from which they leave your site is their exit page.

Page view   Often referred to as hits, a page view is when a user views a page.

Reach   The number of individuals who have seen a particular story.

Repeat visitor   A user who visits a site twice or more in the same recording period. You want to encourage these.

Spike   A spike is when your site suddenly receives a dramatic increase in traffic. This will usually be related to a piece of content you've recently posted.

Stickiness   Usually refers to a piece of content that keeps users engaged on your site.

Time on page   The amount of time a visitor spends on one page before leaving. The higher the time on page, the more the chance the user has engaged with your content.

Traffic   This is a generic term referring to the number of visits, unique users and page views your site has.

User   A visitor to your site. This is not always an individual person as different browsers and devices are counted as separate users.

URL   Uniform resource locator, a unique address to access your site. Often referred to as a web address.

Visit   A visit starts when a user arrives on your site and ends when they leave your site, regardless of how many pages they engage with.

Unique user   The number of users who have accessed your site within a recording period, typically a month. Repeat users are only counted once.

Reach v. Impact: engaging an audience, rather than just finding one

The KPIs you choose to focus upon will ultimately have a big impact on the journalism you end up producing. In their infancy, news websites focused heavily on page views, reach and monthly unique visitors. This was because those metrics are simple, easy for everyone to understand and attractive to advertisers. Page views and visitor numbers became the industry staple, in a similar way that circulation and readership were for newspapers and listeners and viewers are for broadcasters.

As a result most managers in the sector encouraged reporters to seek page views where they could find them and attract more and more new users to visit the site. This resulted in newsrooms increasingly being accused of producing clickbait, where headlines deliberately overplayed the story to get a user to read it. But constructing a business model based solely around attracting traffic without the quality to back it up is a short-term game. There is a real danger your bounce rate will remain high and a high percentage of your visitors will visit once, never to return.

To thrive as a sustainable news outlet you need to build a returning customer base. You need your audience to decide if your journalism is worthy of their time. Therefore you need to find out what makes your audience tick. As journalism professor Jeff Jarvis sees it, aiming for impact rather than hits 'starts with listening to the public's wants, needs, and goals so we can measure our success ultimately against whether those goals are achieved.'[8] Jarvis argues that building for the future involves listening to your audience and identifying how you can be useful to them.

This is why you need to prioritise building a community of readers. Not only will a community sustain your news site through regular use – even if those traffic figures are initially lower than you'd hoped for – but you can also get insights from them as you continue to develop your site. This feedback adds qualitative detail to the quantitative data you are analysing, which will help you put those figures into context.

What KPIs should you measure?

The KPIs you choose to measure should fit in with your objectives for the site, and it is likely these will shift during the project's development. Realistically, your initial indicators of success are likely to be page views and monthly unique visitors and your newsroom targets should be set accordingly. The reason for this is you first need to attract an audience to your site, which will involve raising awareness of your existence and your journalism. Impressive figures will also make it easier for you to implement your business plan.

However, while pursuing this strategy you need to be continually aware of your bounce rate. If this remains stubbornly high it suggests your journalism is failing to deliver or is inconsistent. This is a problem, as you are potentially losing readers and will have to attract new visitors to replace them just to stand still. If you find yourself in this situation it's advisable for the newsroom to focus on the quality of content and suspend its targets until more of your visitors begin engaging with your journalism.

Once your site has developed into a semi-sustainable business you should consider altering your KPIs. Indicators of this maturity would be a relatively regular number of unique monthly views and consistent income. This suggests that you are well established and the community you have set out to target is aware of your site. In this instance, altering your KPIs to prioritise engagement over reach would reflect your new priority – deepening your existing audience's use of the site.

To do this you should switch to KPIs that focus on time on page and the entry/exit page for visitors to your site. This alteration should make your traffic less volatile and reduce your bounce rate. Prioritising stickiness in the content you produce will assist in keeping your audience on your site. This switch to deepening engagement among readers has already occurred among several UK publishers, who have prioritised increasing the amount of time visitors spend on their sites.

This shift will allow you to be more creative and innovative in the journalism you aim to produce. If your newsroom is prioritising engaging, high-quality content it offers a better environment for reporters, encouraging them to remain committed to the project, and should capture more time and attention from your existing audience. As Tony Haile, CEO of Chartbeat, states:

> If a quality publisher wants to be successful they should stand in front of their team and say 'I don't give a damn about whether we can squeeze one more click from our audience today. I just want them to come back tomorrow.'[9]

Ultimately, in order to become a sustainable news outlet you need your target audience to keep returning. Some newsrooms are going even further and want to identify how their journalism impacts on readers, from making them healthier to being more empathetic towards others.[10] Your best chance of having a positive impact on your audience is by setting long-term KPIs that prioritise a high standard of journalism over an ever-increasing flow of traffic.

Maintain your instincts

As important as analytics are to digital newsrooms, you should avoid the temptation to let your numbers trump everything else in your decision-making, otherwise you could end up in a digital cul-de-sac. Making metrics central to the newsroom created some issues at Gawker, as writers admitted to sticking to formats that had attracted traffic in the past, posting frequently to keep their figures high and avoiding articles that took longer to produce.[11]

Identifying the types of stories that will attract visitors to your site is crucial as it signposts your way to sustainability, but it shouldn't overrule your site's mission. More than most professionals, journalists rely on their gut. News values and a belief in serving the public interest have always framed the way journalists have worked and you should avoid shelving these instincts. You will need your instincts to serve the mission you have set yourself as a start-up and provide your target audience with a clear indicator of the quality of your journalism. Academic Dr An Nguyen put this well:

> People come back and forth [from] a certain news site in part because they trust – or at least expect – that the content on the surface is the outcome of a sound, reliable judgement of what is important and relevant to them.[12]

This judgement is becoming increasingly important in the post-publication period. The placement of articles on your site, adding new content, adopting different social media techniques and altering headlines have all become routine adjustments for newsrooms as they seek to increase audience interest. As a publisher you have to decide when to trust the numbers and what to alter. Sort your stories from least to most viewed to establish which stories haven't been read; once you've done this you can work out why.[13]

Thinking mobile first

If you are aiming to be a successful publisher your platform needs to prioritise mobile users. The 20 billionth mobile phone was sold in 2016[14] and four out of five news websites already receive more traffic to their mobile site than their desktop one.[15] This audience on mobile is predicted to keep increasing; this was demonstrated by Google's decision to alter its search algorithm to prioritise mobile-friendly sites.[16]

Crucially this surge in mobile usage will see the platform overtake print and TV as the biggest UK advertising market. Half of the near £9 billion spent on digital advertising will be spent on mobile by the end of 2016.[17] Part of advertisers' attraction to mobile is due to location-based advertising. This identifies where people are using their phone and shows them targeted messages. Although still in its infancy, this technology has the potential to become a regular feature in our lives. As entrepreneurial journalism expert Mark Briggs states: 'This is the holy grail for local advertisers: to reach potential customers at the precise moment when they are looking for your type of product or service and are in your neighbourhood and ready to buy'.[18]

The audience shift from desktop to mobile has occurred quicker than the original move from print to online. In two years the Huffington Post went from 17 per cent of its page views being on mobile to 67 per cent,[19] meaning their mobile users quickly become their priority. This rapid revolution in consumption has led to a shift in culture, with the *New York Times* temporarily stopping staff accessing its desktop site[20] and Buzzfeed's content management system forcing journalists to read their stories as they appear on mobile before they can publish; such is the platform's importance.[21]

The purpose of these approaches is to confront journalists producing content with the reality of the audience engaging with it. As a reporter you will probably be sitting in an office with a reasonably-sized monitor, whereas the majority of your audience is snatching a few minutes on their phone while commuting on a train, in a queue at the bank or second-screening while watching television. Failing to serve the mobile audience is no longer a viable business decision for any newsroom.

Legacy publishers across Europe are increasingly experimenting in the mobile market by launching arms-length news start-ups, with a sense of autonomy from their main title. In Germany Ze.tt, BYou, Bento, Kompakt and Orange are aiming at the millennial mobile market in a similar manner to Ampp3d in the UK. The freedom of being an internal start-up appears to have created space for experimentation with different formats. The Kompakt newsroom produces short, snappy content, with a particular focus on science and technology, whereas Ze.tt has developed a site where activism and strong viewpoints play a key part in the news agenda.[22] These platforms demonstrate how long-standing publishers are beginning to alter their approach to news to satisfy the demands of their contemporary target audiences, from the design of the site to the topics that are covered.

Aspects to prioritise

- Keeping things simple is vitally important when producing content for mobile. So you should ensure the text is large enough for people to read and there are regular paragraphs to break it up.
- You should consider producing 'snackable' news, i.e. short stories of around 100–150 words that readers can read quickly to find out about a topic.
- Ensure that graphics and images work across a range of platforms – for example, consider the layout on the iPhone, an android phone, a tablet and desktop. Screenfly or mobiReady are useful websites that demonstrate how your content looks on a wide range of devices. You should also consider how it works on a variety of different browsers.
- Target video and images. It is better to show your audience the story rather than tell them. Using these platforms also opens up new, better opportunities for advertising.

Stuart Heritage is the founder of Hecklerspray and co-founder of Luv&hat. He now writes for the Guardian.

Starting Hecklerspray helped me to learn about writing headlines, structure and SEO. I would run 500-word stories on the hour every weekday between 10 a.m. and 5 p.m., trying to build an audience and make it look like a big website. But I was quite burnt out towards the end of the day.

Our main source of traffic, I quickly worked out, would be the entertainment section of Google

FIGURE 7.1 Stuart Heritage

News. So I decided to make it my main gatekeeping source as well. If a story was doing well on Google News Entertainment, or better yet on the actual Google News homepage, I'd write a story about it, ram it full of keywords to a degree that'd get me penalised these days, and submit it to Google News.

Often we'd make the page. On the rare occasion that we'd be the top link on the top story of the Google News homepage, which happened a maximum of ten times, we'd get 100,000 hits an hour and the site would crash. It was gaming the system, really, but it worked.

Often, I'd have to write them all myself, so every day was just a frantic churn of writing. The stories needed to be funny, too, so that was added pressure. But it taught me how to work to deadline, and how to react to the news agenda nimbly, even if it did fully exhaust me for five years.

Around 1.5 million people a month were reading it. It developed a band of loyal readers. It allowed me to build up a portfolio of work and I ran it for five years. I started writing for NME and was named as one of the fifty most influential people in UK media by the *Independent*. The *Guardian* also named Hecklerspray in a top fifty rundown.

I learnt on the job and built things up for myself. I bet on myself and it turned out. Make your own website, it's so easy. You can design it and sell advertising. You can make it your job from nothing. You've got total control over the entire direction of your career.

I missed having control so I started a website called Luv&hat with my partner. We've built it into something that pays money and been commissioned for eighty podcasts by Audible. It's amazing. If you have the power to make something for yourself it means more.

It's very important not to give up. Make your own stuff and show them. You have more power to make something outside the traditional structures of the media industry, more than at any time in the history of journalism.

Engaging your community of readers

Audience involvement was limited in the traditional mass-market media business model. Readers had their say in letters pages, could ring in or were welcome in reception to inform a reporter about a story, but by-and-large researching and producing articles was left to journalists. Feedback usually came when it was a hit with the editor or there was a problem.

The advent of the internet has made it much quicker and easier for audiences to engage with journalists. Part of any modern reporter's job is to manage their online interactions, which has provided an opportunity for those reporters more adept at cultivating their audience. Once you have built an audience you need to find a way for the newsroom to maintain a running dialogue with them. This not only ensures they feel more involved in the journalism being produced, but it can also result in audience suggestions that improve the quality of the story.

The advantage of writing for a specialist or hyperlocal site is that your audience already has at least a basic knowledge about that topic; otherwise they wouldn't be visiting your site. There are several ways you can use this insight.

When you decide on the topics you are planning to cover in the week ahead you can include them in a post on your website or social media account; you could even produce a short video explaining why you are covering them. This gives your readers an insight into the process of producing your content. BBC Sport sparked a huge increase in its social traffic by revamping the Facebook page of its flagship show *Match of the Day*.[23] A key part of this approach has been short videos where host Gary Lineker reveals the show's running order to fans hours before it starts.

Newslists have always been closely guarded secrets in newsrooms and it does offer the competition an opportunity to know your plans; however, exclusive stories can always be held back. The pitfalls are outweighed by the opportunity for your audience to get involved. This will yield useful advice, but more importantly it encourages them to return to read the completed story and become invested in the site.

This was certainly the experience of the *Guardian* when it embarked on its open newsroom experiment in 2011. Dan Roberts, then the paper's national news editor, believed that 'Whatever competitive advantage may have been lost by giving our rivals a clue to what we were up to was more than made up for by a growing range of ideas and tips from readers.'[24]

Avoiding traditional barriers between journalists and readers is a crucial step in encouraging communities to develop a sense of ownership of a news website. You should actively take steps to promote this ownership, as it fosters interaction between readers. Will Perrin, founder of Kings Cross Environment, a hyperlocal blog based in London, has seen his site bring together a diverse range of contributors who share an interest in their area:

> They talk and they chat, it's creating bridging capital between people who would otherwise never connect in a community. We see all kinds of bonding social capital created through photos, local history, local events, where people come together around a point of reference.[25]

Developing this sense of belonging in an online space over a common passion is a powerful driver when it comes to increasing audience interaction. This is demonstrated by the sustainable nature of established internet forums: in many ways these online spaces have become virtual local pubs. This interaction provides a sense of gratification for visitors and encourages them to return regularly. Developing similar types of interaction is crucial to developing a sustainable news site.

The role of the audience engagement editor

Newsrooms are increasingly turning to audience engagement editors in a bid to get their content in front of the largest audience possible. This initial purpose of the role, or similar sounding ones, is to become a virtual paperboy or girl, using analytics and social media to amplify the impact of the stories being produced by the newsroom. But it also requires the ability to listen to the audience, both by examining and reacting to metrics and responding promptly to comments and tweets.

This little-understood role has becoming increasingly important in digital newsrooms. It is often staffed by a reporter experienced enough to take on a senior role but young enough to be savvy across a variety of digital platforms. Internally it is their job to identify how and when to reach readers, by examining analytics and identifying trends around audience behaviour. They are a 'vessel between the audience and the staff' that aims to identify ways of making complex content relatable to readers.[26]

Readers expect more from journalists in the digital age. Newsrooms have never been as willing to engage by answering the individual questions their audience are posing. Engaging with the audience requires the ability to adopt an authoritative but friendly tone, encouraging conversation but also knowing when not to respond.

Experimenting with new tools, live blogging major events or breaking news, leading efforts to curate content and recruiting community bloggers are also tasks that often fall under their remit.[27]

When you are organising your start-up, the audience engagement editor is a role you should give particular attention to. It requires identifying an adaptable, inventive and competent all-rounder, but doing so will greatly improve your chances of your target audience engaging with content and returning in the future.

Using chat apps to engage

The way publishers relate to their audiences will continue altering as technology evolves. The usefulness of platforms can only truly be identified through experimentation. For example, the German tabloid *Bild* used the January 2016 football transfer window as an opportunity to try out sending readers transfer rumours via Facebook Messenger.[28]

The *New York Times* used instant messaging service WhatsApp to keep its readers briefed on the visit of the Pope to Latin America in 2015. Users signed up to receive text, pictures and video messages on the chat app, which has 1 billion monthly active users. However, despite high engagement the paper said it suffered technical glitches: 'The interest in receiving Pope updates over WhatsApp was so overwhelming that the app was unable to keep up with the sheer volume of chats we received … There were also challenges in unsubscribing users'.[29]

Despite these issues you should find, as a smaller, niche publication, that WhatsApp provides a direct way to engage your audience when reporting on a big event. When the BBC covered the 2014 elections in India it posted around twenty times a day to the platform.[30] You can even use the platform to spark a conversation between readers, as the *Guardian* did in 2016 with its coverage of the challenges facing millennials around the globe.[31]

Using WhatsApp increases the chances of the content you are posting being read by the audience, as you are contacting them directly. Your messages will appear as a push-notification, which means it will be instantly visible on their phone. Using a chat app also opens up funding streams as you can potentially include some advertisements within your coverage.

View non-involvement as a positive

Finding a way to engage with your audience is obviously crucial for any newsroom. But it shouldn't be your ultimate ambition. You should be aiming to develop a culture where your audience identifies as a community and can converse together without you even taking part.

Why is this important? Because every time journalists have to spark a debate or encourage interaction it involves devoting time away from your primary objective – investigating, interviewing and producing news content. The more organic and natural this process becomes, the easier it becomes for the newsroom. If you consider the letters pages in newspapers, historically debates went on endlessly between readers with little oversight, and publishers benefitted as a result.

If you can get to a stage where readers regularly use *your* platform to discuss issues raised in *your* journalism then the site is likely to be thriving. Not only does it suggest your reporting is engaging that audience, but that your site is benefitting from increased repeat traffic, which is a primary objective for long-term sustainability. Obviously you have to monitor and moderate the views appearing on your platform in a fair and transparent fashion, but overall, being able to take a backwards step is a positive sign.

Use your analytics to build growth

Building an audience for news has never been an easy task. If anything, the internet has made this process significantly easier for independent publishers. As writer Chris Anderson says: 'Top-down messaging is losing traction, while bottom-up buzz is gaining power.'[32] In other words, word of mouth and peer recommendations carry far more weight in the digital age. If you produce a high-quality news website and promote your content regularly on social media, people will visit it, return regularly and tell others about it.

Analytics are a tool that allow you to develop a greater understanding of this audience. They are not the sole focus, but they can prompt you to adopt different newsroom practices to suit their behaviour on your site. They can help you to identify a certain time that is the best to post or topics that attract the highest level of interest. Used correctly, the metrics and dimensions will help you to maximise the impact of your journalism.

The reality is that no commercial operation can waste time producing material their audience isn't interested in. You need to be decisive and pragmatic in targeting areas where you can succeed. Regardless of the KPIs you choose to focus upon, audience figures of some description need to be central to these discussions. They will also help you to produce realistic and relevant targets for the future, which will help to drive growth without demotivating everyone involved.

Your audience is out there. Now you just need to go and find out what they actually want, as opposed to what you think they want.

Further reading

Cherubini, F and Nielsen, R (2016) *Editorial analytics: How news media are developing and using audience data and metrics*. Reuters Institute for the Study of Journalism. Available at: reutersinstitute.politics.ox.ac.uk

Notes

1 Cited in Cherubini, F (2015) *Trends in newsrooms: Analytics, audience development and the newsroom*. World Association of Newspapers and News Publishers.
2 Marshall, S, cited by McNally, P (2014) *12 social media tips, tools and techniques to help journalists work better*. NewsRewired.
3 Petre, C (2015) *The traffic factories: Metrics at Chartbeat, Gawker Media and the New York Times*. Tow Centre for Digital Journalism.
4 Memo cited in Ponsford, D (2015) *Journalists to be given personal online audience growth targets after job cuts at Trinity Mirror Midlands*. Press Gazette.
5 Greenslade, R (2015) *One Trinity Mirror sentence that spells the death knell of journalism*. The Guardian.
6 Wong, K (2015) *Making it through the startup 'trough of sorrow'*. Forbes.
7 Cited in New York Times (2014) *New York Times innovation report*.
8 Jarvis, J (2014) *Geeks bearing gifts: Imagining new futures for news*. Albany, NY: SUNY Press.
9 Haile, T (2013) *Cargo cults or the Wright brothers? Metrics can improve newsrooms but only if the culture is ready*. Gigaom.
10 Silverman, B (2015) *Numbers, numbers everywhere*. Nieman Lab.
11 Petre, *The traffic factories*.
12 Nguyen, A (2013) *Online news audiences: The challenges of web metrics*. In *Journalism: New Challenges*. Fowler-Watt, K and Allan, S (eds). Bournemouth University.
13 Robinson, J, speaking at the World Association of Newspapers and News Publishers (WAN-IFRA) conference in Washington DC, cited by Edge, A (2015) on Twitter.
14 Evans, B (@benedictevans) *Some time this year, the 20 billionth mobile phone and the 5 billionth PC will be sold*. 12 January 2016, 10:26 p.m. Tweet.
15 Mitchell, A (2015) *State of the news media 2015*. Pew Research Centre.
16 Google (2015) *Finding more mobile-friendly search results*. Official Google Webmaster Central Blog.
17 Sweney, M (2015) *UK mobile ad spend 'to overtake print and TV'*. The Guardian.
18 Briggs, M (2012) *Entrepreneurial journalism*. London: Sage.
19 Nielsen, R (@rasmus_kleis) *In 2 years, HuffPo went from 18% mobile PVS to 67%. This is as big a shift as from print to desktop digital, and much faster*. RISJ lecture, 23 November 2015, 5:51 p.m. Tweet.
20 Bilton, R (2015) *How publishers are trying to build mobile-first cultures*. Digiday.
21 Nielsen, R (@rasmus_kleis) *Janine gibson says BuzzFeed CMS makes journos read stories as they'll appear on mobile, because news HAS to work on mobile*. RISJ lecture, 23 November 2015, 6:34 p.m. Tweet.
22 Wang, S (2015) *Young money: How German legacy publishers are chasing millennial audiences*. Nieman Lab.
23 Hurst, C (2015) *Match of the Day hits 3 million Facebook fans*. About the BBC Blog. BBC.
24 Roberts, D (2011) *Lessons from our open news trial*. London: The Guardian.
25 Scarbrough, H (2014) *Reflections on building your audience*. Cardiff: Centre for Community Journalism.

26 Powers, E (2015) *The rise of the engagement editor and what it means.* Mediashift.

27 Buttry, S (2012) *Engagement editors: an emerging important job in digital first newsrooms.* The Buttry Diary.

28 Hazard-Owen, L (2016) *Axel Springer's Bild is testing news delivery via Facebook Messenger.* Nieman Lab.

29 Ingber, H and Minsberg, T (2015) *Sharing news of WhatsApp, an international desk experiment.* New York Times.

30 Barot, T (2014) *How BBC News covered Indian elections on WhatsApp and WeChat.* BBC College of Journalism.

31 Fishwick, C (2016) *It's #notjustyou: millennials share their secret fears.* The Guardian.

32 Anderson, C (2009) *The longer long trail.* London: Random House.

8

YOUR SMARTPHONE AS YOUR BEST REPORTING TOOL

With Lindsay Eastwood

Utilising your smartphone as your main piece of reporting kit is cost-effective, makes you more mobile and means you are always ready to publish.

We have already discussed how smartphone use amongst audiences is impacting on the way journalism is being consumed – now we are going to outline how it is changing the way reporters produce and publish content. A decade ago recording sound required an audio recorder, shooting footage involved a video camera, and taking high-quality images was largely the domain of photographers. But technological advances have changed all that.

Nowadays journalists are being sent out equipped with smartphones. Why this sudden change of tack? Convenience and cost are the main drivers. If you can give a reporter a smartphone rather than specialist, expensive kit and still produce quality journalism then it makes financial sense for the publisher. Using smartphones across platforms demands a varied skill set from journalists, but it offers them more variety when it comes to deciding how to tell a story; sometimes pictures illustrate it best, powerful quotes may come across better as audio, and when action is unfolding video is the obvious platform.

Indeed, possibilities are now expanding far beyond these three basic options. When it comes to video footage you can now decide if you want to livestream onto your platform or straight into Facebook, you can slice it into GIFs or make it into a package using iMovie and quickly upload to the web. And the added advantage is, as anyone who has dragged heavy video equipment to a job will tell you, that a smartphone is considerably lighter.

The capabilities of our phones are constantly evolving and expanding. This chapter tells you how to get the best out of your smartphone in the current climate, but as a modern journalist you need to make sure you keep on top of advances in technology and apps to ensure you keep providing your audience with the best possible standard of reporting.

Preparing your reporting toolkit

A big advantage of your phone being your main reporting device is that most people take their phones everywhere. This means that if you are 'off-duty' you can cover a breaking news story as professionally as you would be able to if it was a scheduled event. This is also why within minutes of any big news story occurring in a public place, social media is swamped with user generated content; digital technology has made us all potential producers. Following a plane crash at the Shoreham Airshow in August 2015 the BBC ran pictures and video from spectators who were recording the event.[1]

As journalists you need to be more aware than members of the public of the ramifications – both legal and ethical – of instantaneously publishing content, an issue we will touch upon more in Chapter 10. Your reputation as a news outlet and individual journalist is on the line every time you publish. As a professional you also need to develop a better understanding of the kit you are using.

Filming on smartphones is resulting in a series of positive side effects for newsrooms. Journalists at Dutch broadcaster Omrop Fryslan have found filming with phones is a lot less intimidating for interviewees and it allows them to produce more personal stories.[2] At TV Leman Bleu in Switzerland it has allowed stories to be reported quicker and improved accessibility compared to bigger kit.[3]

The iPhone

iPhones are generally considered the best equipped phones for journalists. We will focus primarily on using them, but most of the wide ranging guidance in this chapter will also be applicable to android phones. When using any smartphone, as a journalist you need to be particularly aware of its remaining *memory* and *battery*. This is vitally important because if your phone runs out of memory you can't save any more content and if it runs out of power it will simply switch off.

In addition to your smartphone, it is advisable to keep the following equipment in a bag close at hand:

- A portable external phone battery and charger. You should also fully charge your phone prior to leaving on a story.
- A monopod or compact, light tripod that fits your phone. Monopods are attachable poles that allow you to achieve a more stable shot than using your hands, especially if you are conducting a video interview.
- A pair of headphones that will attach to the phone.
- An external microphone. Lavalier clip-on mics for the iPhone are available at a nominal price and don't require a battery. Alternatively the IRIG mic pre-amp, which costs slightly more, will allow you to use both radio and boom mics.[4]

- Spare batteries, if your microphone requires them.
- Your trusty pen and pad.

To preserve your phone's memory once you are on a job, you should delete all the images and video you no longer require, creating more space to take more. If you are shooting video you should put the phone in airplane mode in its settings before starting. This ensures someone contacting you won't disturb filming. After shooting your footage you should use the headphones to listen back to the audio you've recorded. You won't be able to hear it while you're recording.

Apps

With more than 50,000 new applications being released every month,[5] you need to educate yourself about those that will be helpful to you as a journalist. The apps below – which are available at the iOS app store – are a mixture of tried and tested, low cost tools that you need to have as a digital journalist, and a few curve-balls that may help you experiment with your reporting. You need to regularly make yourself aware of new apps. Visiting appshopper.com, investigating categories within the iOS App store/Google Play store and logging onto journalismtools. io are crucial in this regard. These tools are transient and better ones will eventually appear on the market. You should always have a backup tool and monitor if each apps' producers are still updating it.[6]

Audio

(i) Voice Record Pro will allow you to record a high standard of audio.
(ii) Ferrite Recording Studio both records audio and supports multi-track editing.
(iii) AudioBoom and Soundcloud allow you to embed playable audio into your news site.

Moving footage

(i)   FiLMiC Pro allows you to shoot high definition, advanced video.
(ii) Periscope facilitates livestreaming video.
(iii) iMovie allows you to create news packages, which then need uploading to YouTube. Pinnacle Studio is an alternative to iMovie.
(iv) You can add text to a video with Gravie.
(v)   GIPHY Cam allows you to shoot GIFs, while GIF Toaster helps you create GIFs from pre-shot video.
(vi) Hyperlapse from Instagram enables you to shoot varying speeds of time-lapse content.
(vii) PicPlayPost embeds multiple videos, GIFs and images into collages.
(viii) Quik makes short video, which works well on social media.

Static images

(i)   Camera+ and Pro Camera 8 can help you shoot high-quality photographs.

(ii)   Diptic allows you to display images in a variety of collages.

(iii)   Over lets you alter pictures and add text or an image.

(iv)   Annotate allows you to annotate images.

(v)   Video2Photo extracts screen grabs from video.

(vi)   Storyo can turn images into a picture story.

Added extras

(i)   Social – Facebook, Twitter, Snapchat, Instagram.

(ii)   Messaging – WhatsApp.

(iii)   News – Dependent on specialism but BBC News and Sky News cover the mainstream UK news agenda.

(iv)   User generated content – Banjo lets you monitor geographic areas for social media content. You as the reporter need to verify it.

(v)   Copyright protection – Marksta adds a watermark to your images.

(vi)   Teleprompter – The video teleprompter app allows you to record and read your script to camera at the same time.

(vii)   Animation – VideoScribe Anywhere helps you tell stories through animations.

We will focus on several of these apps, particularly the video and audio ones, throughout this chapter. Avoid overloading your phone with too many free apps, as studies show paid apps use less battery and processing power and don't usually contain adverts.[7] To get the best from an app you should get to know it, learn its shortcuts and read the manual.[8] Once you have prepared your reporting toolkit and downloaded the apps we can move onto why and how journalists increasingly need to use these tools.

Using your phone to take high-quality images

All modern journalists – not just the digitally savvy ones – are expected to be able to use a smartphone to take pictures, particularly when it comes to images of breaking news. Advances in picture quality mean that most people can take a good, if not award-winning, picture with one.

Pictures that capture action unfolding work particularly well online; the traditional posed photo just doesn't work on a website. It looks stilted and does nothing to add to the story. So take a snap of the subject of the story doing something. Even better, take a sequence of pictures – it's much more natural and tells the story a lot better.

An advantage of working online is that you have space to display images. If you have a reporter at the scene of a breaking story, using images to show how the story is unfolding demonstrates that you are at the scene and at the heart of what is happening. But if you're using pictures, include captions. How can the reader hope to understand the story if they don't know what they're looking at?

Taking better images with the iPhone

Following a few simple tips can help you take some fantastic images. Press the camera icon on your iPhone to access the camera screen, make sure the white text says 'Photo'; when the camera is in stills mode the circle on screen will be white. You should then turn on HDR, which stands for High Dynamic Range. It's along the top of the screen, so just tap it before snapping. This helps to boost the light and dark, giving you a clearer image.

Focus

An out of focus image is no use to anyone, so before taking any pictures you need to set the focus. This is done in the same way you do when shooting footage. Tap the screen on the intended subject of the image and you will see a yellow box appear; this will focus the shot on this aspect. If you are using HDR you may find you get a better quality shot if you choose a darker part of the target image to focus upon. If you have time, experiment with the focus to find the best shot.

The flash isn't necessarily always your friend. It can provide a welcome boost of light or overexpose the subject depending on the subject of your picture. Therefore you should flick it on and off to assess the impact. Once you feel confident in your photographic ability, download Camera+ and/or Pro Camera 8 to take your pictures to the next level.

FIGURE 8.1 Image of cups that demonstrates how to focus a smartphone camera

Editing

You can enhance your pictures quickly and easily. Go to your camera roll and find your picture. Go to edit, in the top right hand corner of the screen. This opens up a series of options:

- Auto-enhance, which is a magic wand icon, will help boost the saturation and contrast. It may make the image look more professional.
- Red eye reducer, which is shown by an eye icon, which reduces the appearance of red eye in any people in the image.
- You can change the aspect ratio or rotate the image by pressing the rotation square icon.
- A filter can be applied to the picture by pressing the three interlinked circles icon.
- The colour can also be adjusted by clicking on the circular dial icon.

Key tool: Pixlr Editor

You should use Pixlr Editor, which is available online, if you need a more advanced editing tool to crop your images, resize them or change their file format. Think of Pixlr as a free, less advanced version of Adobe Photoshop. It does the overwhelming majority of tasks any online journalists could need it to do. As *Time* magazine puts it: 'Pixlr isn't Photoshop. But for a free tool that works entirely within your browser, it replicates a remarkable percentage of Photoshop's most important image-editing tools, and does it very, very well.'[9]

Pixlr has a function that allows you to select the quality, and therefore size, of the images you are creating. This can be extremely handy when too many large pictures are slowing down your site. Once you have finished editing your images, either with Pixlr or on your smartphone, you can upload them directly to your site or to your social media and photosharing accounts.

Increasing importance of broadcast in digital journalism

The way we use the media is fundamentally shifting. Millennials, who are aged between 18 and 34, watch significantly less television than older generations and devote the time 'saved' to digital devices.[10] The way this group behaves is a glimpse into the future of our media consumption. But the fall in TV consumption doesn't necessarily mean young audiences have had enough of broadcasting; it's more about the linear way it is scheduled and physically watching it off a television. There is a digital landgrab going on and visual content is playing a central role in it.

Facebook Live, which was launched to every user in spring 2016, is the latest disruption in this field. The platform – which is building on the success of Periscope – is still in its early stages but the social media giant is encouraging users to try it, prioritising live streams in newsfeed and encouraging heavyweight publishers, like

Buzzfeed, the Huffington Post and the New York Times, to utilise it.[11] Smaller newsrooms are following suit, and if you have the resources to produce succinct, engaging content, and a big enough Facebook audience to make it worthwhile it is worth experimenting with. BBC West Yorkshire Sport has seen a big jump in its audience figures after swapping Periscope for Facebook Live for their pre-match previews, with video views reaching 10,000.[12] However, broadcasting is draining on resources, so you need to closely monitor the impact of every broadcast. It's impossible for small newsrooms to compete on every platform.

The big initial success of Facebook Live was a 44-minute broadcast by Buzzfeed where two staff tied rubber bands around a watermelon until it exploded. The broadcast, which was shot on an iPhone with tripod, has been watched by 10 million people – more than 800,000 people watched it live – and attracted more than 320,000 comments from readers.[13] This level of engagement was unexpected and helped identify that suspense, audience interaction and events viewers can join at any time are crucial to attracting people.[14] News sites are likely to prioritise crowd-pleasing entertainment to maximise their audiences. But using Facebook Live does not mean you are guaranteed a massive audience as the platform has also come under fire for the lack of visibility and findability of news on its platform. Some broadcasters feel this makes it difficult for audiences to access their content.

Nick Garnett is the North of England reporter for BBC 5 Live. He reported on the Charlie Hebdo *massacre and the Nepal earthquake using his smartphone.*

FIGURE 8.2 Nick Garnett

The greatest strength is Facebook's audience but they haven't worked out how to utilise that and focus it so that people can actually find out what is going on. If you put in a search term for Justin Bieber there is no ranking and no system so you would know who [is reporting the news] and whether it can be trusted. That is what they have to address. Twitter is working because it's pushing quality content up [through Moments] rather than down. It's almost as if they've launched [live streaming] without doing the background work and I can understand why they have done that.

As a news delivery method it is OK, but as a way of knowing what you are going to get it's awful at the moment. It will change, but it needs to change soon. It can be a watermelon and it can be serious news but it would just help people who are trying to find the serious news if they knew where to go. It would also help them if they are trying to find a watermelon.

Video storytelling is also spiking. Upworthy prioritised the platform and saw its Facebook video views shoot up from 5 million to 200 million a month in just a year.[15] It demonstrates that viewers are prepared to engage with video online when it is offered to them. It can explain complex stories quickly, such as the *New York Times*' interactive which explained how debris from missing Malaysian Airlines flight 370 ended up washing up on the island of Reunion,[16] and provides an appealing alternative to audiences. BBC Online produced *Pint-sized Ashes*, short daily packages mixing audio highlights from their radio coverage of England's 2015 series against Australia with cartoon images because competitor Sky Sports held visual rights. It ended up attracting a bigger audience than the satellite broadcaster's TV coverage.[17]

The increase in video audiences is mirroring the expanding mobile audience, which means packages should be produced primarily for mobile users. You should also be aware that audiences on social media are less likely to listen to the soundtrack on a video, so if you are planning on posting your videos there directly you may want to consider using text captions to tell the story and attaching a copyright-free audio backing track. This approach puts a lot more emphasis on your images to tell the story. However, if you want to produce packages primarily for your site, which remains the best option – particularly at the outset, when you are seeking to establish your brand and drive traffic to your site – then you should prioritise interviews.

Using your phone to record high-quality video

When you are shooting video about a story you need to ensure it is visually stimulating and the audio you record is of a high quality. Most stories should include either an interview to camera or a vox pop. You should be aware that pressing buttons on the camera can make the phone wobble. Although increasing amounts of video are currently shot vertically, you should set up your phone to shoot *horizontally*. This ensures your video is shot on a longer screen (16:9 aspect ratio) and avoids letterboxing – having a black box around your video.

As stated above, make sure the phone is fully charged, extraneous images and video are removed from your library, and airplane mode is switched on before you start shooting. Tap the camera icon; you should now see on the screen what your camera is pointing at. If you want to, you can reverse the lens to record yourself. This is useful if you want to record a piece to camera. If you do, make sure you look at the lens, not the phone itself. Then slide the white writing near the *white* circle to video. When you select video mode the circle will go *red*.

Before starting you want to ensure your smartphone is attached to a monopod or tripod. This will stabilise your shots. More advanced mobile journalists might invest in a gimbal or shoulder pod.[18] If you don't have these you should try to brace yourself on a solid surface, like a wall, or alternatively tuck your arms into your sides. Due to its size it is very difficult to zoom or pan with a smartphone so you should get yourself in a good position to film before pressing Record.

FIGURE 8.3 This is how you shoot video using a monopod

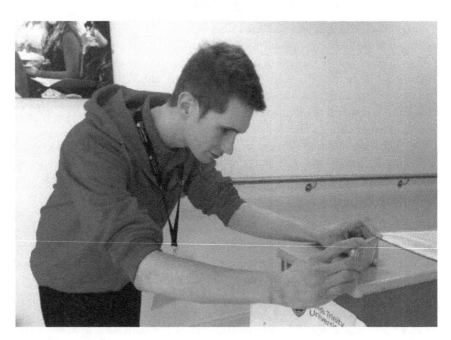

FIGURE 8.4 Bracing yourself can provide stability while shooting video

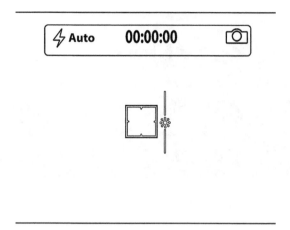

FIGURE 8.5 How to adjust the exposure on the camera

The camera has automatic focus and exposure (brightness). This means it will make assumptions about what you are aiming to film, as it has no brain, so you need to tell it what you want to focus on. Ensure the focus is on the main protagonist, i.e. the interviewee or focus of the story, and not an item in the background, by tapping the screen on their face. This also allows you to adjust the exposure, or brightness.

A yellow box will appear and you will notice the camera adjust. Slide the sunshine symbol to alter the exposure. To lock the focus and exposure – thus stopping it changing – tap the yellow box. Text will appear above it saying ae/af lock. To remove the lock, tap it again.

Hit the red button *prior* to starting the recording. This will give you a few sections of 'pre-roll', which makes it easier to edit afterwards. At the end of recording allow a few additional seconds before pressing stop; again, this will assist the editing process. If you find it easier you can use the volume buttons on the side of the phone rather than the red button to start and stop recording. Once you feel comfortable with your filming try downloading FiLMiC Pro to produce more advanced footage.

Lighting

You need to be aware the camera doesn't function as well in low lighting conditions because the lens is small. You can turn on the flash, which is helpful for close-up shots, but if it is still too dark you need to move location or introduce more lighting, for example a torch or car headlights. If you have an additional iOS device to hand you can download the SoftBox Pro app to act as an additional light.[19] Avoid shooting into the light; keep any sunlight, windows or bright lamps behind you. Otherwise your interviewee will look like a silhouette or the background will be overexposed.

FIGURE 8.6 Avoid shooting into the light

Operating the camera

To produce professional looking footage it is best to keep the camera still and let the subject move through the frame. It makes it easier to edit if you start with an empty frame, the subject then enters frame and leaves frame. Panning, going from side to side, or tilting, up and down, is difficult to pull off successfully with a smartphone as the movement can make it wobble. If you want to do that within your piece you should practise before you start recording. Plan where you want the shot to start and end and try to achieve a steady speed and motion. Start and finish the pan/tilt with a steady shot lasting a few seconds; this will make it easier to edit and offer you more options. Most pans should last no more than five seconds.

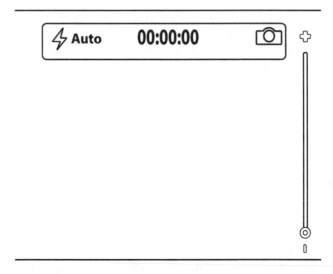

FIGURE 8.7 The slider on the smartphone allows you to zoom. However, this is difficult to do smoothly

FIGURE 8.8 Think about what is in the background of your shot

You should avoid zooming while filming. If you do need to use the zoom then pinch the screen and the zoom slider will appear. It is very difficult to achieve a steady zoom, so try to avoid this. Even if you zoom in to take a 'still' shot the zoom will amplify any wobbles. You can achieve the same effect as zooming by filming a wide shot, from further away, and then physically moving closer and filming a tight shot.

A good piece of footage will include a variety of shots – wides, medium shots, close-ups and shots from a range of angles. Think carefully about what you can see in the frame. Line up the side of the camera with walls and straight lines in the background so the picture looks level. Avoid big empty spaces or ugly objects in a room, like plug sockets and doorframes. Make sure your interviewees don't appear to have trees, lampposts or architraves sprouting from their heads.

Sound and interviews

This is where your external microphone will come in handy. Wind noise and noisy backgrounds are a problem, as they will drown out the sound you want to record. For the best results, record sound in a quiet spot, preferably somewhere sheltered, and get the camera as close as possible to the source of the sound. Check the sound has recorded afterwards.

Aim to record soundbites, because your storage and battery life are limited. Speak to the interviewee before recording to get extra information. Choose an interesting background for your interview, but not one that is too distracting or noisy. Don't use the same background twice or else it will look like a jump cut – this is when the subject unexpectedly moves due to an edit.

Eyelines

These are the rules for conventional TV-style framing, and correct framing can be difficult to achieve with a smartphone. You need to position the phone on a slight angle so that you can see the screen but also get the framing and eyeline right. It takes practice to master this skill.

Use tight framing, showing the interviewee's head and shoulders, or closer, as the sound quality will be better. There needs to be looking/talking space – you should be able to draw an imaginary speech bubble in the space in front of the interviewee's mouth in the direction they are looking. The side of the frame should not be directly against their mouth with lots of space at the back of their head.

Don't position the interviewee too far to one side of the screen, particularly if the background is dull, as there will be too much empty space.

Don't give too much headroom, i.e. empty space above their head.

We need to see both eyes, otherwise the interviewee appears in profile.

FIGURE 8.9 This is good framing for an interview

FIGURE 8.10 Here the interviewee is too far to the left

FIGURE 8.11 Your interviewee needs to be looking at you

The interviewer should stand as close as possible to the side of the camera lens and ask the interviewee to look at them, so their eyeline is slightly off camera. The camera lens, the interviewer's eyes and the interviewee's eyes all need to be on the same level, otherwise it creates a feeling of inferiority or superiority.

FIGURE 8.12 Your interviewee needs to be on the same level as you

Alternate the side you ask your interviewees to stand at if you are placing their interviews back-to-back in the edit. This is a common consideration when it comes to shooting vox pops. Here are a few interviewing tips:

- Make sure you ask open questions to encourage better answers.
- Avoid talking – simply smile to encourage them to talk, don't nod or your shot will be shaky.
- Don't breathe heavily. Your face should be close to the camera to achieve correct framing. It will pick up your breathing.
- Ask questions in a clear, loud voice in case you want to include them in the edit.
- The most interesting and watchable interview clips are usually emotional or opinionated. The video can be accompanied by text, so in most cases, especially human-interest stories, it is better to see emotion and read facts.

How to create a video package on your phone and upload it online

Key tool: iMovie

iMovie is an iOS video editing app, which means it is available on the iPhone and iPad. It is a crucial newsroom tool as it can help you produce high-quality news packages quickly.

Editing your footage using iMovie

When you have finished filming, go into the iMovie app on your phone. Tap Video to view the footage you have filmed. Tap Projects, or Theatre, to create a new package, followed by the + icon. Then select Movie, as the Trailer option is there to help create a cinematic trailer. Next you are asked to select a Theme. You should only choose 'Simple' here. Finally tap Create Movie in the top right. If you want to know what all the icons mean at any point tap the ? icon.

To import footage into the timeline tap the Film/music icon. All your film clips will appear; in broadcasting this footage would be referred to as your rushes. Tap on the footage you want to import; it will be highlighted gold.

Then various options appear:

- Arrow down = import footage straight into timeline.
- Play = play footage.
- Audio gauge = import the audio only.

When you already have footage in your timeline you can use the next three options, but remember to slide the long white cursor to the correct position on the timeline first:

- Box on box = selected footage is inserted as overlay, to go over the top of existing video. You might use this for 'cutaways'; these are visuals you show to break up long shots in packages.
- Box in box = selected footage appears in a small box.
- Split screen = selected footage appears in the right half of the screen and existing footage on left.

How to edit your footage

1. Trimming

To scroll through your video, slide your finger faster along the timeline. To trim the footage, tap the timeline. It turns gold around the edges and two gold pins appear at each end.

Slide these gold pins to the desired edit points. It isn't always obvious the pin is moving in the timeline, but if you look in the viewing window you

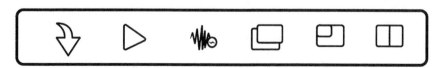

FIGURE 8.13 These are your choices when you import footage

FIGURE 8.14 This is how your timeline will look when you are editing footage

will see the footage move. If you want to cut out a middle section of a clip, get the white timeline cursor to the right spot, double click into the timeline and swipe your finger downwards to 'add an edit' or 'split' the clip. Double click on a clip and select delete – the waste bin – to cut out anything you don't want. To undo any action tap the reverse arrow symbol or shake the phone violently.

2. Reorganising footage

You can change the order in which the clips appear. To do this, tap and hold the clip and drag it to the required spot. However be careful: if you drag it up into the main screen it will go into the bin.

3. Adding transitions

Try to achieve a good edit using simple cuts and overlays rather than transitions. However, if you have a 'jump cut', where you have cut out the middle of an interview and the footage jerks, and you haven't filmed any cutaways, you may need to add a transition.

Double tap the transition icon, the little box on the timeline between the clips, and a variety of options will appear:

- I/None = Simple cut
- Star/Theme = fast dip to black, complete with weird sound effect.
- Triangles/Dissolve = mix first image with next
- Wipe 1/Slide = next image slides in, with four options for direction.
- Wipe 2/Wipe = first image wipes out, with four options for direction.
- Barcode/Fade (two options) = black flash or white flash.

When producing a news report the *white flash*, which is located in the fade menu, is the recommended transition.

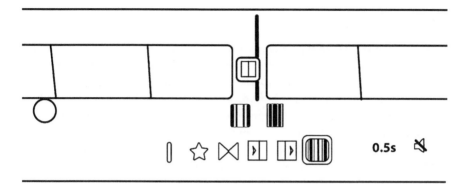

FIGURE 8.15 This is the transitions menu

Adjusting audio levels

To adjust the audio levels in iMovie, double tap the clip to make it gold and hit the speaker icon. There is no audio level monitor so you need to use your own judgement about levels. Due to the position of the microphones, audio you record in an interview will probably be quieter than a voiceover. It is probably best to err on the side of caution and boost the audio levels between 100 and 200 per cent for interview clips. You want the audio to be as clear as possible, as online viewers may be watching it in places where there is background noise. Remember to also adjust the audio on cutaways.

Recording a voiceover

Get the white cursor to the point where you want your voiceover to start. If you tap the microphone symbol you will see a black sound meter. Tap record, and after the countdown speak into the bottom of the phone as the microphone is by the charger hole.

If you are happy with your voiceover, tap accept. If the voiceover isn't in the right place on the video, tap the purple slab and hold it and you can slide it to the right spot. If you need to trim it, tap it once and use the gold pins. If you want to edit out a chunk in the middle, tap the footage and then tap the scissor icon in the bottom right and select Split.

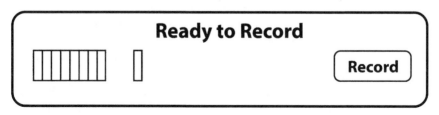

FIGURE 8.16 This menu appears when you are about to record a voice-over

Adding captions and titles

First select the area of the clip where you want the title to appear – it is best to bring it in a second or two after the person starts talking and leave it up for about five seconds. Then make a 'split' to mark the 'in and out' for the caption.

Tap the T icon (text) at the bottom. Choose a text style. They are all white writing in a mixture of lower and upper case, some have more than one layer, and only a few are appropriate for news. Tap in the viewing pane to type your caption. You can choose whether you want it in the 'centre' of the screen – usually only used if you want to put an opening title on your film – or 'lower', which is best for name captions. But your caption placement may be determined by your shot, as captions require a dark enough background to display the words.

Uploading your video to YouTube

Once you have finished editing your video tap the upload icon. You then need to enter your YouTube user name and password. Enter a title for your film; this will appear when it is published so name it carefully. Think about search engine optimisation and check your spellings. Enter a brief description; this will also be published. Scroll down and choose a category – this should normally be News & Politics.

Scroll down and select a size. This should be HD – 1,080p. Choosing private will allow you to get someone to check the footage before it goes out. When you select public, it becomes available to everyone. Then tap share. It will then take a few minutes to export the movie and upload it to YouTube. From YouTube you can embed the video in your site. Additionally, YouTube has its own video editor at youtube.com/editor.

Using your phone to record high-quality audio

Adding audio into your posts can be a great way to encourage visitors to your website to delve deeper into the story. If you have written a news story based on an interview you have recorded, including the full interview allows the reader the option to listen to everything the interviewee said. You can also conduct a vox pop – gaining the 'voice of the people' – to identify how the public feels about the issue you are reporting on.

Audio is an ideal platform for vox pops as the audience can hear different people speaking. You can also do away with written pieces completely and focus on audio packages. In these, you introduce the story as the reporter, speak to interviewees – putting both sides of the issue if there is division – and summarise the issue at the end. This style of package is particularly popular on stations such as BBC Radio 5 Live.

Podcasts are also enjoying a spike in popularity a decade after they initially began appearing. The number of Americans who listen to a podcast every month has nearly doubled since 2008,[20] and the medium fits the current consumer desire for on-demand media available on mobile phones. The advantage for an entrepreneur seeking to serve a niche audience is that podcasting offers a low-cost way to serve listeners. If a passionate host can attract an audience it also offers the opportunity to sell targeted advertising space.

Conducting an audio interview

As with any interview you need to do your research and prepare questions for your interviewee. To gain a high quality recording you may want to invest in an iPhone microphone, possibly an iRig MicCast, to boost the quality of the audio. Choose the location of the interview carefully. A place with too much background noise will cause you problems. You may want to record background noise that is relevant to your interview afterwards. As respected journalist Mark Briggs says: 'It is always a good idea to search for those sounds that will help you describe the setting. Are power tools being used? Is it a busy office with lots of chatter and phones ringing?'[21] Try to record more than ten seconds of these natural sounds without interruption. They will be beneficial when it comes to editing your audio.

Before recording put your phone in airplane mode. During the interview try not to speak too much, especially over your interviewee, as this will all be recorded. And if you remember hearing a fantastic quote, jot it down so you can go back to it later. You should record your interviews in Audio Record Pro or, as a back up, your phone's Voice Memos. If you have internet access you can record straight to Audioboom. But if you upload your audio to the internet make sure the rough recording is not instantly available to your audience.

Editing your audio

You can put a package together on your phone using the Ferrite Recording Studio. If you prefer to edit audio on desktop the best package you can use for editing is Adobe Audition. However, a comparable downloadable, free open-source alternative is Audacity.

Audacity is available for both Mac and PC operating systems and there is a series of tutorials in an Audacity wiki online to help you get the best out of it. It will allow you to edit a sound clip, create a package or record a voiceover. When editing you should identify the best clips from your interview and delete the rest. If aspects of the conversation bore you, they will bore people listening. Alternatively, if you have five minutes of an amazing, captivating interview you should probably run it in full.

When editing you need to normalise audio levels and ensure your recording is in stereo, so you can hear it in both headphones. Ideally it should be exported as an MP3 file. To make it available on your site upload it to Soundcloud or Audioboom and embed it into your post. Additionally, uploading to Clammr, the world's biggest short-form audio community, can promote your content to a wider audience.

Keeping an eye out for the next tool for news

Finding inventive ways of telling stories to mobile audiences is set to be a key issue for newsrooms in the next decade. Virtual reality is the next journalistic frontier, particularly for established media giants like the *New York Times*,[22] who – along with Google Cardboard and Vrse – are producing immersive video content for early adopter audiences. VR allows audiences to experience the reality of war-torn countries like Syria without distractions.[23] But it remains to be seen whether audiences will buy into VR content en masse, and whether the cost of producing this type of immersive footage will put off small newsrooms.

The disruption caused by technological advances has sparked an era of unconstrained journalistic creativity. Italian start-up Graphic News, which launched with a team of four, tells audiences a story a week using cartoon slideshows.[24] 442oons produce cartoon parodies of the week's football action for its 700,000 YouTube subscribers.[25] Hard news is being told in new ways too; when the Tampa Bay Times wanted to demonstrate how bad public schooling for black students was in Pinellas County, instead of writing about it they studied data from the state's board of education to produce a slideshow of twenty-five different graphs supporting

Christian Payne is a specialist in creative technology, using tools for digital storytelling. He runs his own website, blogging as Documentally.

Keeping up to date is about reading as many articles about journalism as possible. I use platforms such as Instapaper to ensure if I can't read something at the moment but it's relevant and interesting to me I can archive it and read it on my

FIGURE 8.17 Christian Payne

other devices. Then it's ready for when I have time to read it.

I follow and connect with a lot of people in mobile journalism. I go to conferences so I can experiment hands-on. If that object fits my workflow and improves on an existing tool then I'll consider shifting over to it. I didn't leap into 360 [degree video]. I waited until there was a device that was small enough for me to carry around.

If I had gone out and invested in six GoPros and a rig to shoot video it would have been very heavy duty and affected how much other work I could do. Go slow, incorporate it into your workflow, and if there is an improvement focus on it. The story is the most important part of what I do. I don't want to get the story to fit the tools, I'm using the tools to fit the story.

the argument.[26] The investigation, called 'Pinellas Failure Factories', won a raft of awards and led to a public investigation.[27] As Mariana Santos, director of interactive and animation at Fushion, says, journalists 'need to experiment and dare to do things in a way that hasn't been done before'.[28]

Journalists will be serving a demanding digital-native consumer group in the future. There will be fourteen times more video traffic within five years, when it will account for 70 per cent of all mobile data traffic. Of 16–19 year olds, 45 per cent currently spend an hour or more per day on YouTube and viewers find buffering more stressful than standing on the edge of a cliff.[29] As Rebecka Cedering Angstrom, from the Ericsson Consumer Lab, says: 'We are at the beginning of a media transformation. There are new behaviours, new users and new technology being developed.'[30]

But as a journalist you need to be sure – whether it is a fully equipped TV studio or a smartphone you are using to produce news – that the story remains at the forefront of your thoughts. As multi-award winning journalist Scott Rensberger says: 'Storytelling is the most powerful thing in the world – it connects the dots of our communities.'[31]

Notes

1 BBC (2015) *Shoreham plane crash: Seven dead after Hawker Hunter hits cars.* BBC Sussex.
2 Vellinga, W (2016) *Mojocon.* Dublin.
3 Keller, L (2016) *Mojocon.* Dublin.
4 Willett, M (2016) *iPhone sound recording for video review.* YouTube. Leeds Trinity University.
5 Eema, E (2016) *Mojocon.* Dublin.
6 Settle, M (2016) *Mojocon.* Dublin.
7 Ibid.
8 Eema, E (2016) *Mojocon.* Dublin.
9 McCracken, H (2013) *50 best websites 2013.* Time Magazine.
10 Pakman, D (2015) *May I have your attention, please?* Medium.
11 Wang, S (2016) *Facebook Live is swallowing the world (or, at least, users' attention) this time with Facebook Live video.* Nieman Lab.
12 Jones, G (2016) *LTU Media Fest.* Leeds.
13 Gesenhues, A (2016) *Buzzfeed's exploding watermelon video proves Facebook Live is no joke.* Marketing Land.
14 Valinsky, J (2016) *One month in: Four things the New York Times has learned using Facebook Live.* New York Times.
15 McNamara, C (2016) *Thanks to you all, Upworthy has 200 million reasons to celebrate.* Upworthy.
16 New York Times (2014) *How missing jet's debris could have floated to Reunion.*
17 Agnew, J (@aggerscricket) *More people watched BBC TMS pint sized Ashes than the TV coverage of the whole series.* 24 August 2015. 7:23 a.m. Tweet.
18 Eagen, M (2016) *Mojocon.* Dublin.
19 Ibid.
20 Vogt, N (2015) *Podcasting: Fact sheet.* Pew Research Centre.
21 Briggs, M (2013) *Journalism next: A practical guide to digital reporting and publishing.* 2nd edn. London: Sage.
22 Rosenbaum, S (2016) *Virtual reality and journalism: Can they get along?* Forbes.
23 Jones, S (2016) *Mojocon.* Dublin.

24 Bassan, V (2015) *Graphic news: Comic journalism is going mobile-first in Italy.* Journalism. co.uk
25 442oons (2016) YouTube homepage.
26 Lash, N (2015) *Why Pinellas County is the worse place in Florida to be black and go to public school.* Tampa Bay Times.
27 Walsh, M (2016) *Tampa Bay Times series on Pinellas District's failures wins top investigative prize.* Education Week.
28 Albeanu, C (2015) *'We need to be bold and not fear failure': Q&A with Mariana Santos.* journalism.co.uk
29 Ericsson Consumer Lab (2015) *10 hot consumer trends for 2016.*
30 Cedering Angstrom, R (2016) *Mojocon.* Dublin.
31 Scott, C (2016) *Why storytelling 'is still everything' despite new journalism tools and technology.* Journalism.co.uk

9

USING SOCIAL MEDIA TO PROMOTE YOUR WORK

Social media platforms have become central to building an online audience for start-ups. What is the best way of ensuring your story ends up attracting the widest possible audience?

The rapid rise in our social media use is one of the defining shifts of the past decade. We all have instant access to our entire network of friends and family, tailored news based on our preferences and the platform to tell our audience exactly what we think about any issue.

Social media has overtaken entertainment as the UK's favourite online activity. In the UK, 32 million Brits have a Facebook account and 15 million have a Twitter handle.[1] On average, more than 30 minutes of the near 3 hours every UK resident spends online every day is spent on social media.[2] This has led to social replacing direct access and search as the largest source of traffic for news websites, accounting for between 30 and 50 per cent of external visits.[3]

Readers are increasingly engaging with stories recommended by their online contacts, resulting in each piece of journalism increasingly having its own individual trajectory. According to Simon Milner, Facebook's policy director for UK and Ireland, 'You're much more likely to read a story, no matter who the publisher is, if it's been recommended by a friend.'[4]

Digital newsrooms, such as the Huffington Post and Buzzfeed, that produce around 1,000 posts a day between them, have an increasingly symbiotic relationship with social media platforms.[5] These news outlets produce content for social platforms in return for gaining traffic. In return this keeps huge audiences entertained and engaged on social media.

It is a fundamental shift in how the news is delivered and demonstrates why legacy newsrooms are finding it harder to command their traditional authority in a fragmented digital world.

As an entrepreneurial journalist you should be aware that social media offers a golden opportunity to get your content to your audience for free. For a start-up, social media is a quick and effective way of announcing yourself to a wider audience.

However, you first need to identify:

- Which platforms you are using and why you have chosen them.
- How these platforms will help develop your audience share.
- How you are planning on putting that into practice.

In short you need a social media strategy, and this chapter will help you develop one.

Which platforms are you using and why?

Finding your audience

There is a multitude of social media platforms available but you only have a limited amount of time. So you should start by identifying which social media platforms your target audience is most likely to use.

The importance of selecting the right social media platform was demonstrated in the 2015 UK general election. Despite 47 million political tweets being sent during the campaign, Twitter's youthful left-leaning audience failed to encourage more young people to vote in the election.[6] By comparison the right-wing Conservative party focused its attention on bigger numbers of older voters on Facebook and were returned to office with then Prime Minister David Cameron proclaiming 'Britain and Twitter are not the same thing.'[7]

A key demographic for analysing the future of social media is the millennials. This group, aged between 18 and 34, are important because they are the first generation to have grown up with regular access to computers, mobile phones, and therefore social media. They are the tester generation and their behaviour is shaping the development of the digital world.

Linear forms of entertainment, particularly television, are losing significant millennial audience share due to a shift to mobile devices. As the *New York Times* observes, the millennial audience no longer watch the evening news, they have a sense of 'if something is important, it will *find me*'.[8]

As a result 88 per cent of American millennials get their news from Facebook and 33 per cent from Twitter. The amount of time they spend online ensures that 69 per cent of them keep up with the news daily and, crucially for entrepreneurial journalists, 40 per cent of them pay for at least one news-specific service, app or digital subscription.[9] This growing acceptance that news costs money *could* ensure the survival of digital journalism in the future.

The millennial audience is proving difficult for legacy media to penetrate, which provides further encouragement for start-ups. In a study of fifteen major US news sites, only Vice and Buzzfeed attracted more than half their audience from the millennial age group.[10] As a result they are extremely appealing to advertisers, as demonstrated by Vice selling three years of advertising for its new TV network before it even existed.[11]

Evidence suggests the social media use of trailing (or younger) millennials is becoming increasingly fragmented. Although Facebook remains the dominant platform for them, Instagram and Snapchat have surpassed Twitter in terms of audience share.[12] As a result these visual social platforms are becoming increasingly attractive to advertisers.

However, if you are seeking pre-millennial readers it is likely Facebook will become your most crucial social platform. It will offer you the best opportunity to get your content in front of large number of people in the 35+ age bracket. Baby

---

Anna Doble is online editor for Radio 1's Newsbeat, *and former head of online at Channel 4 News.*

Eighteen months ago, *Newsbeat's* core team were radio-focused. Today they are digital journalists able to shoot and edit video and craft distinctive online content for 16–25 year-olds while remaining at the heart of Radio 1 and 1Xtra's on-air news. It seems obvious, but creating genuine multimedia journalists has been key to our transformation – and will remain the key as we continue to adapt our ways of storytelling to young audiences.

FIGURE 9.1 Anna Doble

Newsbeat also ramped up its original journalism, looking at previously untouched subjects from the rise in young men with 'bigorexia' (muscle dysmorphia) to dating app addiction, the death of clubbing and the spike in self-poisoning by teenage girls. *Newsbeat's* reporting put the audience front and centre, allowing them to tell their stories around difficult topics, and we experimented with new formats including podcasts, YouTube mini documentaries and animation.

Increasingly we'll be making bespoke content for platforms – from Instagram to Snapchat – and creating content in 'social corridors' which connect information-saturated young audiences with the things the BBC stands for: accuracy, balance and trust in its new coverage. The mechanics of the site – the share tools, the visual boldness, the fresh look and feel, the quiz modules, the embedded social content – matter enormously, but creating routes into our content will likely become the journalists' primary challenge.

boomers and members of Generation X have been attracted to Facebook in huge numbers in recent years as it allows them to keep up to date, and in some cases reconnect, with friends and family.

Twitter v. Facebook: how different platforms require different approaches

Facebook

Facebook's size is its biggest draw for an entrepreneur keen on building market share. As founder Mark Zuckerberg sees it: 'The value that people get [from Facebook] is how much information everyone is sharing'.[13] Facebook has 1.3 billion active monthly users[14] and its users share around 2.5 million pieces of content every minute.[15] In addition, Facebook Messenger has an additional 500 million active monthly users.

The phenomenal growth of the platform over the last decade has resulted in it becoming by far and away the largest social media platform, and it is difficult to see it being displaced in the near future.

This is primarily down to Facebook's ability to adapt to the market. Facebook prioritised its mobile app to such a point in 2013 that it shut off its desktop website to focus employees on improving it. It is an approach the *New York Times* replicated two years later. Now all mobile users spend more than 80 per cent of their time in-apps, and 'concentrating on social and messaging has allowed Facebook to completely dominate mobile ... The killer-app of the mobile generation is the platform for self-expression and communication'.[16]

The introduction of Facebook Instant Articles is being closely monitored by publishers. It offers advantages to small newsrooms as they can use the platform to access big audiences on Facebook, and a Wordpress plugin is already available to assist technologically. Publishers are entitled to all the revenue they generate from ads in Instant Articles, if they sell them. Otherwise they can take 70 per cent if they rely on Facebook to sell their ads through their advertising network.[17]

Giving more control over publishing to Facebook is a risk, as it is likely to drive more traffic away from your website. However, the French newspaper *Libération* reported its readers were spending 33 per cent more time reading their articles and they had seen a 10 per cent boost to their follower numbers on Facebook after two months of producing Instant Articles.[18]

How can promoting your content on Facebook benefit you?

The most common reasons people give for using Facebook are seeing what their friends are discussing, finding content that entertains them and looking for interesting articles/links. Promoting your content through Facebook allows you to access the vast number of users who are interested in news but not engaged enough to leave a social network to find it.

It allows you a mechanism to deliver the news directly to their newsfeed. The rewards for creating enticing content are potentially huge. In the UK, 97 per cent of adults with a social media profile say they use the site. A fifth of those users say they visit Facebook more than ten times a day,[19] demonstrating that the platform has a significant number of very engaged users, keen and ready to share their thoughts.

Having a Facebook page for your site allows you to really connect with these engaged users, build an audience and share content. Avoid connecting personally with your audience; you want them to engage with your brand. The older half of the millennial audience, aged between 25 and 34, is the largest demographic on the site with around a quarter of users in this age range. It is increasingly where significant numbers of this demographic will go to find out what's happening.

Twitter

Twitter's strength lies in its simplicity. It is a micro-blogging platform giving you 140 characters to disseminate information to your followers. It allows you to create a tailored newsfeed by choosing accounts to follow, makes you aware of trends and provides instant access to a diverse database of hashtags, key terms and individuals.

More than 300 million people a month use Twitter and around 350,000 tweets are sent per minute. Although this is not in the same league at Facebook, its users are extremely engaged, with around half of them signing in each day.[20] Twitter has quickly become a staple tool in the newsroom due to its ability to distribute short snippets of news to the audience immediately. In short there might be a much bigger audience on Facebook but Twitter is the best place to find people heavily engaged in news. Additionally, more than eight out of ten Twitter users access the platform on their mobile, which is more than Facebook users.[21]

How can promoting your content on Twitter benefit you?

Unlike Facebook, which primarily operates in networks, Twitter is 'essentially an overwhelming firehose of crowdsourced data'[22] and is therefore a relatively open platform. This creates more opportunity to directly access individuals and encourages greater sharing of links, video, images and conversations.

A key benefit of Twitter is it 'allows you to see who is "following" you (and who they are following), making it part social network. This makes it particularly useful for making contacts.'[23] If you create content that appeals to your followers often they will re-tweet it. This is when your content starts to travel beyond your immediate network of followers: now it is appearing on the accounts of additional followers. When tweets go viral in this manner it can dramatically increase your audience reach.

A Twitter account becomes more valuable the more followers it has. This is because tweets or re-tweets from that account appear on more newsfeeds, increasing the opportunity for engagement with the content being distributed. You need your content to appear on as many of these high-value accounts as possible.

Attracting young audiences: Snapchat and Instagram

Snapchat and Instagram, two social media platforms that rely on visual content, are increasingly becoming mainstream media battle zones. This is because they are attracting young, wealthy, primarily female audiences who are moving away from television. Both of these platforms are demanding from a journalistic point of view but they offer the potential to grow your operation and generate income in the future.

Snapchat

Snapchat allows users to take images and record video before adding text and drawings on them. Although best known for its quickly disappearing pictures, Snapchat now offers the chance to produce longer stories, allowing journalists to use it to provide alternative, fun coverage for a younger demographic. The platform offers an opportunity for creative news outlets to compete and reach audiences on their own account through its My Story option. These stories disappear from the platform after 24 hours but you can archive them.

Just under half of Snapchat users in America are aged between 18 and 24. Compare that to Facebook and Twitter where less than 20 per cent of users fall into that category.[24] Snapchat is also enjoying tremendous growth, buoyed by its success in the youth market. It tripled its number of daily video views from 2 billion to 6 billion in half a year in 2015.[25]

There are drawbacks for start-ups, though; Snapchat has an inbuilt media section called 'Discover', which gives all its users instant access to a handful of established journalistic brands that produce content for it on a daily basis. The platform has also recruited a team of journalists itself to cover the 2016 US presidential election, suggesting it may begin producing its own journalistic content.

Instagram

Instagram is a social network that allows stories to be told through pictures or up to 15 seconds of video. It has an engaged audience of around 300 million active users, which has grown rapidly in the last two years. Instagram has three times the active users that Snapchat has and it is used by almost two thirds of all American teenage girls.[26]

The visual quality on Instagram is generally higher than Snapchat as users upload more content to the platform. Instagram retains content, making it a longer lasting and less demanding platform for journalists to work on. Hashtags are used to navigate around the site and these trend in a similar manner to Twitter, although the platform is actually owned by Facebook.

Mainstream UK news organisations, like BBC News and the *Guardian*, have adapted to Instagram's audience by using their accounts to tell often overlooked human-interest stories from around the world. Plans for a Snapchat-style stories feature on Instagram were revealed in August 2016. This will create story slide-shows, which last for 24 hours, from images and video content. They will appear in users' main feeds to drive interaction with them.[27] This move is intended to increase Instagram's appeal to younger users and diminish Snapchat's unique selling point.

How can these platforms help develop your audience share?

Recent research suggests two thirds of Twitter and Facebook users believe those platforms serve as a source for news,[28] a figure that has risen significantly in recent years. Alongside the specific audience they attract, each social media platform has its own specific method of working. This impacts heavily on the way you go about promoting your site and driving engagement with your content.

How to promote your content on Facebook

You should launch a Facebook page for your news site alongside promoting your content from your personal account. Your stories should appear on your Facebook page as soon as they have been posted on your site. Don't include too much information on the Facebook post if you want the audience to click on the hyperlink to visit the content on your site.

You want to create a community around your page. To build this avoid using the page as a purely promotional tool; instead interact with the audience. Have conversations, and if you are aware of other material that will interest them share this too.

You should also find and tap into existing Facebook groups that are relevant to your specialism. These are likely to be populated by engaged users, offering an ideal opportunity to grow your audience. This tactic is particularly valuable when running a hyperlocal site as it allows you to interact with residents, giving the opportunity to promote content, find out about new stories and gain feedback on the site.

Key tool: Facebook Insights

Facebook Insights allows you to access key analytical information about posts on your Facebook page. This free tool, which is activated once your page has thirty likes, tells you how many people have seen your posts, engaged with them and liked, shared or commented on them. You can also identify how many people have watched the videos you've posted.

It also provides key information about your audience. It tells you the age, gender and location of your readers. You can also establish when your audience is online; this will help you post content at the right time. All this allows you to build up a stronger profile of your audience, allowing you to target your core demographic in future content. This information is also crucial for your advertisers.

You can establish whether any external sources are linking to your Facebook page, which will allow you to identify any unexpected source of readers you should be catering for. You can also monitor the pages of your competitors and pay to extend the reach of your posts on Facebook.

Paid social media promotion

For a small price you can boost the reach of your Facebook posts among your target audience. This option is particularly helpful for start-ups as it is cost-effective and can be aimed at your target audience. InvestigateWest in America invests around $12–18 per story in Facebook promotion to reach an additional 6,000 to 8,000 people.[29]

When promoting your post you can choose the age of the people who will see it, their location, crucial for hyperlocal sites, and their interests, which is crucial for specialist sites. The post will also stop being promoted when you've reached your budget limit.

If Twitter is proving your best social platform you can target people by promoting your tweets in a similar manner. You will only be charged when users interact with your tweet or follow your account.

How to promote your content on Twitter

As a start-up you should promote content on the personal accounts of your team as well as your site's Twitter account from the start to raise awareness of your news site. But your main tactic should be aiming to piggyback on popular, existing Twitter accounts to increase the reach of your content. Draw up a list of influential people or organisations with large Twitter followings based on the specialism or location that you are writing about.

If you want someone to see your message you should include their Twitter handle in your post. If you can get your content re-tweeted by an account with hundreds of thousands (or even millions) of followers then it will appear on thousands of timelines. The re-tweet also implies the account holder has judged your work to be of a high standard and comes with their implied seal of approval.

If you are covering an event you should always include relevant Twitter hashtags to make your content more visible. When covering sport these are likely to be the initials or nickname of the team involved; conferences often have their own hashtags and industries their own acronyms. You should also include the Twitter handles of the event, organisation or team you are covering – but be aware they will receive a notification about this so expect critical coverage to be challenged.

Additionally, keep an eye on relevant trending topics as including these in your posts will increase the visibility of your content. But don't include irrelevant trending phrases, as your tweet will be perceived as spam.

Key tool: Twitter Analytics

Twitter Analytics is a tool that allows you to measure audience engagement with your tweets. It is free to use and once you have set it up it will begin recording data. It measures how many people have seen your tweet (impressions), how many people engaged with your tweet in any way (engagements) and the percentage of the people who saw your tweet who then engaged with it (engagement rate).

The data you receive will help you identify which of your tweets has been popular online, allowing you to tailor your content to your audience. Experimenting with different ways of scripting your tweets and including a variety of content within them will help you identify which type of tweets are most successful with your audience.

Twitter as a newsgathering resource

Following a lot of people on Twitter often results in your own follower count increasing, but in this case your timeline will get very busy. All this information may be a great resource but it makes it difficult to identify the content you are particularly interested in. To solve this problem you should use Twitter lists, which are a great way of filtering the information you are receiving. They allow you to focus on content from a small number of the accounts you follow.

For example, if you are running a hyperlocal blog you should have separate lists for:

- Public services – emergency services, council(s), courts, key local councillors, MPs, schools/colleges and hospital trusts.
- Sport – local clubs and organisations, prominent sportspeople and regional/ national administrative bodies.
- Community – voluntary organisations and charities, prominent figures, local campaigners and key businesses.
- National news sources and competing regional news outlets.

Organising your news sources in this way allows you to focus when there is a breaking news story that requires your attention, and encourages you to produce a balanced range of hard news, community and sports stories.

To create a list, go to your profile page and click on the Lists tab on the left-hand side. Click 'create list' and then give it a descriptive name. You can decide if you want the list to be public – allowing other users to subscribe to it – or private, so only you can. Some lists, like a list of your advertisers, you may want to keep private so your competitors don't see them.

To add people to your list click on the cog icon next to the follow button on their profile page. Select add or remove from lists and then choose a list to alter. You don't need to be already following that account. To see tweets from accounts on your list you need to click lists again on your profile page.

Twitter is also a database you can use to search for interviewees. If you want to find a doctor in your area to interview them about changes in the National Health Service you can type 'doctor' in the search box and then go to more options and click 'near you'. This will give you all the accounts of people with 'doctor' in their Twitter bio.

If you are running a specialist site you can use the advanced search to find people related to those specialisms in cities across the world. This would be extremely helpful if you were running a technology news site and a product was being launched in Beijing and you want to find an interviewee at the launch.

Building and promoting content on Snapchat

Most stories on Snapchat are told by combining both images and video clips, both of which appear on-screen for ten seconds. Utilising both formats varies the content in the package and allows you time to explain some aspects of the story when static images are on-screen.

When constructing your story remember your audience only has ten seconds to read any writing – so keep it brief. Snapchat thrives on creativity and humour so your first stories on the platform should be light-hearted. Covering hard news on the platform requires an adept understanding of your target audience.

Plan your package out on a storyboard before shooting it, as you would with a video package. This will give you an idea of the type of shots you want to get. To build your story press the + button at the bottom of the screen after shooting your first snap.

Remember, the major drawback on Snapchat is that your content will disappear after 24 hours, so after completing your package you need to cross-promote your story on other forms of social media and on your news site immediately. Ensure you archive your past Snapchat stories before they disappear from the platform.

Creating and promoting content on Instagram

On Instagram either static images or video footage can be used but not both together. The video clips can be slightly longer than Snapchat – 15 seconds rather than 10 – but must be used on their own rather than built into longer packages.

As a result if you are posting video content you should edit it together before uploading it to Instagram, the same way you would when uploading to YouTube. Whether you are using a static image or a video you need to consider how you will identify your content to your audience. You should either create a graphic within the visual or alternatively ensure your caption includes all the necessary information to complement your content.

As the audience is less youthful on Instagram it is a more natural home for hard news content, so it is easier to cover serious topics. When posting content include key hashtags and search terms when appropriate. Integrate your Instagram feed on your Facebook page to creating instant social cross-promotion; and you should also install an Instagram widget on your site's homepage.

Putting this planning into practice

Writing style on social media

When posting on social media as a news organisation is it important to strike a balance between authoritative and approachable. You need to ensure standards are maintained, so ensure words are spelt correctly and in full, keep your personal opinions out of the post and avoid using first-person pronouns such as I, we and us. If you want to come across as an objective, reliable news organisation you need to stick to the facts.

Try to write in full sentences, although this can be difficult with character limits, and get the key information across to your reader. If you need to post twice to give your audience the whole picture, this is better than missing elements out or trying to cram everything into one post. If you post information or quotes from another news outlet it is vitally important to attribute these; you shouldn't be presenting content from another source as your own.

If you include images on your post, caption them to include names, explain what is happening and where. Videos should also have a synopsis to describe the content.[30] Your standards shouldn't slide just because you are posting on social media rather than on your own site.

But you also need to engage

Alongside developing your reputation as a well-respected news source you need to demonstrate the ability to respond. This is often a problem for the small teams involved in start-ups who often resort to the old-media tactic of broadcasting their stories on social media but failing to engage with the audience afterwards. As a J-Lab study of 200 news start-ups found, newsrooms need to develop these interactions further.[31] A heavily engaged audience usually leads to greater opportunities to raise revenue in the future.

Developing a two-way relationship with their audience on social media has reaped rewards for reporters at the *Liverpool Echo*, who have consciously developed their social platforms into a community; this has involved prioritising human-interest stories on Facebook and remaining 'mindful' that people visit the platform to engage with family and friends. 'We will do our best to engage with people as much as possible and do our best to respond to tip-offs and to encourage general interaction.'[32]

Breaking news on social media

The speed of social media has had significant implications on breaking news. You need to ensure you get breaking stories online as soon as possible or you will lose audience share to your competitors. The best way to avoid this is to first break the news – even if you have limited information on it at the time – and then follow it up.

If you are going to follow this technique of posting news snaps you have to ensure your source, more than one in most cases, is solid before posting it to all your social media platforms. Once you have done this be sure to write up the completed story as quickly as possible and link this to the initial information.

Writing engaging content

The content you are posting has to engage the audience on that particular social media platform. This involves experimenting until you find a successful formula. This involves altering the text you include in the post, the image you use, whether a video, audio or any other multimedia is embedded or not, and alerting other accounts on the platform to your post.

The size of the audience on Twitter and Facebook means you can often tell quickly whether a story is likely to drive engagement. If your first post falls flat, experiment with a different method of attack and remember the techniques that bring you the most success with your target audience. Your long-term plan should be to encourage people who become aware of you on social media to access your site directly; this should increase their engagement with other content on the site.

Sparking an emotive response to your content is one way to engage your audience. You have to grab their attention in a similar way a powerful intro or image does or a shocking piece of multimedia. An effective way to do this online is to personalise your post to suit a section of your target audience. For example, if you are a hyperlocal site writing about a rush hour traffic jam you could title your post 'If *you* were late to work this morning this is why' before including your link and an image. Alternatively, if you are writing about education for an audience likely to include parents you might write 'Where in the county does *your* child have the best chance of getting good grades?'

You have to give your reader a concrete reason to engage with your content. Eye-catching statements and posing questions are two approaches, although you should attempt to pose open questions, suggesting you will give a well-rounded answer. Posing closed questions within your content, suggesting a yes or no answer, is typical of so-called clickbait and may put off your audience.

Don't just write for clicks

The biggest difference between clickbait and news is that journalists should deliver on the promises in their social media posts and headlines. Clickbait exists to drive instant audience clicks, not to encourage repeat visits. Your journalism should be about building an audience and encouraging people to come back and see your content time and time again. As Mic Wright, editor at digital news start-up The Malcontent, says:

An entertaining or provocative headline *isn't* clickbait, a story that fails to deliver on the headline's promise is clickbait. A story that was written because the writer was thirsty for clicks more than interested in writing about the topic *is* clickbait.[33]

If you aim to produce good journalism for your audience you should never be afraid of the accusation that you are producing clickbait. You are merely using a technique to encourage people to read your story in the first place; it is the digital equivalent of standing on a street corner behind a billboard shouting out the day's headlines and inviting people 'to read all about it'. But the debate around clickbait is complex and not limited to start-ups.

In August 2015 one fan of the popular gaming series Football Manager posted a story on Reddit about a game that ran 1,000 years into the future. The *Guardian*, a respected UK news outlet, ran an article about it in the Football section of its website two days later. Does The *Guardian* writing about a fan playing a computer game suggest a lowering of editorial standards to attract traffic in the football off-season? Or does the fact the story was shared more than 6,000 times imply they were right to cover it?

Similarly, six months earlier a heated office argument about the colour of a dress alerted Buzzfeed's social media manager Samir Mezrahi to the potential debate to be had amongst their audience. He then posted about it on Twitter – drawing instant click throughs, re-tweets and debate – before posting several times in different ways on Facebook, all within fifteen minutes.[34] The ensuing viral argument about whether it was black and blue or white and gold led to Buzzfeed receiving its highest number of onsite visitors at any one time.

Both of these stories were trivial but attracted audience engagement. However, you should maintain consistent editorial standards in your work.

Include images in your social media posts

When working on Facebook and Twitter people are more likely to engage with your content if you include an image in your post. So ensure you include an image with most social media posts. You should also attempt to vary the images you use when re-posting content for the second or third time.

This can be particularly challenging for small newsrooms or those covering breaking news, but there are several free tools available to help solve the problem. Canva allows you to use templates to overlay pictures with text quickly with custom sizing to fit a variety of social media platforms. Recite allows you to create images for social media using quotes, and Over is an app that offers the chance to put a variety of fonts onto your image.[35] You can also upload a Creative Commons image, if its licence permits it.

If you prefer an offline option you can download Lunchbox from US-based National Public Radio. It contains two programs that allow you to create images containing text blocks. If you need to resize an image to fit your post use the

Social Image Resizer Tool as it will size your picture to fit a variety of social platforms.

If you want to add a GIF (a short video clip) to your page you can shoot one with the Giphy Cam mobile app or Cloud App, which works on Macs, to allow you to upload screencast GIFs.

Think like a business

From a publisher's point of view you want your content to act as a gateway to your journalism. You want to encourage audiences to visit your site to increase visitor numbers and drive future engagement. To ensure you are doing this protect your intellectual property. Add a logo, watermark or ident to your pictures and video to avoid them being run without permission by competing websites. Watermark.ws is an online option that will allow you to attach a watermark and Waterbug, which is part of the NPR Lunchbox suite, will allow you to work offline.

Tagg.ly will allow you to add a logo and metadata to a picture or video to assert it belongs to you. Including a promotional jingle on your audio would achieve the same result.

Key tool: Hootsuite

Hootsuite is a free dashboard that allows you to pull in information from your social media accounts. You can use it to create streams of content that can be monitored simultaneously. It allows you to keep up-to-date with conversations around topics, hashtags or lists you have created. It is also a simple way to monitor your competitors' output on a daily basis. Hootsuite allows you to post content to all your social media channels at the same time, reducing the time it takes to distribute your content. It also offers the chance to schedule your posts to go out at the optimum time to engage your audience.

Best time to post content

You need to experiment to discover the best periods for engagement with your own individual target audience, but there is some general guidance about the best times to post across different social media platforms. When it comes to Facebook, midday is generally the best time to post content. This is because the audience can read it at lunchtime but the content will still be fresh on their newsfeed in the evening. Users of Facebook tend to be linked to fewer accounts that on Twitter so it is easier for your content to stay accessible to the audience.

Twitter is a transient platform so you need to post your content within the five minutes your audience is online or they will miss it. If you are aiming to reach a professional adult audience then you should be aiming to tweet your stories out around 8 a.m., lunchtime and 5 p.m. These are times when people are commuting or often at their desk eating their lunch.

Content on Snapchat only has a 24-hour shelf life so most news outlets produce daily content tied to the day of the week, similar to a newspaper. If you adopt this approach you should upload the next day's content either close to midnight or early the following morning. A study of 61,000 Instagram posts found the best time to post content on the platform worldwide was at 7 a.m. and 10 p.m., as this is a peak time for users to be engaged but few are posting images.[36] However, if you are looking for a regional, rather than specialist audience, this advice will be less relevant.

The future

Newsrooms are getting used to engaging with audiences on their own terms; the era of expecting readers to consume everything you produce and identify what they are interested in is over. The way you promote your content on social platforms is crucial. Buzzfeed racks up a staggering 5 billion views per month of its articles and videos, which it promotes on thirty different platforms. Less than 5 per cent of its 3 billion monthly video views are on Buzzfeed.com.[37]

Social media has become such a huge part of our relationship with the news that some digital newsrooms have even decided to become homeless. NowThisNews has shifted its entire focus onto social media, leaving its homepage adorned with the message 'Homepage. Even the word sounds old. Today the news lives where you live.'[38] The page includes links to its eight social platforms.

Although this approach seems drastic it demonstrates where you should be investing time and resources as a digital entrepreneur. Create distinctive content, focus on its production and social distribution and innovate on the formats you produce.[39] If you can do this, your content will increasingly thrive on social media and develop a community of readers, and a sustainable business model can begin to take shape.

Notes

1 Source: Statista.
2 Internet Advertising Bureau UK (2015) *Definitive time people spend online – 2hrs 51mins a day.*
3 Maymann, J (2015) *Re-shaping the online media industry.* Speech at the Reuters Institute, Oxford.
4 Ciobanu, M (2015) *Responding to digital change: Insights from the Huffington Post.* Journalism. co.uk
5 Maymann, *Re-shaping the online media industry.*
6 Byrne (2015) *Getting engaged? The relationship between traditional, new media and the electorate during the 2015 UK general election.* Oxford: Reuters Institute.
7 BBC News (2015) *Cameron: 'Britain and Twitter are not the same thing'.* BBC.
8 New York Times (2014) *New York Times innovation report.* New York.
9 Figures from Media Insight Project (2015) *How millennials get news: Inside the habits of America's first digital generation.* American Press Institute and the Associated Press–NORC Center for Public Affairs Research.
10 Comscore data cited in Doctor, K (2014) *The newsonomics of the millennial moment.* Nieman Lab.

11 Ives, N (2015) *Vice TV network has already sold three years' worth of ad time, CEO says.* Ad Age.
12 Lenhart, A (2015) *Teens, social media and technology overview.* Pew Research Center.
13 Penenberg, A (2009) *Viral loop: The power of pass-it-on.* London: Sceptre.
14 Kemp, S (2015) *Digital, social and mobile worldwide in 2015.* We are Social.
15 James, J (2014) *Data never sleeps 2.0.* Domo.
16 Pakman, D (2015) *May I have your attention, please?* Medium.
17 Marshall, J (2016) *Facebook's Instant Articles advertising fixes win over publishers.* Wall Street Journal.
18 Grangier, X (2016) *Libération on Facebook's Instant Articles.* LinkedIn.
19 UK figures from OFCOM (2015) *The communications market report 2015.*
20 Kemp, *Digital, social and mobile worldwide.*
21 Fitzgerald, B (2014) *Data point: Social networking is moving on from the desktop.* New York: Wall Street Journal.
22 Basta, V, cited by Mason, P (2015) *Twitter works just fine: But for investors, anything except total market domination is a disaster.* London: Guardian.
23 Bradshaw, P and Rohumaa, L (2011) *The online journalism handbook.* Harlow: Pearson.
24 ComScore figures, cited in Kafka, P (2015) *Here is the chart that explains why media companies are obsessed with Snapchat.* Re/code.
25 Matney, L (2015) *Snapchat reaches 6 billion video views, tripling from 2 billion in May.* TechCrunch.
26 Lenhart, *Teens, social media and technology.*
27 Constine, J (2016) *Instagram launches 'Stories,' a snapchatty feature for imperfect sharing.* Techcrunch.com
28 Barthel, M, Shearer, E, Gottfried, J and Mitchell, A (2015) *The evolving role of news on Twitter and Facebook.* Pew Research Center.
29 Robinson, J J, Grennan, K and Schiffrin, A (2015) *Publishing for peanuts: Innovation and the journalism start-up.* Open Society Foundation's Programme for Independent Journalism.
30 Lin, M (2015) *A Twitter guide for journalists.* Mulinblog.com
31 Schaffer, J and Polgreen, E (2012) *Engaging audiences: Measuring interactions, engagements and conversations.* J-lab.org
32 Reid, A (2014) *10 social media tips for local news organisations.* Journalism.co.uk
33 Wright, M (2015) *This isn't clickbait: Why you shouldn't hate Buzzfeed but should think more about the media.* The Next Web.
34 Avirgan, J (2015) *Podcast: How Buzzfeed made #thedress go viral.* FiveThirty Eight.
35 Buffer (2015) *23 tools and resources to create images for social media.* Medium.
36 Beres, D (2015) *Here's the best time to post a photo on Instagram.* Huffpost.
37 Moses, L (2016) *With a bet on platform strategy, Buzzfeed faces business challenges.* Dididay.
38 NowThisNews (2015) *Homepage.* Nowthisnews.com
39 Marconi, F (2015) *The rise of 'homeless' media.* Medium.

10

THE BOUNDARIES YOU MUST NOT CROSS AND REMAINING ETHICAL IN THE JOURNALISTIC WILD WEST

With Nigel Green

Which laws do you need to be aware of if you are going to publish independently? And how can you ensure your newsroom remains ethical when fictional stories are increasingly dressed up as fact? This chapter contains some initial advice to get you started.

Let's start by making one point clear. A media lawyer did not write this chapter. If you are in a mess or worried that you could be, the first rule of media law is to seek legal advice. This chapter is, however, informed by a wealth of experience as a crime reporter, having covered numerous difficult investigations stretching back to 1985.

This has involved facing a fair few threats of legal action – and worse – but emerging having never been sued, prosecuted or censured by regulators. Most reporters will tell you that *McNae's Essential Law For Journalists*[1] remains the best book on the market when it comes to outlining the wide variety of legal risks you are likely to face. You should order one for your office.

While that will cover extreme detail, this chapter will provide an overview, geared towards you as an entrepreneurial journalist embarking on your career and in need of rapidly learning the basics. Experience shows you what really matters and what is really likely to bite you amongst the endless chapters written on media law and regulation.

Those brave enough to enter the industry these days have to be sharper and more self-reliant. An impulsive or thoughtless post on social media can be costly or, in extreme cases, end in prison. Previous generations working on national and regional newspapers or in TV had the safety net of in-house lawyers. Today's independent journalists are unlikely to have such a luxury, although an informal network of legal experts offering free advice is developing online.[2] But there are also basics that were important all those years ago and are still important today.

The reporter's responsibility is to be accurate and not be afraid of standing their ground when necessary. Just because someone says you cannot do something, does not automatically mean you cannot.

UK civil courts: defamation – the basics

Even after changes in the law designed to protect free speech, defamation is still arguably the biggest threat faced by journalists. It is a complex topic that could take up chapters but the following advice aims to keep you safe, while still allowing you to tackle controversial stories. For a start, unless you want to look stupid, do not talk about slander when you mean libel. They both fall under the umbrella term of defamation – a statement that harms the reputation of an individual or a company. A layperson may tell you libel is written, while slander is spoken. That is not entirely correct.

Libel is permanent – written in a newspaper, an e-mail or a social media posting but also any comment that is broadcast on television, radio or even in a theatre. Slander is transient – perhaps a comment made in a pub or between friends. Libel is far more likely to factor in any claim against a journalist, not least because it is easier to prove that the statement has been made. However, slander still presents something of a risk for reporters. For example, when researching an allegation that a politician is cheating on his wife, it may not be wise to discuss the claim with his colleagues, neighbours or friends if they are not already aware.

How to stay safe

First, make sure that what you write is accurate. If it is, the chances of you being successfully sued are greatly reduced. Second, try to get more than one side of the story. Do not view the world in terms of 'innocent victims' and 'bad guys'. Stay impartial and go that extra mile to get a response from the 'bad guys'. This is not just the right thing to do; it will also help keep you safe.

If, when you approach the 'bad guys', they put the phone down on you or shut the door in your face, e-mail or write to them to give them the right of reply – or at least be able to prove you tried. If there are holes in your story, you want to know before it is published or broadcast.

So for example, John Smith tells you a doorman at Brown's bar beat him up and you telephone the bar and a nervous member of staff replies: 'No comment.' However, after e-mailing the bar, the manager contacts you to tell you they have CCTV of Mr Smith waving a knife around. While you may not want to back down just because someone threatens legal action, you may want to ask yourself: 'Is the story worth the hassle?'

It is important to remember that the claimant is also taking a massive risk. If you think you or someone you know has been libelled, think long and hard before taking legal action – particularly if the comment is merely posted on social media by someone with few followers and even less money. There are countless examples of

Gavin MacFadyen is director of the Centre for Investigative Journalism. He recommends that newsrooms severely scrutinise contentious stories.

I believe there should be multiple eyes on stories – particularly a big investigation. You can get drawn into stuff. You have to subject your evidence to the same scrutiny as the bad guy.

In investigations where people are going to sue you or hurt you, you have to make damned sure that

FIGURE 10.1 Gavin MacFadyen

the quality of information is good and that means you have to trust the people you work with. We have all been betrayed by freelancers who cut corners or didn't do what they said they did because they are working on limited time and resources.

Legal advice is very important in this country because of the danger of libel, but it can't be just left to a lawyer. Journalists are often just as good as lawyers in looking at evidence.

Since contributing to this book, sadly Gavin MacFadyen died of a short illness in October 2016. He was a strong believer in investigative journalism.

those who have lost millions of pounds and had their reputations further damaged because they wanted their day in court.

What does a claimant have to prove?

First, they have to prove that the statement is defamatory. In short, this means their reputation has been damaged. Obvious examples would be to say someone is a liar or a thief or incompetent at their job. Second, they must prove that the statement referred to them. Media law students are correctly warned that this does not mean that the claimant has to be named. They can sue if it can be 'reasonably understood to refer to them'.

Although there is no set number, journalists should be careful about making defamatory statements against relatively small groups of people. For example, it would be unlikely anyone could sue if someone wrote about a Leeds lecturer stealing from students, because it could refer to hundreds of people. However, if someone wrote that a Leeds Trinity University journalism lecturer stole from students, a dozen people might have a case.

Third, the claimant must prove the statement was published to a third party. If you send a personal letter, an e-mail or direct message to someone accusing them of something, you will be safe. But if you copy others in, you are venturing onto thin ice. An online story, broadcast or social media posting would obviously constitute publication to a third party. While caution is always advised, it should be stressed that courts do not look favourably on claimants who sue over a statement that only a handful of people have read or heard. Judges have described postings on social media, blogs and readers' comment sections as 'pub talk' or 'not worth the candle'; meaning not worth the court's time.

Prior to the 2013 Defamation Act, there was a fierce campaign to change defamation law in the UK. Journalists and other writers felt the law was too heavily tilted in favour of the claimant and this had led to a 'chilling effect' on free speech. Many hailed the introduction of the Act in early 2014. At the time of writing, it is still bedding in. However, it would be naive to think it will remove the threat to journalists. Indeed, the *Press Gazette* reported a 60 per cent rise in libel claims in 2014, although it acknowledged that this could merely be a blip.[3]

One of the most important changes brought in by the Defamation Act 2013, is that the claimant must prove 'serious harm'. A company must prove they have suffered or are likely to suffer 'serious financial loss'. At the time of writing, it is still unclear exactly how serious such harm needs to be. However, it is important to note that certain false allegations, of activities such as terrorism or paedophilia, are so serious that a court would assume the claimant has been seriously harmed.[4]

Ruth Collard is a partner at Carter-Ruck Lawyers. She believes the Defamation Act of 2013 has had an impact on the number of claims.

There is certainly a degree of caution in advising claimants to sue – unless there is a very serious allegation, widely published, or where there is some incontrovertible damage. In recent years there has definitely been more mediation – much more emphasis by the courts to work to resolve things. It's always in the client's interest to try to settle.

I would be very wary of advising someone to sue [an independent journalist] because they would have to spend vast sums of money but aren't going to get it back if they are successful. The same is true of an individual blogger, and you must ask if they really caused you serious harm.

FIGURE 10.2 Ruth Collard

Defamation: the main defences

The first line of defence is truth. This used to be known as justification and was always regarded as a difficult defence. Under civil law, you only have to prove your case on the balance of probabilities but it is for the defendant to prove the statement they make – not for the claimant to prove that it is not true. This brings us back to the basics. Make sure you try to get the other side of the story, before you publish or broadcast.

Try to avoid adjectives in your articles. You may be able to prove that a manager sacked a disabled employee but, if you refer to the manager as 'heartless', can you prove it? You may be able to prove that a senior police officer's statement is incorrect – but does that mean they are 'dishonest'?

Another key defence is honest opinion, formerly known as fair comment or honest comment. This defence covers published opinion and is often run alongside another defence, such as truth.[5] The key points when running an honest opinion defence are that it is the honestly held opinion of the person making it and it was based on facts or a privileged statement. Privilege is outlined below.

So here are two examples that wouldn't be covered by honest opinion:

- A damning restaurant review where the claimant could prove that the journalist actually thought the food and service were good but wrote a bad review because they had a personal feud with the owner.
- A sports journalist writing that goalkeeper John Smith is 'useless' and should be sacked because he let in seven goals, when before the game, Smith was injured and was replaced by Peter Brown.

The most secure defence is absolute privilege, which covers all statements given in court and inquests. The journalist does not need to worry about whether the statement is true, so long as their report is fair, accurate and contemporaneous. To ensure your report is fair, if a defamatory statement is made, always try to balance it up by making clear that it is only an allegation and, if appropriate, include that the person concerned denies it.

Ensuring your report is accurate may seem obvious but, during the heat of battle when covering a court case, it is easy for a journalist to mix up names or misquote what was actually said. Contemporaneous merely means that you should be published or broadcast 'as soon as practicable'. Do not lose sleep over this. Even if you delay publishing or broadcast, you are protected by qualified privilege.

Qualified privilege is similar to absolute privilege but the requirements are that your report needs to be fair and accurate, without malice and in the public interest.[6] Qualified privilege covers a wide range of meetings and documents but those most likely to be encountered by journalists include public meetings, such as local authorities, official police statements and press conferences.[7]

Moderating readers' comments

While this may seem like a minefield, in most respects it is the same as any other material you would consider carrying. The main risk is libel but, while the 'repetition rule' applies and you can still be sued for publishing someone else's defamatory comments, the Defamation Act 2013 gives you increased protection.

You need a 'report and remove' system and a 'robust' written complaints policy, possibly via a 'Report Abuse' button.[8] Before users can post comments, they are required to include their names and contact details and be warned their details will be divulged if they post anything defamatory. This – in theory – is supposed to shift the onus from the operator to the person who writes the offending comment.

Staff should be trained to deal with complaints and react promptly – preferably within 48 hours. They also need to keep written records of complaints, with the dates and times of actions taken. There is obviously a balancing act between allowing users to be outspoken but, if in doubt, the operator should remove the comments to ensure they are safe.[9]

Always think before you re-tweet a comment. While the chances of being sued may be slim, court cases such as that involving Lord McAlpine and Sally Bercow show that they are all too real.[10] One of the key changes of the Defamation Act 2013 was the introduction of the section 5 defence, which is designed to protect responsible website operators from being sued for comments posted by others.

Covering criminal courts in the UK

There is little dispute that coverage is now just a small fraction of what it was in the 1980s, when crime stories were in high demand and readers of regional newspapers wanted to know what their neighbours had been up to. Journalists were familiar faces in courts and often knew the barristers, solicitors, clerks and ushers, and could usually rely on an unofficial tip on which cases were the most interesting – and help to plug any gaps.

Now there are often just one or two reporters in the crown court and on most days the magistrates' court is totally uncovered. The unfortunate side effect of this is that court staff are generally less familiar with the media. While most are friendly and helpful, some are ignorant of the laws and guidelines. Court staff have wrongly told trainees they cannot write the names of defendants because they are 'confidential', while others have said they can take notes – so long as they do not use the information outside court.

There is also a common misconception that you cannot take notes without the permission of the court. This is wrong, although it is usually wise to turn up early and introduce yourself to the usher and clerk before proceedings start.

Another irritating issue that now arises is the argument over what exactly is a 'bona-fide' (i.e. genuine, lit. 'in good faith') journalist. This term – used in laws dating back nearly a century – belongs to a bygone era before there were independent journalists. Having a press card can help when faced with officiousness. Details are available from the UK Press Card Authority. Journalists who have faced problems have also been helped after contacting the HM Courts and Tribunal Service press office.[11]

It is also worth knowing that, under rule 5.8 of the Criminal Procedure Rules, journalists and any other members of the public can contact a court to get information on a case they may not have been able to attend in person. This may be invaluable to a reporter who has received a tip that a particular person recently appeared in court but may otherwise be struggling to confirm the facts.

If you do this within six months, you can do it with a simple verbal request, perhaps over the phone or in person and you do not have to give a reason. If more than six months has elapsed, you need to put it in writing and give an explanation.[12]

Contempt of court

The Contempt of Court Act 1981 is designed to ensure that those accused of criminal offences receive a fair trial. Our legal system is supposed to prevent juries being swayed by what journalists write or broadcast. No journalist has been imprisoned for contempt since 1949 but, in theory, you could be jailed for up to two years. More likely, you could be on the receiving end of a very large fine and, under the Courts Act 2003, even face having to pay the costs of a new trial.

So, with such a heavy punishment, it can be unnerving that the Contempt of Court Act 1981 does not spell out precisely how you could prejudice a trial. The key point is that once a suspect has been arrested, proceedings are 'active' and you must not publish or broadcast information that could create a 'substantial risk of serious prejudice'. This may seem vague – and it is. However, when checking a story always ask yourself: 'Is that really likely to create a substantial risk of serious prejudice?'

You are running the biggest risk of breaking the law if, once a suspect is arrested, you publish or broadcast the defendant's previous convictions or evidence which suggests they are guilty, including descriptions or pictures of the offender and defendant if identity is an issue.[13] As always, when deciding how far to push the boundaries, ask yourself: 'Is it worth the risk?'

Journalists often complain that, while they have to tread carefully, social media users have frequently – and in huge numbers – been able to flout the law. However, the attorney general, Dominic Grieve QC MP sought to clamp down on all offenders in 2013 and served notice on sites such as Facebook and Twitter, as well as traditional news outlets.[14]

Children and sexual offences

Always tread carefully when reporting on, interviewing or taking pictures of children. In particular, the law is strict when covering criminal cases involving those aged under 18. Most juveniles accused of a criminal offence appear before a youth court. Only 'bona-fide' journalists are allowed to cover youth courts, and should you be allowed to remain in the court, you must still remember that, unless the court lifts reporting restrictions, under section 49 of the Children and Young Persons Act 1933, you cannot identify the defendant or anyone else involved who is under the age of 18.

Remember that identification is not restricted to naming them. You must also avoid other information that could lead to their identification, such as address, school or a photograph. Obviously, identification of a parent or relation would also identify the youth – and thus break the law. Away from court, while there is no law to prevent you identifying children or interviewing them, various regulatory codes urge journalists to tread carefully.

Victims of sexual offences are afforded lifetime anonymity; this extends to anything that is likely to lead to their identification by the public, not just their name. Almost all offences with a sexual element are covered by this ban.

Copyright: avoiding a hefty bill for using images and video

Prior to the digital age newspaper journalists operated a pretty cavalier approach to copyright. It was usual to pick up 'collect' pictures of the victim or the killer when conducting 'death knocks'. Yet it was rare that money changed hands for such pictures or copyright was even acknowledged when the pictures were used. It was usually only in high-profile cases where the owner was a professional or someone who knew they could make money, that pictures were paid for.

However, that doesn't mean journalists should not know and stick to the law, not least because the general public has become more streetwise when it comes to knowing that – on major stories at least – their pictures and interviews may be worth money.

Copyright law is designed to protect anyone who creates a work of art – be it a photograph, painting, piece of music or writing. Ripping off someone else's work is deemed to kill such creativity. The Copyright, Designs and Patents Act 1988 – which came into force in 1989 – means that the copyright of a photograph belongs to the person who took the picture.

There are exceptions, including situations where those employed by media usually sign over such rights in their employment contracts. While re-tweeting or embedding a tweet or Facebook post does not break copyright law, that does not mean you can lift other people's photographs for your own use, such as on your website. Journalists have become increasingly reliant on user-generated content (UGC) in recent years, and pictures and video gathered by others can be useful. However, if the material is sent to you, it is important that you agree any conditions, such as free use, before you publish or broadcast.

The right to take pictures

This is an issue that, worryingly, affects many journalists. Take out a camera – particularly one with a large lens – and start taking photos or filming in a busy street and it may not be long before someone asks if you have 'permission' or tries to stop you.

Sadly, police officers are often the biggest offenders – despite chief officers supposedly issuing guidance. The web is awash with videos of photographers being hassled by police and security guards who do not know the law. The law is simple. There is nothing to stop you taking pictures or filming in a public area.

There are two key points to remember. First, make sure it is a public area. While shopping centres and train stations are open to the public, they are likely to be private property. Second, make sure you cannot be accused of breaking another law. One of the most likely allegations you could face is obstruction. This does not just mean physical obstruction – rather that the journalist has prevented the officer from doing their job.

Another likely charge is that the journalist's actions amount to a breach of the peace. Thus, it is crucial that the journalist remains calm and cannot be accused of behaving badly. Neither a police officer nor anyone else has the lawful power to delete pictures and they need a court order to seize them.

The National Police Chiefs' Council (NPCC) – formerly the Association of Chief Police Officers (ACPO) – issues advice to frontline officers, who are supposed to recognise that journalists have a job to do,[15] although some would argue that this message often does not get through. While journalists should always know their rights and stand their ground where needed, it is always worth asking: 'Is the picture worth the hassle?' Regardless of whether you are right legally, getting attacked or arrested means a lot of stress and wasted time.

Data protection: what to avoid

This may not be the sexiest area of media law but it is becoming increasingly relevant. As the law of defamation has supposedly swung in favour of the journalist, solicitors working for the rich and famous are increasingly looking to exploit data protection as a line of attack. As Ruth Collard, a partner at Carter-Ruck Lawyers, says: 'The Data Protection Act is increasing in importance. The Information Commissioner is now showing more teeth.' The 1998 Act is designed to protect people's personal information. All organisations holding people's personal information are obliged to register with the Information Commissioner.

The person who is legally responsible for holding the information is known as the 'data controller'. Generally this will be a media organisation rather than an individual journalist. Freelance journalists and bloggers working on their own could be classed as data controllers and should register with the Information Commissioner.[16] Although it would be naive to suggest that every freelancer or blogger does this, it should be remembered that you could be fined for not doing so.

There are several reasons why you should at least know the basics of this law. First, if you are holding someone's personal information, you need to keep it secure. Think very carefully about how you store information or carry it around. A stolen laptop or a dropped USB stick could be embarrassing and costly – particularly if the information is not password-protected.

Second, under section 55, anyone can commit a criminal offence if they obtain someone's personal information illegally. This would include obtaining information about someone by deception, hacking, exploiting poor security or unauthorised leaks. However, the Information Commissioner's guidelines state that a journalist would only be prosecuted if it were in the public interest.[17] This would in theory protect a journalist exposing, for example, criminal or anti-social behaviour. Third, if you are holding someone's personal information, they may have the right to access it via a 'subject access request' (SAR).

At this point, it is worth noting that you also enjoy this right. You may want to know what information a public body such as a police force, or a private company, holds on you – although you may have to pay a small fee. If a journalist or blogger receives a request from someone they have information on, they may be able to rely on section 32, which exempts journalists from having to co-operate, so long as you are actually planning to run a story, you reasonably believe it is in the public interest, and co-operation will hamper your work.

Crucially, always be aware that in releasing information, if you release someone else's personal information you could be breaking the law. Finally, you need to be aware that organisations, such as police forces, sometimes wrongly use the Data Protection Act as a reason not to release information. The Information Commissioner makes it clear that the act does not ban the release of personal information if it is 'justified in the circumstances'.[18]

How to maintain ethical standards in your newsroom

Ethics has become an increasingly prevalent buzzword in British journalism in the last few years. However, it remains a piecemeal concept that depends entirely on your primary platform, a potentially unsustainable situation in an increasingly digital and globalised era.

Prior to the phone hacking scandal – which led to the closure of the *News of the World* in 2011 – the conduct of the press had been overseen by the Press Complaints Commission (PCC), which set an editors' code of conduct for its members to follow. The subsequent Leveson Inquiry, which investigated improper conduct by news organisations, nearly led to newspapers facing statutory regulation. However, post-Leveson the newly created Independent Press Standards Association (IPSA), which is supported by most of the national and regional press and aims to be a stronger regulator, oversees the sector and operates the same code of conduct as its predecessor. IPSO has promised more prominent apologies and can fine publishers up to £1 million.[19] While their Editors' Code of Practice is regulation rather than law and only applies to those who have signed up, all journalists should be familiar with the code – not least because they could be supplying material for companies who are IPSO members.

Alternatively, broadcasters are overseen by the Office of Communications (Ofcom), which has the power to fine broadcasters up to £250,000 or 5 per cent of its revenue and the ultimate sanction to suspend the licence of commercial broadcasters.[20] Those wanting to work in broadcast media should be at least familiar with the basics of Ofcom's code of practice. It is lengthy and complicated but the key part is section five, which demands that stories be impartial. Unlike newspaper reporters, TV and radio journalists should not take sides politically.

One area that remained almost untouched by the Leveson Inquiry was the internet. Lord Leveson's one-page summary on the internet stated that it didn't operate to ethical standards and therefore audiences would not necessarily believe what they read online. He said: 'Some have called it a "wild west" but I would prefer to use the term "ethical vacuum"'.[21] Leveson's distinction between the ethical standards required by legacy media – because, in his view, audiences are more likely to believe them – and digital journalists may suit legislators who are wary of regulating a platform that doesn't recognise borders, but it does little to assist start-up digital publishers and the subjects of their stories, who will want the same redress to stories that they have access to offline.

Therefore the remainder of this chapter will seek to offer guidance on four key aspects you need to consider if you are aiming to be a responsible publisher in the 'Wild West' online. These are all areas highlighted by the Online News Association in its social newsgathering ethics code.[22] Ultimately you need to work to standards you feel are appropriate and openly and prominently state what those standards are to your audience in a statement or self-governing code of conduct, possibly housed on your site's 'about' page.

Accuracy

This is your primary concern as a news organisation. Almost three quarters – 72.6 per cent to be precise – of complaints to the now defunct PCC resulted from the fact that complainants felt the story was inaccurate.[23] However, complaints are not the only problem caused by inaccuracy; if your audience begins to believe your stories are inaccurate it will impact on their trust in your organisation. Therefore if you are going to claim something is true, you damned well need to know it is.

However, if you are a small news organisation there are obviously times when you do not have a reporter on the ground to validate all the facts. So therefore you need to begin building a bank of trusted sources, both traditional reliable individual contacts and other news publishers who have an established reputation. Then in cases where stories break you can make a calculated judgement on whether to run with a story.

If you decide to run a piece of aggregated news, where the story is broken by another news organisation, you should include a prominent hyperlink to the story and make it clear to your audience who produced it. Transparency is key in this respect, as we'll address below. But you need to be aware that if you run a story, regardless of whether it states 'X is reporting …', that you can't just pass the buck if the story falls down. As a publisher you have taken a conscious decision to trust that news source, so you are still gambling with your own reputation if you were wrong to do so. Finding additional sources of your own to bolster an aggregated story will reinforce your belief in its accuracy, in addition to just being good practice. If you merely plagiarise content from other news organisations you will quickly be found out.

Not that good intentions alone will save your news organisation from mistruths. According to Max Read, former editor of Gawker, the amount of hoax news online is continually rising: 'Already ankle deep in smarmy bullshit and fake "viral" garbage, we are now standing at the edge of a gurgling swamp of it.'[24] The only way to avoid getting caught up in this chain of misinformation is to conduct your own verification of stories. Journalist Craig Silverman identified a series of bad practices allowing hoax news to flourish in his academic report, *Lies, Damn Lies and Viral Content.*[25] These included newsrooms applying little or no fact checking, hinting in copy that unsubstantiated rumours are fact, and failing to follow up the story later on. This lax culture, which has developed due to chasing traffic with stories that are 'too good to check', has made newsrooms far too easy to hoax. As a result, Silverman recommends journalists investigate the publisher who broke the story, its history or potential motivation for pushing it, and which other news outlets are running it.[26]

User generated content and privacy

User-generated content (UGC) has grown massively in recent years and that growth has led to its own risks. Journalists from bloggers right up to those working for international media giants are now relying on ordinary readers, viewers and listeners posting comments, reviews, photos and videos. All too often those contributors – including guest columnists – have little if any knowledge of the law or regulation. Others may be malicious cranks or hoaxers.

The use of user-generated pictures raises a range of issues. While the vast majority of people you deal with will be honest, you should always remember that a photo might not be what the contributor claims it is. In 2015 alone news organisations were caught out by images purporting to be of the Nepal earthquake, the terrorist attacks in Paris and the story of a man documenting his journey from Senegal to Spain on social media at the height of the European migrant crisis.[27] There are also complex ethical considerations: the killer of American journalists Alison Parker and Adam Ward uploaded footage of their murders to social media, and both Facebook and Twitter were criticised by British MPs for allowing it to autoplay on their platforms.[28]

In a small newsroom, monitoring social media may be the responsibility of your audience engagement editor – more on this role in Chapter 7 – and they need to be the external eyes and ears of your newsroom. Using Tweetdeck or lists of trusted sources on Twitter will provide you with a constant stream of information. When you search for reactions from bystanders in the wake of an incident consider the words people at the scene will use, for example 'me' or 'my' as they relay their personal experience[29] and check the location on their tweet. You should rely on the experience of your editorial team to assess if content feels genuine and put a template in place for contacting people via social media to ask for the right to use it.[30]

There are several ways of checking if a picture is genuine. You could use Google's reverse image search – images.google.com – or similar services like Tineye, Fotoforensics and Exifdata. You should use these if you have any suspicions that the picture has been copied, tampered with or was not taken when and where the contributor claims. Remember that copyright will usually belong to the photographer who took the picture. Often they will be willing to let you use the picture free of charge, but if not, ensure you agree a price in advance. Otherwise you leave yourself open to being sued for breach of copyright. Recent cases have led to payments in the tens of thousands of pounds.

While there is no copyright in facts, if you were to use substantial written work, such as a review or an interview, without consent, you could also be in breach of copyright. Do not make the mistake of thinking you can steal a photograph and use it because you are only a small news website and the photographer is unlikely to know. Professionals can and do use software to trace where their pictures have been used.

Similarly, when stories break, journalists will often plunder people's personal social media accounts in the search for pictures. Large media organisations will bear the risk of being sued for breach of copyright but a small newsroom can ill-afford such an outcome. Likewise, be aware that lifting pictures from someone's Facebook account could be regarded as a breach of privacy. If you are given permission to use an image or video ensure that in the caption you credit the person who took it and the platform it was taken from.

Ned Rocknroll, the husband of actress Kate Winslet, was granted an injunction against the *Sun* which banned it from using pictures of him partially naked at a family party.[31] The pictures had actually been available to see on his Facebook account but the judge ruled there was no public interest in them being used more widely.

Another trap to be avoided is the false assumption that pictures which breach someone's privacy can be used if someone else took the picture. Intrusive or graphic pictures, perhaps of someone in pain at the scene of an accident, could be ruled to be in breach of their right to privacy under Article 8 of the European Convention on Human Rights. They are also likely to fall foul of regulatory codes, although obviously these only apply to those newspapers who have signed up to IPSO and broadcasters covered by Ofcom. The obvious answer to such privacy issues is to try, where possible, to get the person's consent.[32]

This also applies when livestreaming material, particularly if you are in a public location.[33] Ask yourself: Is it a place where passers-by might have a reasonable expectation of privacy? Do you have parental consent to be filming children? If you are at the scene of an accident, how can you ensure that graphic – particularly disturbing – content doesn't appear on the broadcast? Siobhan Heanue, an ABC broadcaster on location in Nepal during an earthquake, refrained from livestreaming footage following the disaster due to the graphic scenes she saw.[34]

If you are handling data you need to be keenly aware of how much of it is disclosed to your audience. You need to make responsible, editorial judgements when collecting and publishing information and reflect on your overall journalistic standards. You can't just put all of it out there without thinking about the consequences.[35]

Transparency

Transparency has become an increasingly important virtue for news organisations since going online. The rolling nature of the internet means that many stories are reported on as they develop, rather than just one or two daily versions being produced to fit newspaper deadlines. The reduced production time and lack of considered revision this can bring increases the chances of incorrect information reaching the audience, at least at first. Breaking news is particularly vulnerable to this, an example being several erroneous initial reports related to the shooting of twenty children and six adults at Sandy Hook Elementary School in 2012.[36] The desire to get to the truth quickly, the pressure this places on journalists and sources, and social media reports of varying reliability can all contribute to incorrect information being released.[37]

Although your checks should ensure incorrect information isn't published in the first place, in instances where mistakes occur it is crucial to be honest with your audience. It is better to admit a temporary error than ignore it, change the story hoping no-one will notice and persist with a claim that you didn't get it wrong in the first place. In 2015 the *Guardian* made more than 2,600 corrections to online stories[38] but it still maintains its reputation as a journalistic heavyweight; in part due to its readiness to address these errors. Its practice of correcting factual errors with a footnote explaining the original mistake is one you should consider adopting.

Similarly, if a story relies on figures gathered by a pressure group fighting for change, your audience deserves to know that. It assists your credibility if you are being honest about your sources. As author Tom Rosenstiel says: 'Acknowledging your relationship to the information is an essential step in establishing why people should believe you. Without it they should be suspicious.'[39]

This transparency should also extend to financial matters. The financial side of running a small newsroom is tricky to say the least; nevertheless you need to heavily guard the impartiality of your coverage. If you promote an advertiser in your news stories – excluding branded content or advertorials – or withhold negative coverage of that company, your reputation as a news outlet will be damaged. This is often easier said than done. In 2015 Buzzfeed admitted three posts on its site were deleted due to their advertisers complaining about their content;[40] and the *Telegraph*'s chief political commentator Peter Oborne resigned citing concerns about the paper's coverage of HSBC.[41]

Conclusion

This chapter has set out the basics on how journalists can avoid falling foul of law, on regulation, and on ethical standards you can stick to. Media law is the most important topic a young journalist can learn. You may not be studying to be a media lawyer, but a good knowledge and understanding of media law will encourage you not to run away from potentially risky stories.

There are countless rich, powerful or corrupt people out there who will use their privileged position to prevent ordinary members of the public from finding out what they want to keep secret. There are others in officialdom who, nervous of their own jobs or simply unsure, will play safe and tell journalists that they cannot do something they are perfectly entitled to do. It may sound sanctimonious, but the future of journalism – and even democracy – relies on reporters and photographers who know their rights. Make sure you do.

Useful websites

* Reporting restrictions in the criminal court: judiciary.gov.uk
* *McNae's Essential Law for Journalists*: mcnaes.com
* Press Gazette: pressgazette.co.uk
* UK Press Card Authority: ukpresscardauthority.co.uk
* ONA Social Newsgathering Ethics Code: toolkit.journalists.org/social-newsgathering

Further reading

Dodd, M and Hanna, M (2016) *McNae's essential law for journalists*. Oxford: Oxford University Press.
Silverman, C (ed.) (2014) *Verification handbook: A definitive guide to verifying content for emergency coverage*. Maastricht: European Journalism Centre.

Notes

1 Dodd, M and Hanna, M (2016) *McNae's essential law for journalists*. Oxford: Oxford University Press.
2 Townend, J (2011) *Navigating digital publishing law without a 'night lawyer': An exploration of informal legal support networks*. Cultural Policy, Criticism and Management Research, 5: 27–46.
3 Hutchings, C (2015) *Despite a 60 per cent jump in libel cases last year, it is too early to judge the new Defamation Act*. Press Gazette.
4 Turvill, W and Press Association (2014) *Libel appeal versus Sunday Mirror dropped in first test of Defamation Act 'serious harm' test*. Press Gazette.
5 Dodd and Hanna, *McNae's essential law for journalists*.
6 Ibid.
7 Defamation Act 2013: chapter 26, *Defences*. legislation.gov.uk
8 Ponsford, D (2014) *Six things all journalists need to know about the Defamation Act 2013 (which is now in force)*. Press Gazette.

9 Dodd and Hanna, *McNae's essential law for journalists.*
10 Press Association (2013) *Lord McAlpine libel row with Sally Bercow formally settled in High Court.* The Guardian.
11 Turvill, W (2015) *Government agency intervenes after reporter barred from taking notes in magistrates court.* Press Gazette.
12 Dodd and Hanna, *McNae's essential law for journalists.*
13 Ibid.
14 Gov.uk (2014) *Attorney general to warn Facebook and Twitter users about contempt of court.* gov.uk
15 National Police Chiefs' Council (2010) *Communication Advisory Group, guidance 2010.* National Police Chiefs' Council.
16 Information Commissioners' Office (2014) *Data protection and journalism: A guide for the media.* ico.co.uk
17 Ibid.
18 Ibid.
19 BBC News (2014) *Press watchdog IPSO will 'damn' deliberate rule-breakers.* BBC News.
20 OFCOM (2013) *Procedures for the consideration of statutory sanctions in breaches of broadcast licences.* ofcom.org.uk
21 Leveson, B (2012) *Leveson Inquiry: Report into the culture, practice and ethics of the press.* pp. 736–737.
22 ONA (2016) *ONA Social newsgathering ethics code.* toolkit.journalists.org/social-newsgathering
23 Cole, P and Harcup, T (2010) *Newspaper journalism.* London: Sage.
24 Read, M (2014) *Gawker 2015.* sausage.gawker.com
25 Silverman, C (2015) *Lies, damn lies and viral content: How news websites spread (and debunk) online rumors, unverified claims and misinformation.* Tow Centre for Digital Journalism.
26 Ibid.
27 Rusk, D (2015) *How the internet misled you in 2015.* BBC News.
28 Rawlinson, K (2015) *Virginia shooting: Facebook and Twitter told to rethink autoplay video.* BBC News.
29 Victor, D (2015) *The one word journalists should add to Twitter searches that you probably haven't considered.* Medium.
30 Bell, F (2015) *Get it out of the door fast … and right: First draft news.* Medium.
31 Halliday, J (2013) *Judge banned Sun using Ned Rocknroll photos to protect Winslet's children.* The Guardian.
32 Banks, D (2013) *The legal risks of UGC.* mediahelpingmedia.org
33 Llewellyn, S (2016) *Mojocon.* Dublin.
34 Heanue, S (2016) *Mojocon.* Dublin.
35 Bell, E (2012) *Journalism by numbers.* Columbia Journalism Review, September–October, 48–49.
36 Warren, L and Stebner, B (2012) *'It was my brother. I think my mother is dead. Oh my god.' Moment accountant sibling of school shooter saw himself mistakenly named as killer on TV in case of mistaken identity.* MailOnline.
37 Clark, R, in McBride, K and Rosenstiel, T (2014) *The new ethics of journalism.* London: Sage.
38 Nelsson, R (2015) *How we correct the record in the Guardian archives as well as on our pages.* The Guardian.
39 Rosenstiel, T (2013) *Why 'be transparent' has replaced 'act independently' as a guiding journalism principle.* Poynter.
40 Stack, L (2015) *Buzzfeed says posts were deleted because of advertising pressure.* The New York Times.
41 Oborne, P (2015) *Why I have resigned from the Telegraph.* opendemocracy.net

INDEX

Page numbers in *italic* denote figures and those in **bold** denote tables.

ABC (Audit Bureau of Circulation) 5
Abeyie, Joanna *78*
'Accelerated Mobile Pages' (AMP)
  (Google) 9–10
ad blockers 10, 30, 35, 37
Adobe Audition 143
advertising: campaigns 5, 8, 10, 31–2; key
  terms 30; native 25, 30–1; networks 29;
  as PR 83–5; pre-roll ads 32; revenue
  23, 25; as source of income 29, 105;
  transparency 176; UK market 116
Advertising Standards Authority (ASA) 31
Altman, Sam 80, 88
Ampp3d 50, 116
analytic data 79, 83, 110–15, 121, 153–5
Anderson, Chris 59, 60, 121
Apple 10, 30, 126
apps 51–2, 120–1, 126–9, 131, 138–42,
  159–60
Audacity 143
audience: contribution of 7, 121; coverage
  styles and 44–5, 50; customer relations
  84–5, 99; demands of 112; engagement
  113–15, 118–21, 153, 157, 158;
  feedback 80, 86, 100, 105–6, 114;
  'gatewatching' 7; growing your 73,
  79–80, 82, 104, 109–22, 118; and
  innovation 40; local communities 63;
  'managing' 9; personalisation of news
  54, 95–8, 105; potential 59; readers'
  comments 105–6; relationships with

8–9, *78*; research 60–1; size of 6, 57, 72;
  and social media 148–50, 152–3, 155
audience engagement editors 9, 110,
  119–20
audio content 32, 66, 126, 142–3, 160
audits 85–6
Axel Springer (publisher) 35

Ball, James 50
Baquet, Dean 18
Bassan, Valerio 44
BBC (British Broadcasting Company):
  audience 6, 12, 61, 77; and hyperlocals
  65–6; *Newsbeat 149*; regional *64*; social
  media use 120, 152
BBC Radio 5 Live 142
BBC Sport Online 100, *101*, 119, 131
Belam, Martin *48*
Bell, Emily 9
Bell, Martin 79
Berger, Jonah 42–3
Blendle 35
Blizzard (magazine) 34, 62
Blockbuster 41
blogs 31, 44, 100, 110, 120, 144
Boyer, Brian 45
Bradshaw, Paul 98
breaking stories 8–9, 176 *see also* content
Briefing, The 105
Briggs, Mark 116
Brixton Blog 64

Brock, George 6
Bruns, Alex 7
Burchett, Wilfred 56
Bureau of Investigative Journalism (BIJ)
    34, 35
Burkeman, Oliver 82
burnout 82
business models 4, 5, 22–37, 87
business plans 2, 23, 67, 76, 87
Buzzfeed: business model 5; business plan
    2; and clickbait 159; community posts
    43–4; content management system
    (CMS) 116; datasets 49; and Facebook
    Live *130*; and native advertising 30–1;
    and social media 12, 147, 161; and viral
    content 41–2
Buzzsumo 110

Cairo, Alberto 50
camera, smartphone as 124–9
Campus London *71*
Canter, Lily 17
Canva 159
Cedering Angstrom, Rebecka 145
Centre for Investigative Journalism *165*
charitable status 35
Charity Commission 35
Chartbeat 110–11, 115
'Chicago's Million Dollar Blocks' 53
citizen journalism 7, *71*, 99, 125
City Talking, The 36
civil law 167
Clammr 143
clickbait 158–9
Collard, Ruth *166*, 171
Colling, Mike 10
Columbia Journalism Review 9
Common Space (news site) 58
communities, grassroots 35, 43–4, 63,
    64–5, 72, 88
competitors 29, 40, 66, 75, 110
contempt of court 169
content: access 86; accuracy of 173–4;
    aggregating 102–3; audio 32, 66, 126,
    142–3, 160; and ethics 167; evergreen
    97–8; high quality 61–2, 159; for mobile
    users 116; online 94–9; planned 87,
    95–7; reactive 98–102, 157–8, 176;
    social media 153–4, 156–8, 160–1;
    sponsored 31; written 103
content management system (CMS) 92–3,
    116
Cooke, Matt *71*
copyright 170–1, 175

cost analysis 25, 76–7
court reporting 168–70
Creative Commons images 159
crowdfunding 27, 32–3, 58
Crowdtangle 8
customer relations 84–5, 99

Daily Dot, The 106
Daily Mail 6, 46, 60
Daily Telegraph 33, 176
data, analytical 79, 83, 110–15, 121,
    153–5
data protection 171–2
Dataminr 8
datasets, public sector 48–53, 61–2
Datawrapper 51–2
Dawson, Ross 5
De Correspondent (Dutch news website) 9
defamation 164–8
digital: skills 16–17, 36–7; subscribers 4, 11,
    14, *14–15*, 32–4
digital firms 87–8
Digital News Report 11–15
diversity, in journalism 78
Doble, Anna *149*
Doctor, Ken 7
Documentally *31*, *144*
Double Click for Publishers 29
Dropbox 24

'e-lancing' services 81
e-mail newsletters 105
editing footage 138–43
El Español (digital news website) 32
Engaging News Project 105
enterprise centres 88
ethical standards 79, 163–77
Eurostat 49
Evernote 24, 96
Exifdata 175
experimentation 41, 45, 112, 116–17, 120
eyewitness media *71*

Facebook: BBC Sport Online 119; ethical
    standards 174; posting content 160; as
    social network 13; users *83*, 99, 147; v.
    Twitter 150–1
Facebook Insights 153–4
Facebook Instant Articles 9–10, 150
Facebook Live 129–30
Facebook Messenger 120, 150
failure, business 89
Ferrite Recording Studio 143
financial costs 23–27, 87

financial sources 25–7, 29, 105
Finn, Andrew 104
Fiverr 81
FixMyStreet 63
focus groups 86
Fotoforensics 175
Francis, Matt 52
Freedom of Information Request (FOI)
49, 62
funding 18, 25–7, 31–5, 63–4, 88, 121 *see
also* financial sources; grants

game-building platforms 45–8
Garnett, Nick *130*
Gawker 111, 115
general election, UK (2015) 65, 148
GIFs 103, 124, 126, 160
Gladwell, Michael 1, 40
Glamour (magazine) 106
glossary terms: advertising 30; website 92,
112
Google 9–10, 66, 88, 116, 175
Google Adsense 29
Google Analytics *83*, 110–11
Google Cardboard 144
Google Docs 24, 49
Google News 117–18
Google News Lab *71*, 88
Google Play 126
grants 27, 34
Graphic News 144
grassroots journalism 62–6, 72
Greenslade, Roy 111
Greenwald, Glenn 72, 78
Gross, Bill 58
Grothaus, Michael 105–6
Guardian: audience 33, 119; audience
editors 110; and clickbait 159; datasets
49; factual errors 176; financial pressure
22; and Instagram 152; pre-roll ads 32;
visualisations 53; website 5–6
Guido Fawkes 60

Hacks/Hackers (grassroots community) 72
Haggerty, Angela 58
Haile, Tony 115
Hannache, Stephane 99
Harding, James 2
Hawkins, Mike 45
Heanue, Siobhan 176
'Hearables' (earbuds) 54
Hebe Media 36
Hecklerspray *117–18*
Heritage, Stuart *117–18*

HMRC 28–9
Hootsuite 160
'hot takes' 100
Huddersfield Examiner 65
Huffington Post 2, 43–4, 49, 102, 116,
147
human rights 175
hyperlinks 94, 99
hyperlocal journalism 62–6, 81, 86, 119,
153, 155 *see also* Lincolnite, The

idea building 56–67
Idealab 58
'identity' posts 42
images *see* photos
iMovie 124, 138–42
Independent 5
Independent Media (South Africa) 81
Independent Press Standards Association
(IPSO) 172
infographics 52–4
InsideClimate News 60
Instagram 152, 156–7
intellectual property 160
Intercept, The 78
Internet Advertising Bureau (IAB UK) 10,
30
internet, arrival of 4–5
investigative journalism 34, 164–5
Ionescu, Daniel *64*
iOS software 10, 30, 126
iPhones 125–6, 143

Jarvis, Jeff 2, 114
Johnson, Stephen 70
journalismtools. io 126

Kang, Martha 50
Key Performance Indicators (KPIs) 103,
111, 113–15
key terms: advertising 30; website 92, 112
Kickstarter 19, 82
Kings Cross Environment 119
Kleis Nielsen, Dr Rasmus 18
Kompakt 116

LaFrance, Adrienne 41
Laterpay (payment tool) 35
Leach, Anna 50
legacy media 29, 36, 61, 77, 148–9
legal advice 27–8, 163–77
Leveson inquiry 173
libel 164, 165
Libération (newspaper) 150

Lincolnite, The 58, *64*, 65, *83*
Linkins, Jason 43–4
liveblogging 100–2
Liverpool Echo 157
livestreaming 65, 126, 175–7
Lunchbox 159

McAdams, Mindy 103
McCandless, David 52
MacFadyen, Gavin *165*
McGuire, Sean 6
McNae's Essential Law For Journalists 163
Mail Chimp 105
MailOnline 5, 31, 60, 67, 99
Malcontent, The 62
Marburger, Joey 46
market analysis 73–5
market research 75
marketing 73–5, 82–6
Marshall, Sarah 106
Matter VC *71*
MC&C (media agency) 10
media law 163–77
metadata, use of 54
Meyer, Robinson 41
Mezrahi, Samir 159
Microsoft Excel 49
Microsoft Office Live 24
Milkman, Katherine 42–3
'millennials' generation 35, 116, 129,
    148–9, 151
Milner, Simon 147
mindset, journalistic 56–8
minimum viable product (MVP) 76–7
mission statements 78
Mitchell, Amy 19
mobile users 6, 46, 50, 116–18
Moran, Chris 110
Moskovitz, Dustin 82
motivation 57–8
multimedia coverage 96, 98, 110, 117, 124,
    149

naming 76
national insurance 29
National Qualification in Journalism (NQJ)
    17
Naughton, John 5, 10
NCTJ (National Council for the Training
    for Journalists) 15–16, *71*
Netflix 31, 41
New Day 5
New York Times: audience 105; and Blendle
    35; financial pressure 22; finding talent

88; mobile users 116; native advertising
    31; popular content 45; report on
    digital talent 1; virtual reality (VR) 144;
    visualisations 53; WhatsApp 120
newsroom diaries 95
NewsWhip 8
Next Web, The (TNW) 36
Nguyen, Dr An 115
niche markets 59–60, 66–7, 72–3, 97
Nolan, Hamilton 67
non-profit journalism 34–5
NowThisNews 161
NPR Digital Services 96
NRS (National Readership Survey) 6
NUJ (National Union of Journalists) *71*

Oborne, Peter 176
Ofcom (Office of Communications) 6, 173
Office for National Statistics 49
'open journalism' 11
OpenX 29
Over (app) 159
Ozy 105

Payne, Christian *31*, *144*
paywalls 11
Penenberg, Adam 42, 44, 60
Peretti, Jonah 42, 43
Periscope 129–30
Perrin, Will 119
personalisation of news 54
Pew Research Center 19
photos: apps for 53, 127, 129; checking
    authenticity 175; right to take 170–1;
    from smartphones 127–9; and social
    media 159–60; website 94
Picktochart 53
Pinterest 81
Pittman, Bob 112
Pixlr Editor 129
plugins 92–4, 106
podcasts 32, 142–3, *149*
Politico 60
Poucher, Graham *84*
Press Complaints Commission (PCC) 172,
    173
Prince's Trust 23
privacy 174–6
private limited companies 27–8
project planning 75–6, *84*
ProPublica (US non-profit) 34, 80
public sector datasets 48–53

Quartz 105

Ramirez, Pedro J. 32
Read, Max 174
readers' comments 168
Recite 159
regional newspapers 58, 63, 75
regional specialisms 66–7
Rensberger, Scott 145
reputation, building a 77–9, *84*, 91, 104, 125
ResPublica (think tank) 10
Reuters Institute 11–15
revenue, online 14, 23, 25, 35–6, 150
Riddle.com 45
Ries, Eric 76–7
Roberts, Dan 119
Rocknroll, Ned 175
Rostance, Tom *101–2*
Rusbridger, Alan 8, 11
Rutenberg, Jim 8
Ryley, John 6

Sambrook, Richard 6
Santos, Mariana 41, 145
Schlosberg, Justin 10
Screaming Frog (content audit tool) 86
Search Engine Optimisation (SEO) 94, 96, 97, *117*
self-employment 27–9
sexual offences, reporting of 170
Shapiro, Michael 102
Shared Count 110
Shirky, Clay 4
Silbermann, Ben 81
Silicon Valley 3
Silver, Nate 72
Silverman, Craig 174
SimilarWeb 75
Sinek, Simon 78
Singolda, Adam 18
skillset, journalistic 14–17, 36–7, 56, 59–60, 71–2, 81
Sky News 6
Sky Sports 131
Skype 24, 86
Slack (messaging tool) 25
slander 164
smartphones 12, *12*, 30, 124–9, 124–45, 142–3 *see also* apps; video footage
Snapchat 18, 152, 156, 161
Sobel Fitts, Alexis 9
social enterprise 35
Social Image Resizer Tool 160
social media: audience 148–50, 152–3, 155; breaking news on 157–8; content on 157, 158–9, 160–1; different

approaches used 150–1; and feedback 86; and freelancers 81; images 159–60; monitoring and tracking 8, 13, 75, 110, 145, 153; news and 5, 6, 11, 103; as newsgathering resource 155–6; posting on 79, 157; promoting content 154, 156–7
social networks *13*, 151
software solutions 23–4
Sorrell, Sir Martin 11
sources, news 7, 49, 155–6
South Leeds Live 33
Speigler Online 81
STEP analysis (marketing) 73–4, **74**
Storify 98
storytelling 42–5, 94–9, 103–4, 106, 176
Stray, Jonathan 54
students, university 87–8
styles of coverage 44–5, 50
subscribers, digital 4, 11, 14, *14–15*, 32–4
Sun, The 11
Sunday Times 11
sustainability 37, 57–8, 76, 79–81, 111, 114
Sutcliffe, Kevin 95
SWOT analysis (marketing) 74–5, **74**, 85–6

Tableau Public 52
Tajani, Antonio 89
Tampa Bay Times 144–5
taxation 28–9
Taylor, Matt 25
television 6, 11, 12, 102, 129, 148
Three (mobile carrier) 30
Times, The 11, 25
timing, of business launch 58
Tineye 175
toolkits, reporting 125–6
Tow Centre for Digital Journalism 9
traditional skills 15–17
training 17, 36–7, *71*, 85
transparency 106, 173, 176
Trello 24
Trinity Mirror 5, 46, *71*, 111
Trisolute news dashboard 66
Twitter: ethical standards 174; live blogging 42; as newsgathering resource 155–6; posting content 160; promoting content 154–5; users 82, 147; v. Facebook 150–1
Twitter Analytics 155

university enterprise hubs 88
Upper Calder Valley Plain Speaker 64–5
Upworthy 131

Urban, Tim 104, 105
user-generated content (UGC) 170, 174
USP (unique selling point) 61, 62, 63, 67, 104
UsVsTh3m 46–7, *47*

VandeHei, Jim 14, 20
VAT (value added tax) 29
Verge, The 106
Vice (news channel) 95, 106
video apps 126, 131, 138–42
video footage: eyelines 136–8; high quality 131; iMovie 138–42; lighting 133; operating 134; pre-roll ads 32; Snapchat 156; sound and interviews 135–6; taking 124; voiceovers 141; YouTube 142
virtual reality (VR) 144
visualisations, effective 50–4
Vogt, Nancy 19
vox pops 138, 142
Vrse 144

Wait but Why 104–5
Wall Street Journal 106
Washington Post 14, 46, 97–8
Watermark 160
web traffic services 75
website, building a 76–7, 92–4, 112
West Leeds Dispatch 63
WhatsApp 120
Wilson, Jonathan 62
Winnipeg Free Press 36
Wired (magazine) 34, 46
Wordpress 92–3, 100, 110–11
Wright, Mic 62, 158–9

Yorkshire Evening Post 36
YouGov surveys 22, 30, 77
youth courts 169–70
YouTube 13, 31, 142

Ze.tt 116–17
Zuckerberg, Mark 18, 150